ANGLICANS AND CATHOLICS IN DIALOGUE ON THE PAPACY

Anglicans AND Catholics IN Dialogue ON THE Papacy

A Gift for All Christians

Russel T. Murray, OFM

Paulist Press
New York / Mahwah, NJ

Library of Congress Cataloging-in-Publication Data
Names: Murray, Russel T., author.
Title: Anglicans and Catholics in dialogue on the Papacy : a gift for all Christians / Russel T. Murray, OFM.
Description: New York : Paulist Press, 2017. | Includes bibliographical references and index.
Identifiers: LCCN 2016051084 (print) | LCCN 2017015709 (ebook) | ISBN 9781587685668 (ebook) | ISBN 9780809149605 (pbk. : alk. paper)
Subjects: LCSH: Popes—Primacy. | Episcopacy. | Anglican Communion—Relations—Catholic Church. | Catholic Church—Relations—Anglican Communion. | Anglican/Roman Catholic International Commission.
Classification: LCC BX1805 (ebook) | LCC BX1805 .M87 2017 (print) | DDC 262/.13—dc23
LC record available at https://lccn.loc.gov/2016051084]

ISBN 978-0-8091-4960-5 (paperback)
ISBN 978-1-58768-566-8 (e-book)

Published by Paulist Press
997 Macarthur Boulevard
Mahwah, New Jersey 07430

www.paulistpress.com

Printed and bound in the
United States of America

In memory of Professor Margaret O'Gara (1947–2012).
Joyful scholar, dedicated teacher, and faithful servant of the Lord,
may she forever enjoy the blessed unity for which she
fervently prayed and confidently labored.

CONTENTS

Contents

ACKNOWLEDGMENTS

No book is born of a single set of hands. It is conceived, develops, and takes life through the contributions of many people. Acknowledging the assistance and wisdom of those who enabled me to bring this work to life is one way, however small, of thanking them for their guidance and encouragement.

The first stage of this process took place at the University of St. Michael's College in Toronto, under the direction of the late Professor Margaret O'Gara, whose depth and breadth of scholarship was surpassed only by her dedication to her students and her love for the one Church of Jesus Christ. A faithful servant of the Lord, may she forever enjoy the blessed unity for which she prayed and confidently labored.

I am also indebted to those who guided me in my research both at the University of St. Michael's College and the wider Toronto School of Theology, especially the Rev. Dr. David Neelands, Dr. Joseph L. Mangina, and the late Dr. George Vandervelde. A special thanks goes to the late Bro. Dr. Jeffrey Gross, FSC. He never allowed a conversation to conclude without asking me when I would "get that book published, so you can get started on the next one." I suppose I have my proverbial marching orders.

My time in Toronto was followed by four wonderful years at the Washington Theological Union in Washington, DC, where I received no small amount of encouragement, guidance, and support, not only for this book but also for my development as a teacher, a scholar, and a minister of the gospel. Special thanks goes to Dr. C. Colt Anderson; Dr. Angela Senander; the Rev. Dr. John J. Burkhard, OFM Conv.; the Rev. Dr. Vincent DePaul Cushing, OFM; and the Rev. Dr. Louis V. Iasiello, OFM.

I would probably still be wondering whether my draft manuscript was "good enough" if it were not for the encouragement of Dr. Elena G. Procario-Foley, who put me in touch with my editor at Paulist Press, Dr. Christopher M. Bellitto. Dr. Bellitto patiently continued to guide my work even when my Order decided to set my ministerial life off in more than a few unexpected directions. Thank you for all your work.

Further thanks go to the librarians who opened the doors of their collections and fielded my many requests—especially when I was butchering their language. I am thinking especially of the staff of the Centro Pro Unione (Rome), under the direction of the Rev. Dr. James F. Puglisi, SA; the Rev. Dr. Rino Sgarbossa, OFM; and his staff at the Istituto di Studi Ecumenici S. Bernardino (Venice). A special word of thanks is due to the Rev. Dr. Roberto Giraldo, OFM, without whom my year in Venice would not have been possible.

A final, heartfelt word of gratitude goes to my brothers in the Province of the Most Holy Name of Jesus (USA) and to the many Franciscan sisters and brothers, Catholic and Anglican, with whom I am privileged to follow in the footsteps of our Lord, Jesus Christ. May we never waver from this path, for it leads us to the unity for which he prayed and we yearn.

Curia Generale dei Frati Minori
Rome, Italy
June 13, 2016
Feast of St. Anthony of Padua

NAMING THE GIFT

Papal Primacy at the Councils and Beyond

When Jesus came into the district of Caesarea Philippi, he asked his disciples, "Who do people say that the Son of Man is?" And they said, "Some say John the Baptist, but others Elijah, and still others Jeremiah or one of the prophets." He said to them, "But who do you say that I am?" Simon Peter answered, "You are the Messiah, the Son of the living God." And Jesus answered him, "Blessed are you, Simon son of Jonah! For flesh and blood has not revealed this to you, but my Father in heaven. And I tell you, you are Peter, and on this rock I will build my church, and the gates of Hades will not prevail against it. I will give you the keys of the kingdom of heaven, and whatever you bind on earth will be bound in heaven, and whatever you loose on earth will be loosed in heaven."

—Matthew 16:13–19

We had the basilica to ourselves—almost. All but a handful of pilgrims had jostled their way through the bronze doors of St. Peter's and into the vastness of Bernini's piazza, where the newly elected Benedict XVI was leading his first Sunday *Angelus* as pope.

Inside the basilica, everything was cool and quiet. The only sound we could hear was the soft click of the confessional door, as one of the basilica's Franciscan confessors took his turn in "the box." My cousin Jeffrey, who had arrived in Rome only that day, approached the confessional and knelt at the friar's side. As for me, I let my imagination wander about the basilica, soaking in its significance within the Catholic imagination, particularly as it related to the authority of the bishop whom Catholics acknowledge as successor of the apostle whose relics were lying only a few feet from where I sat.

When speaking about the significance of St. Peter's, it would probably be better to speak about its *significances*. There is more than one, and all are arguably as colorful as the 266 popes recognized as the apostle's successors. I find, though, that these meanings tend to cluster into three general groups. The first group tends to see the basilica as symbolic of the permanence, solidity, and apparently static nature of papal primacy. Certainly, this place has grown over the centuries: from Gaius's table to Constantine's *confessio*, from Julius II's grandiose dreams to the realized visions of several artists. All these changes, though, are reflective of the struggle St. Peter's successors have had to realize the primacy entrusted to them by Christ against people wielding a far more mundane authority.

If the first group's understanding of the primacy may be said to be essentially static, as solid and unyielding as the basilica's walls, the second group, ironically, sees the primacy, at least in the form we see today, as dispensable. From its vantage point, the basilica is the complete antithesis of the kingdom Jesus promised to the poor in spirit. It is the existential symbol of a papacy that acts in stark contrast to the One who came to serve, not to be served, and who surrendered his life for the life of the world. They are thrilled to see Pope Francis washing the feet of prisoners, refugees, women, and Muslims on Holy Thursday, just as they rejoiced to see him move out of the Apostolic Palace into the more modest confines of the Casa Santa Marta. Now, if he would only dispense with the Apostolic Palace altogether....

Admittedly, these groupings are caricatures, but precisely as caricatures they represent the two ends of an extremely wide spectrum of opinion among Catholics regarding the primacy that the

Catholic Church claims to belong by divine right to the Roman Pontiff. What is more, from their respective ends, these groups draw attention to the vast, third group that lies between them. This is a group that, for all its variety, tends to see the primacy as being much like the basilica itself, that is, as something inherently capable of growing and changing. Seen from their vantage, the primacy is a thoroughly dynamic reality whose contours are discerned in the light of two sets of encounters: (1) the encounter between the Church's faith in Jesus's proclamation of the kingdom and the history within which it must struggle to live this faith, and (2) the encounter between the gift of the primacy and the other, innumerable gifts that the Spirit bestows upon the people of God for the building up of their life as Christ's Body, his Church. This is a primacy that, for all its permanence, is no stranger to change, and that, for all the contrasts and contradictions that exist between the popes who wielded it and the simple fisherman from whom they have claimed to derive it, strives to fulfill the Lord's charge to tend and feed his flock (see John 21:15–19).

With these thoughts swimming in my head, I watched my cousin rise from his knees in the transept where Vatican I once sat and across from the mortal remains of the pope who convened Vatican II—"Good Pope," now "Saint" John XXIII—and wondered about the challenges lying ahead for the pope out in the piazza and the changes he may have to make to his office in order to meet those challenges. (His resignation was not among my musings, however unsurprised I was when it was announced.) What effect will they have upon the ways future popes will understand the primacy they claim? What is more, what effect will this have upon the ways we will understand and receive—or reject—this claim: my cousin and the confessor before whom he had been kneeling; the pilgrims jostling for a better view of papal apartments; the millions of Christians throughout the world who continue to live apart from one another, in spite of their common love for the Lord; the untold billions of people who look at us and see only more of the division and derision that marks our world?

Of course, I do not know what the answers to these questions will be. No one does! I am sure about one thing, though: the answers will be found only through the graced process of discerning, in light of our faith and the signs of the times in which we live it, what lies at the heart of the Lord's gift of the Petrine primacy of the Bishop of Rome. For this, a thorough (not to mention fearless) grasp of the past is indispensable. It provides us with a fuller understanding of the primacy that our forebears in faith have bequeathed to us. What is more, it enables us to appreciate the fact that this process of discernment is not something we need to invent ourselves. It is, as the third group above appreciates, part of our heritage as Catholics. We need only embrace it, firm in the belief that the Lord who established a primacy in St. Peter will open our eyes to see more clearly and understand more effectively what he wills it to be, both for our sake and for the sake of the gospel.

It is in the service of just such a belief that I shall turn my attention to the discernment of the primacy conducted by the bishops of the First and Second Vatican Councils. In respective chapters, I shall examine how the doctrines developed at Vatican I were that Council's response to a world that, in the eyes of many, threatened the very foundations of the Christian faith. What is more, I shall also demonstrate how this response was not always correctly understood and faithfully conveyed to the Church, including by those whose responsibility it was to do so. I shall then examine how these doctrines were received by Vatican II, as its fathers sought both to clarify the true meaning of Vatican I and to lay the theological foundation necessary for St. Peter's successors to serve the unity of the entire people of God. I shall conclude this section with a consideration of those areas in which Catholic doctrines of the primacy stand in need of further development, in order for Vatican II's vision to become the Church's reality.

CHAPTER 1

PAPAL PRIMACY AT THE FIRST VATICAN COUNCIL

While we recall with grateful hearts, as is only fitting, [the promise of Christ to remain with his Church and the manifestation of his presence in the guiding work of ecumenical councils] and other outstanding gains, which the divine mercy has bestowed on the Church especially by means of the last ecumenical synod, we cannot subdue the bitter grief that we feel at most serious evils, which have largely arisen either because the authority of the sacred synod was held in contempt by all too many, or because its wise decrees were neglected....Thereupon there came into being and spread far and wide throughout the world that doctrine of rationalism or naturalism,—utterly opposed to the Christian religion, since this is of supernatural origin,— which spares no effort to bring it about that Christ, who alone is our lord and savior, is shut out from the minds of people and the moral life of nations....And so we, following in the footsteps of our predecessors, in accordance with our supreme apostolic office, have never left off teaching and defending Catholic truth and condemning erroneous doctrines. But now it is our purpose to profess and declare from this chair of Peter before all eyes the saving teaching of Christ, and, by the power given us by God, to reject and condemn the contrary errors. This we shall do with the bishops of the whole world as our co-assessors and fellow-judges, gathered here as they are in the Holy Spirit by our authority in this ecumenical council, and relying on the word of God in Scripture and tradition as we have received it, religiously preserved and authentically expounded by the Catholic Church.

—First Vatican Council,
Dei Filius, introduction

I. INTRODUCTION

"The eternal Shepherd and Guardian of our souls, in order to render permanent the saving work of redemption, determined to build a Church in which, as in the house of the living God, all the faithful should be linked by the bond of one faith and charity." With these words the assembled bishops of the First Vatican Council opened *Pastor Aeternus* (PA), the first of two intended constitutions on the Church. They continued by recalling how the Lord had prayed for this unity, both for his apostles and for those who would come to believe in him through their preaching (see John 17:20–21). So it was that Christ sent his apostles into the world to preach the good news and appoint "shepherds and teachers" who would succeed them in this ministry "until the end of time." In order that they and their successors may remain "one and undivided,"

> and that, by the union of the clergy, the whole multitude of believers should be held together in the unity of faith and communion, he set blessed Peter over the rest of the apostles and instituted in him the permanent principle of both unities and their visible foundation. Upon the strength of this foundation was to be built the eternal temple, and the Church whose topmost part reaches heaven was to rise upon the firmness of this foundation. (PA, intro.)

If from these words one were to conclude that the constitution that followed saw the papacy in a brilliantly exalted light, one would be both right and wrong. There is a great deal more to appreciate in Vatican I's understanding of papal primacy than its ultramontane veneer might suggest. To appreciate this, though, one must pause before immersing oneself in the language of *Pastor Aeternus* and seek to discern the mind—or, truer to reality, the *minds*—of the bishops who promulgated it. I shall begin with the cares and concerns of the Bishop of Rome himself, Pope Pius IX, as he looked out at the world beyond his window on the eve of Vatican I.

II. ON THE EVE OF VATICAN I

Liberalism, nationalism, realism, industrialism, capitalism, socialism, democracy: these were the watchwords of the day, and they encompassed a host of powerful ideas and ideals that Pius and his contemporaries confidently believed would lead humanity into a future of unimaginable progress. For some, this confidence was in a future they beheld as clear and beautiful, and progressing inevitably toward a man-made utopia. Others, however, shared Pius's dark and foreboding vision. They beheld a future ruled by uncontrollable forces that would undermine revealed religion, reduce human dignity to industrial capital, and overthrow all sense of political order, and they were confident that such progress would lead humanity straight to hell, figuratively and literally speaking.

It was not as though Pius was simply spinning irrational and reactionary wheels. At the time of election in 1846, and for the first years of his pontificate, he had been hailed a progressive reformer. He and his ideological allies were people who had lived through the aftermath of the French Revolution and experienced the new revolutions that had swept across Europe in 1848–49, including Rome, and they had seen the Industrial Revolution devour both human and natural "capital" in the name of technological progress and increased national and personal wealth. In an age seemingly saturated with the desire for material things, they believed it their responsibility to ask what room remained for the things of the

Spirit. If people believed themselves able to reshape the world in accord with their own wills, what was left to prevent them from also believing themselves capable of explaining away every mystery in the name of progress, including that of God? For God is the great Mystery, in whose divine light the true significance of the created world is recognized and the truth of humanity's nature and ultimate destiny is revealed.[1]

To twenty-first-century, Western-educated eyes, Pius's vision may appear more a matter of histrionics than the kind of considered response one might expect from the chief shepherd of a Church whose institutional memory was over eighteen hundred years old. Yet, one should never underestimate the influence "these trying times" can have upon those living through them. For Pius, the times were not merely trying. They were traumatizing,[2] and in the guise of the *Risorgimento*, they were again marching toward Rome in order to overthrow the Church's divinely established foundation—"if they can."[3] Thus, when in 1867 Pius announced his intention to call the first council in three hundred years, one may as well hear him saying, "The fight is on!" In fact, however, the fight had been on for quite some time.

A. The Papal Reaction to a Changing World

In 1832, Pius's immediate predecessor, Gregory XVI, published the encyclical *Mirari Vos*, which condemned such perceived errors as the freedom of the press, nonmonarchical forms of governance, and the separation of church and state. Gregory spoke with even greater force in the 1834 encyclical *Singulari Vos*, which condemned the most prominent proponent of the "errors" condemned in *Mirari Vos*, Hugues-Félicité Robert de Lamennais. When Pius became pope in 1846, one may say that he picked up where Gregory had left off. In the first decade and a half of his pontificate, Pius published over thirty encyclicals, allocutions, and communiqués condemning what he, in line with his predecessor, saw as the most pernicious errors of the day. This output culminated with his 1864 encyclical *Syllabus Errorum*. In this light, Vatican I cannot be seen as having arrived unannounced. It was the product of a long and bitter struggle against modernity. Indeed, Vatican I may be seen as this struggle's high-water mark.

Why a council? It could not have been a matter of issuing new condemnations. Pius obviously had no doubt about his ability to do that well enough on his own. Moreover, given the sweeping condemnations of the *Syllabus*, one could well ask whether there were any "errors" that had escaped his attention. Why a council? Pius himself offered the answer, in the first question he posed to the assembled bishops.

> Pius, bishop, servant of the servants of God, with the approval of the sacred council, for an everlasting record. Most reverend fathers, is it your pleasure that, to the praise and glory of the Holy and undivided Trinity, Father, Son and Holy Spirit, for the increase and exaltation of the Catholic faith and religion, for the uprooting of current errors, for the reformation of the clergy and the Christian people, and for the common peace and concord of all, the holy ecumenical Vatican council should be opened, and be declared to have been opened?[4]

Regardless of history's verdict upon the fruits of the Vatican I Council, not to mention the means by which they were cultivated, the fundamental reason for Pius's decision to call it was pastoral; it was to renew the Church's faith in the fundamental events of revelation and the significance of those events for its life.[5] Pius's council was an ambitious project, and as is the case with all such projects, it aroused a host of deeply felt and conflicting passions. These passions burned with a particular intensity around the most anticipated item on the agenda: the definition of the Roman Pontiff's universal jurisdiction and infallible magisterium—in other words, papal primacy.

B. The Minds of the Council

When Pius announced that the council would meet at the tomb of the Prince of the Apostles, he was sending a powerful message of support to those calling for papal primacy to be defined as an article of faith. As was the case with the Holy See's long struggle against modernity, Pius and his supporters found themselves walking upon a well-trodden path, one measured not in decades, but in centuries.

Papal claims to primacy have long and storied history. Innocent III's adoption of the title "Vicar of Christ," Boniface VIII's *Unam Sanctam*, even the *Dictatus Papae* of Gregory VII could arguably have been considered recent contributions. In 1799, a theologian and Camaldolese monk named Mauro Cappellari made a contribution of his own: *The Triumph of the Holy See and the Church over the Attacks of Innovators, Who Are Rejected and Fought with Their Own Weapons*. The grandiosity of Cappellari's claim, evident in his book's title, was surprising enough. After all, the papacy was then in the throes of public humiliation and the Church itself increasingly subjected to the wills of secular authorities across Europe. The real surprise, though, came a little over three decades later, when in 1831, Cappellari became Pope Gregory XVI. Now he was in a position—indeed, *the* position—to put his understanding of papal primacy into practice.

Cappellari had written *The Triumph of the Holy See* to refute the position advanced by Pietro Tamburini in his book *The Authentic Idea of the Holy See*. Tamburini had argued for a papacy in harmony with the spirit of the age, one adapted to the idea of popular sovereignty by the application of conciliarist and Gallican principles, which he believed history had finally vindicated. Against Tamburini, Cappellari argued that appeals to history were senseless when it came to discerning the authentic "idea" of the Holy See. The Lord had endowed the Church with everything it needed for its proper governance, and this had remained unchanged in its external forms through the centuries, until its sudden and violent overthrow by the revolutionary forces of *liberté, égalité, fraternité*, beginning in 1789.

The future pope also criticized the belief that the true authority of the Church lay in the power of its convictions to convince free men and women of the truth it proclaims. Instead, Cappellari argued, based on the concept of sovereignty itself, that the Church had the same right as any legitimate government to compel the obedience of its members. To assert otherwise was effectively to compromise the ability of the Church to act upon its divinely established mandate and to leave it open to manipulation by people—and states—committed to the promotion of their own self-interests rather than to the salvation of the world.

This analogy between secular and ecclesial sovereignty enabled Capelleri to argue for the sovereignty of the Roman Pontiff: God, the ruler of the Church, established in the person of the pope, the successor of St. Peter and the Vicar of his Son upon earth, his instrument of sovereign governance over the Church. This sovereignty includes all legislative, administrative, and executive authority, and so is able to demand the obedience of all Christians. Intrinsic to this sovereignty is the ability to teach infallibly, and so demand assent to the "deposit of faith" (*depositum fide*), which God had revealed to the world and entrusted to his Church.

This argument was later developed and advanced by many of the day's leading ultramontanists, including the younger Lamennais and his mentor, Joseph de Maistre, whose basic position was clear and direct: "Christianity rests entirely on the Pope, so that the principles of the political and social order...may be derived from the following chain of reasoning: there can be no public morality and no national character without religion, no European religion without Christianity, no Christianity without Catholicism, no Catholicism without the Pope, [and] no Pope without [the] sovereignty that belongs to him."[6]

De Maistre's line of thought was equally as clear and direct. As he stated in his popular work *Du Pape*, "There can be no human society without a government, no government without sovereignty, no sovereignty without infallibility; and this last privilege is so absolutely necessary that one is compelled to postulate infallibility even in secular sovereignties (where it does not exist) if one is not to concede the ultimate dissolution of the social order."[7]

In the early decades of the nineteenth century, this dissolution appeared to be an all-too-real possibility. Political instability in France; the rise of Prussia; the repression of the Church in Poland, England, Ireland, and Belgium; and the threat to the Papal States posed by the Italian *Risorgimento* caused many Catholics to see the person of Roman Pontiff as both a moral support and a sign of their common identity as Catholics. Thus, as Alexis de Tocqueville noted, ultramontanism's true base of support did not lie in the Apostolic Palace. "The Pope is driven more by the faithful to become absolute ruler of the Church than they are impelled by him to submit to his rule."[8]

By 1867, the year in which Pius announced his intention to convene Vatican I, public sentiment was decidedly on the side of his ultramontanist supporters. As the influential journal *Civiltà Catholica* expressed it,

> We have reached a point today when the war of the godless against the Catholic Church is totally concentrated in attacking the papacy, assaulting both its spiritual and its secular prerogatives. We may even rejoice in this rather than lamenting it, for in this way it is revealed that this is the unconquerable rock....But because the supreme interest of every Catholic lies herein it is also our highest duty to bind ourselves as much as possible to this central point, and this contest involving all in the unity of faith, hope, and reverence for the protection of the see of Peter must be the salvation and the boast of all Catholic Christianity.[9]

This opinion was by no means universal. Among the council's future fathers were bishops who objected to any definition of papal primacy, especially one that conceived of infallibility in terms of sovereignty. Some framed their objections in practical terms, arguing that the sociopolitical climate made any definition inopportune.[10] Others objected on theological grounds. In *On the General Council and Religious Peace*, Bishop Henry Maret, dean of the theological faculty of the Sorbonne, argued that the very concept of unlimited sovereignty was ill-conceived.[11] It effectively divorced the pope from the Church by placing him above it. It denied the legitimate authority of the bishops and opened the way to an arbitrariness of rule unheard of in the history of the Church: absolute, unlimited, and unaccountable. Instead, Maret advocated a sovereignty in which authority was invested in the entire body of bishops united with the pope as its head.[12]

Other bishops were more adamant in their opposition. They saw the claim to universal sovereignty as a heretical interpretation of the Church's Tradition. This opinion was found principally among the hierarchy's conciliarist and Gallican sympathizers, but it also came from bishops sympathetic to ultramontanist claims. They charged that the understanding of papal sovereignty proposed by some of their brothers ran contrary to the very constitution of the Church. As Maret had observed, albeit from a significantly different vantage, such an understanding separated the pope from both the flock Christ charged him to shepherd and from those with whom he shared that charge, that is, the bishops, who, together with him, were the Church's most convincing witnesses to the truth of the Christian faith.

By the time the council opened, its bishops were of three distinct minds: the extreme ultramontanists, supported by Pius, who sought to define infallibility as a personal charism of the pope and an intrinsic aspect of his sovereign authority; the future minority that opposed this definition of papal infallibility; and the majority of bishops who, though fundamentally ultramontanist in their thinking, were also open to the concerns of the minority.[13] It was within this atmosphere that *Pastor Aeternus* would develop.

III. THE DEFINITION OF PAPAL PRIMACY: PRIMACY AT THE SERVICE OF UNITY

Pastor Aeternus opened by declaring that Christ, "the eternal Shepherd and Guardian of our souls, in order to render permanent the saving work of redemption, determined to build a Church in which, as in the house of the living God, all the faithful should be linked by the bond of one faith and charity" (PA, intro.). In order that this unity in faith and charity may be maintained among both the bishops and all the faithful, Christ "set blessed Peter over the rest of the apostles and instituted in him the permanent principle of both unities and their visible foundation" (PA, intro.). This primacy entailed two further affirmations. The first was that this primacy was unmitigated; the second was that it was permanent. These were treated respectively in chapters 1 and 2 of *Pastor Aeternus*, and so established the context within which the council would define the jurisdictional sovereignty and infallible magisterium of the Roman Pontiff.

A. Context: Primacy at the Service of Unity

In chapter 1, "On the institution of the apostolic primacy in the blessed Peter" the council stated, "We teach and declare that, according to the gospel evidence, a primacy of jurisdiction over the whole Church of God was immediately and directly promised to the blessed apostle Peter and conferred on him by Christ the lord" (PA 1). The evidence to which they referred was Jesus's conferral of heaven's keys upon Simon, now called "Peter/Rock," and the Lord's calling him to shepherd his flock. In light of "this absolutely manifest teaching of the Sacred Scriptures, as it has always been understood by the Catholic Church," they declared that Peter was chosen by Christ "in preference to the rest of the apostles, taken singly or collectively" and immediately endowed with "a true and proper primacy of jurisdiction" in his own right, and not as a manner of honor or as having been transmitted to him "through the Church," as "those who misrepresent the form of government which Christ the lord established in his Church" contend (PA 1).

The teaching expressed in chapter 2, "On the permanence of the primacy of blessed Peter in the Roman Pontiffs," flowed from this. Permanence is intrinsic to Peter's primacy. It was established "by Christ's authority, in the Church which, founded as it is upon a rock, will stand firm until the end of time" (PA 2). This is confirmed by the uninterrupted Tradition of the Church and by the time-honored belief that

> to this day and forever [the blessed Peter] lives and presides and exercises judgment in his successors the pontiffs of the Holy Roman See, which he founded and consecrated with his blood. Therefore, whoever succeeds to the Chair of Peter obtains by the institution of Christ himself, the primacy of Peter over the whole Church. So what the truth has ordained stands firm, and blessed Peter perseveres in the rock-like strength he was granted, and does not abandon that guidance of the Church that he once received. For this reason, it has always been necessary for every Church—that is to say the faithful throughout the world—to be in agreement

with the Roman Church because of its more effective leadership. In consequence of being joined, as members to head, with that see, from which the rights of sacred communion flow to all, they will grow together into the structure of a single body. (PA 2)

Peter stands forever as the rock upon which the Savior built his Church. As such, he remains the permanent principle and visible foundation of the Church's unity in faith and charity, and continues to exercise his sacred charge, entrusted to him by Christ, in the person of his successor, the Bishop of Rome, whose office Peter established and sanctified by his own martyrdom. "Therefore, if anyone says that it is not by the institution of Christ the Lord himself (that is to say, by divine law) that blessed Peter should have perpetual successors in the primacy over the whole Church; or that the Roman Pontiff is not the successor of blessed Peter in this primacy: let him be anathema" (PA 2).

The central concern of the bishops assembled at Vatican I was the unity of the Church. While the nature of the primacy was the explicit object under consideration, it was so only in relation to the unity it was established by Christ to serve. Thus, the primacy of the Roman Pontiff could have no meaning apart from the unity of the Church. Unity is primacy's proper end, and, as such, was the proper context within which the bishops discussed the primacy. This is evident from all that follows in *Pastor Aeternus*, however obscure this may at first appear—as it did even to some of the bishops themselves.

B. Primatial Jurisdiction

In the light of its potential (and long since realized) significance for the exercise of their own ministry, it is astonishing to discover how little time the bishops devoted to the question of primatial jurisdiction.[14] Although they discussed the schema of *Pastor Aeternus* between May 13 and June 3, 1870, much of this time was devoted to the question of infallibility. The discussion on jurisdiction lasted only a week, June 6–14. After subsequent debate on infallibility, voting on amendments was held on July 2, 9, 11, and 16. The final vote on *Pastor Aeternus* occurred on July

18, 1870. The canon of its third chapter, "On the power and character of the primacy of the Roman Pontiff," declared,

> So, then, if anyone says that the Roman Pontiff has merely an office of supervision and guidance, and not the full and supreme power of jurisdiction over the whole Church, and this not only in matters of faith and morals, but also in those which concern the discipline and government of the Church dispersed throughout the whole world; or that he has only the principal part, but not the absolute fullness, of this supreme power; or that this power of his is not ordinary and immediate both overall and each of the Churches and overall and each of the pastors and faithful: let him be anathema. (PA 3)

For all the obvious force in its language and tone, this definition did not fulfill the minority's worst fears. Given the council's immediate prehistory, it would have been impossible for the bishops *not* to have defined the pope's primacy of jurisdiction in terms other than that of absolute, monarchical sovereignty—as Pius and his supporters expressly expected they would. Nevertheless, this expectation was not entirely born out in the final text of *Pastor Aeternus*. Certainly, this text was undoubtedly marked by the spirit of its time, but it did *not* define papal primacy of jurisdiction as the kind of absolute, monarchical sovereignty that Cappellari/Gregory XVI believed it to have always been.

    1. Universal, Ordinary, Immediate: The teaching on juridical primacy opened with a series of statements intended to summarize the contents of the constitution's first two chapters:

> And so, supported by the clear witness of Holy Scripture, and adhering to the manifest and explicit decrees both of our predecessors the Roman Pontiffs and of general councils, we promulgate anew the definition of the ecumenical Council of Florence, which must be believed by all faithful Christians, namely that the Apostolic See and the Roman Pontiff hold a world-wide primacy, and that the Roman Pontiff is the successor of blessed Peter,

the Prince of the Apostles, true Vicar of Christ, head of the whole Church and father and teacher of all Christian people. To him, in blessed Peter, full power has been given by Our Lord Jesus Christ to tend, rule and govern the universal Church. All this is to be found in the acts of the ecumenical councils and the sacred canons. (PA 3)

Building upon this, the text went on to state that "by divine ordinance, the Roman Church possesses a pre-eminence of ordinary power over every other Church, and that this jurisdictional power of the Roman Pontiff is both episcopal and immediate." This jurisdiction extends over the clergy and the faithful, "of whatever rite and dignity," both collectively and individually, and all "are bound to submit to this power by the duty of hierarchical subordination and true obedience, and this not only in matters concerning faith and morals, but also in those which regard the discipline and government of the Church throughout the world." In this way, the unity of the Church is achieved, and so becomes "one flock under one Supreme Shepherd." From this truth, "no one can depart from it without endangering his faith and salvation" (PA 3).

It followed from this "supreme power which the Roman Pontiff has in governing the whole Church, that he has the right, in the performance of this office of his, to communicate freely with the pastors and flocks of the entire Church, so that they may be taught and guided by him in the way of salvation." This communication may not be "lawfully obstructed" for any reason. Furthermore, it does not depend upon any "civil power" for its effect. It is authoritative in and of itself (PA 3).

Many bishops raised concerns and objections. However, before any anathemas were issued in their name, precisely what was it that they were being called upon to affirm?

These bishops' fundamental concern was how this "pre-eminence of ordinary power over every other Church" could be reconciled with the ordinary power of jurisdiction each bishop has over his own diocese. If it could not be clearly reconciled, then locals bishops would essentially be nothing more than personal representatives of the Roman Pontiff—vicars of the Vicar of Christ. As Bishop Félix de Las Cases put it,

> The schema seems to aim at nothing else than that the
> Pope is in practice the only bishop of the whole Church,
> the others being indeed bishops in name but in reality
> nothing but vicars....The assertion of episcopal jurisdic-
> tion, ordinary and immediate, over the whole Church,
> sounds very much like that other thing...the Pope is the
> *immediate*, ordinary bishop of every diocese, as much
> that of Gubbio as that of Rome.[15]

According to Bishop Jean-Pierre Bravard, a member of the
council's vocal French minority, such a definition contradicted the
divine constitution of the bishops' apostolic ministry:

> The bishops would appear only...as vicars of the Roman
> pontiff, removable at his will, whereas Christ chose
> twelve whom he called his apostles, and that [sic] all
> of us who are assigned a see, once we have received the
> fullness of the priesthood, had believed that we were
> truly and irrevocably espoused to that see before God
> and that we were bound to it as a spouse.[16]

Still other bishops objected that the description of the pope's
jurisdiction could just as easily be applied to the jurisdiction of
secular rulers. In what sense, then, could it be spoken of as a special gift of a loving God for the unity of the Church? Regardless
of the diverse grounds of their objections, the minority's overriding concern was that the definition presented for their approval
appeared to betray the very Tradition the council had been called
to affirm.[17] To put it another way, the minority bishops were inter-
rogating the council in the name of the Church's Tradition, which
had the Spirit of the Lord himself as its firm and indefectible
foundation. The future of the council turned on the response they
would be given.

Bishop Zinelli of the *Deputatio de fide*, which was charged
with explaining the text of the decree, responded by assuring the
bishops that the proposed definition did not betray the Spirit's
gifts to the Church. The pope's primacy of jurisdiction was not
without limits, and those limits were to be measured by the very
nature of the episcopacy itself.

To the concern that the *universal* jurisdiction described in the text made the bishops, in effect, vicars of the pope, Zinelli affirmed that the episcopal office, with all the rights inherent in that office, exists by divine right. Therefore, it could not be obfuscated or obviated by the pope's primacy of jurisdiction.[18] This authority, "given" by Christ to the Roman Pontiff "in blessed Peter," exists "for the building-up of the Church," not for its destruction (*ad aedificationem Ecclesiae non destructionem*).[19] He stated this explicitly in a response to another of the French minority, Bishop Landroit of Rheims: the bishops are of divine right, they have ordinary and immediate jurisdiction within their respective sees, and it is not in the power of the Bishop of Rome or of the council to destroy the episcopate, or anything else in the Church that is of divine right.[20] Zinelli explained the meaning of "ordinary" in a more "common sense" light:

> All [the jurists professors of Canon Law] call "ordinary" that power which belongs to anyone by virtue of his office, "delegated" that which does not belong by virtue of the office but is exercised in the name of another for whom it is "ordinary." With this explanation of the terms the *Deputatio de fide* considers the discussion closed. For does not the sovereign pontiff hold by virtue of his office whatever powers are his? If it is by virtue of his office, then it is ordinary power.[21]

Nevertheless, the concern was certainly a legitimate one, and Zinelli knew it. It was for this reason, he explained, that the *Deputatio* had inserted a well-known and honored expression of Pope Gregory VII into this section of *Pastor Aeternus*.

> This power of the Supreme Pontiff by no means detracts from that ordinary and immediate power of episcopal jurisdiction, by which bishops, who have succeeded to the place of the apostles by appointment of the Holy Spirit, tend and govern individually the particular flocks which have been assigned to them. On the contrary, this power of theirs is asserted, supported and defended by the Supreme and Universal Pastor; for St. Gregory

19

the Great says: "My honor is the honor of the whole Church. My honor is the steadfast strength of my brethren. Then do I receive true honor, when it is denied to none of those to whom honor is due." (PA 3)

In this light, the service to unity that the Pope's primacy of jurisdiction renders the Church must be seen as existing not *over* and *apart from*, but in relationship *to* and *with* the same service rendered by the episcopate as a whole. What is at issue, then, was not *the* divine right of the Roman Pontiff superseding *a* divine right of the bishops. Rather, it is the issue of *a* divine right proper to the Bishop of Rome in his role as Supreme Pontiff being at the service of *the* divine right of the bishops to govern the faithful entrusted to their care, so as to preserve their unity in Christ.[22] This understanding of the relationship between the jurisdiction of the Roman Pontiff as *universal* primate and that of a local bishop as pontiff of a local church is further evidenced by the fact that the Bishop of Rome is a *bishop*. As such, the jurisdiction he exercises on a universal scale for the sake of the Church's unity is nothing other than that exercised by every local bishop for the sake of the unity of his diocese.

> It must be admitted that *the power of the sovereign pontiff is in reality of the same kind as that of the bishops*. Why not, then, use the same word to indicate the quality of jurisdiction exercised by the Popes and the bishops, and why not speak of episcopal power in the bishops and of the supreme episcopal power in the sovereign pontiff?[23]

Properly understood, the primatial jurisdiction of the Bishop of Rome does not exalt him above his brother bishops. Instead, it places him precisely in their midst. It is only the *quality* of his jurisdiction, given to him by virtue of his being the "perpetual principle and visible foundation" of the unity of the Church and the episcopate, that distinguishes him from other bishops. Whereas their jurisdiction is within their respective sees, his as Supreme Pontiff extends universally, and whereas their acts on behalf of the unity of the Church depend upon their communion with him, he may act independently of them, should the Church's unity necessitate it. This may also be seen when considering the Bishop of Rome in his role as "head" of the "body" of bishops.

> The bishops gathered with their head in an ecumenical council—and in that case they represent the whole Church—or dispersed but in union with their head—in which case they are the Church itself—truly have full power. There would be confusion if we were to admit two full and supreme powers separate and distinct from each other....But we admit that the truly full and supreme power is in the sovereign pontiff *as in the head* and the same power, truly both full and supreme, is also *in the head united to the members*, that is to say, in the pontiff united to the bishops.[24]

There is one—and *only* one—full and supreme jurisdiction within the Church, and it is episcopal in nature. It is in the bishops as a whole, united as a body with their head, and in the head itself—not as a disembodied entity possessed of its own unique power, but always understood with reference to entire body of bishops, by virtue of that which he shares with them, that is, the office of bishop.

While the clarifications offered by Zinelli on behalf of the *Deputatio* were clear enough to allow many in the minority to vote *placet* (i.e., yes) to the definitions of *Pastor Aeternus* on the morning of July 18, 1870, they were also vague enough to avoid committing the majority to too specific a definition of the relationship between the episcopal "body" and its primatial "head." This may have split the more extreme ultramontanists from those who saw any move to separate the authority of the Roman Pontiff from that of his brother bishops a betrayal of the Church's Tradition. The result was what one may call "wiggle room"—the kind of wiggle room that would permit the Second Vatican Council to develop its teaching on collegiality.

2. And Full: With this understanding of jurisdictional primacy in mind, the *Deputatio*'s further explanations of the *fullness* of this universal, ordinary, and immediate jurisdiction followed with relative ease.

"How is an immediate power to be distinguished from a mediate one?" Zinelli asked. "That power is called immediate which may be exercised without having to pass through an intermediary. But is not the Pope able by himself to perform episcopal acts in every diocese, without passing through the mediation of the local bishop? Should he rather get the bishop's permission to confirm, for example, or to hear confessions?"

> There is no reason to fear that in the government of particular churches confusion would result from the fact that this ordinary, immediate power runs alongside the proper power of the bishop in this or that diocese. Confusion would arise if it was a matter of two equal concurrent jurisdictions, but not if one is subordinate to the other. It would certainly be the case if the sovereign pontiff availed himself of his right to perform all episcopal tasks in every diocese every day, and with no regard to the bishop, riding roughshod over what ought to have been wisely decided, he would be using his power *non aedificationen sed in destructionem* and confusion of spiritual leadership would soon follow. But who could imagine such an absurd possibility? Let us all consider the matter calmly. Let us, with confidence in the moderation of the Holy See, be assured that this authority will work for the upholding of episcopal power, not for its weakening.[25]

A clearer statement on the subordinate relationship existing between these two powers may have been more helpful than a simple call for confidence in the pope's discretion. Is the subordination akin to what we now call subsidiarity? Unfortunately, Zinelli does not provide us with a ready answer. However, the simple fact *that* the *Deputatio* had declared that the authority of the local bishop would not in practice be put at risk constitutes an important piece of evidence, and it was with this mind that the bishops voted in favor of *Pastor Aeternus*.[26]

C. Primatial Magisterium: Infallibility

As was noted above, much of the bishops' time prior to voting on the final text of *Pastor Aeternus* was spent discussing papal infallibility. Infallibility was *the* question, and all the bishops knew that the time would come when they would have to offer their own considered responses. In part, this was why Pius had convoked Vatican I. Fortunately, history provided them with plenty to draw upon for those responses.

1. The Root of Infallibility: From at least the fifth century, Rome's bishops expressed little doubt about the definitive character of their pronouncements. However, it was not until the thirteenth century that this character became the subject of serious theological consideration. St. Thomas Aquinas and the Second Council of Lyons both considered the question of papal magisterium. While both clearly granted the pope a definitive teaching authority, neither defined this authority as infallible. The first explicit argument on infallibility's behalf was offered by the Franciscan Peter of John Olivi in 1283, and he did so in the form of a *quaestio*: "Whether the Roman Pontiff is to be obeyed by all Catholics as an infallible [*inerrabili*] standard in faith and morals." Although some historians see in Olivi the theological root of *Pastor Aeternus*, the history behind his *quaestio*—whether Franciscan poverty was truly rooted in the example of Jesus and the apostles—leaves the inquirer with no alternative but to look elsewhere.[27]

This search eventually leads to the thirteenth-century Carmelite Guido Terreni. Terreni's view of papal infallibility was remarkably close to that defined in *Pastor Aeternus*.[28] While one may arguably (if tenuously) claim that the dogma of 1870 was, in essence, being taught as early as 1330, one cannot say that it enjoyed uninterrupted growth and ever-increasing acceptance in the Church. The Great Western Schism (1378–1417), the Council of Constance (1414–18), and the "Articles of the Gallican Clergy" (1682) are evidence enough of this fact. To that, one may add that by the dawn of the eighteenth century, most proponents of papal infallibility were to be found in what would soon enough become the Kingdom of Italy.

To what can the considerable gains made by the promoters of papal infallibility between 1800 and 1870 be attributed? It would be to the same social, political, and religious factors that were promoting an expansive understanding of papal jurisdiction. Thus by 1870, infallibility's moment had arrived. The only question was what kind of moment it would enjoy.

The short answer is a deftly handled, highly nuanced moment. Given the passions surrounding the issue, and amount of time dedicated to addressing them, this should come as no surprise. Satisfying both the majority and, to a large extent, the minority was no mean task. Not only was Pius satisfied, but even Maret felt himself justified in asserting, "The minority has triumphed in its defeat."[29] To understand how this happened, one must consider infallibility in terms of its *subject*, its *object*, and its *act*.[30]

2. The Subject of Infallibility: The fourth chapter of *Pastor Aeternus*, "On the infallible teaching authority of the Roman Pontiff," opened by declaring,

> That apostolic primacy which the Roman Pontiff possesses as successor of Peter, the prince of the apostles, includes also the supreme power of teaching. This Holy See has always maintained this, the constant custom of the Church demonstrates it, and the ecumenical councils, particularly those in which East and West met in the union of faith and charity, have declared it. (PA 4)

If one were to conclude from this statement that the *subject* of papal infallibility is the Roman Pontiff, one would be correct, but *only* if one keeps two things in mind. The first is a distinction, the second a qualification. Before naming these, a few more words from *Pastor Aeternus* are in order.

The Holy See, the "constant custom of the Church," and the ecumenical councils together testify that infallibility was given by the Lord to St. Peter and his successors for one reason: the unity of the Church. As the Fourth Council of Constantinople had declared, "The first condition of salvation is to maintain the rule of the true faith." Unity in faith is constitutive of the unity that the Lord wills for his Church. It was for the sake of this unity that he declared to Simon, "You are Peter, and upon this rock I will build my Church." The necessary effect of this word of the Lord is evidenced in the life of the Church itself, particularly in the lived witness of the local church that Peter's successors led—the church of Rome: "in the Apostolic See the Catholic religion has always been preserved unblemished, and sacred doctrine been held in honor" (PA 4).[31]

While one may not be surprised that the bishops decided to call three sets of witnesses to support their teaching, as opposed to arguing for its veracity against all detractors, one should resist the temptation to read these testimonies as nothing more than an exercise in proof-texting. What the bishops chose to cite reveals a very nuanced understanding of what it was they were actually defining. In other words, while they may have presumed the truthfulness of their claims, common enough for those in communion with the Roman Pontiff, their typically Catholic presumption was not open-ended.

The first set of witnesses consisted of statements from the Councils of Lyons II and Florence. The statement from Lyons II was drawn from the profession of faith demanded of the Byzantine Emperor.

> The holy Roman Church possesses the supreme and full primacy and principality over the whole Catholic Church. She truly and humbly acknowledges that she received this from the Lord himself in blessed Peter, the prince and chief of the apostles, whose successor the Roman Pontiff is, together with the fullness of power. And since before all others she has the duty of defending the truth of the faith, so if any questions arise concerning the faith, it is by her judgment that they must be settled. (PA 4)[32]

The testimony from Florence made much the same point: "The Roman Pontiff is the true vicar of Christ, the head of the whole Church and the father and teacher of all Christians; and to him was committed in blessed Peter, by our lord Jesus Christ, the full power of tending, ruling and governing the whole Church" (PA 4).

The second set of witnesses was none other than the bishops themselves, who

> sometimes individually, sometimes gathered in synods, according to the long established custom of the Churches and the pattern of ancient usage referred to this Apostolic See those dangers especially which arose in matters concerning the faith. This was to ensure that any damage

suffered by the faith should be repaired in that place above all where the faith can know no failing. (PA 4)

Such referrals were an acknowledgment of the "pastoral office" of the Roman Pontiff to ensure that the "saving teaching of Christ should be spread among all the peoples of the world; and with equal care...[make] sure that it should be kept pure and uncontaminated wherever it was received" (PA 4).

The final set of witnesses was that of Rome's bishops in the exercise of their "pastoral" office on behalf of the Church's unity in faith. This was done "as the circumstances of the time or the state of affairs suggested, sometimes by summoning ecumenical councils or consulting the opinion of the Churches scattered throughout the world, sometimes by special synods, sometimes by taking advantage of other useful means afforded by divine providence" (PA 4). Regardless of the means, however, the end was the same:

[to define] as doctrines to be held those things which, by God's help, they knew to be in keeping with Sacred Scripture and the apostolic traditions. For the Holy Ghost was promised to the successors of Peter not so that they might, by his revelation, make known some new doctrine, but that, by his assistance, they might religiously guard and faithfully expound the revelation or Deposit of Faith transmitted by the Apostles." (PA 4)

Thus has the word spoken by the Lord to St. Peter, and through him to his successors, been fulfilled: "I have prayed for you that your faith may not fail; and when you have turned again, strengthen your brethren" (PA 4, cf. Luke 22:32). From this, the council drew its conclusion:

This gift of truth and never-failing faith was therefore divinely conferred on Peter and his successors in this See so that they might discharge their exalted office for the salvation of all, and so that the whole flock of Christ might be kept away by them from the poisonous food of error and be nourished with the sustenance of heavenly doctrine. Thus the tendency to schism is removed and the whole Church is preserved in unity, and, resting on its foundation, can stand firm against the gates of hell.…

Therefore, faithfully adhering to the tradition received from the beginning of the Christian faith, to the glory of God Our Savior, for the exaltation of the Catholic religion and for the salvation of the Christian people, with the approval of the Sacred Council, we teach and define as a divinely revealed dogma that when the Roman Pontiff speaks *ex cathedra*, that is, when, in the exercise of his office as shepherd and teacher of all Christians, in virtue of his supreme apostolic authority, he defines a doctrine concerning faith or morals to be held by the whole Church, he possesses, by the divine assistance promised to him in Blessed Peter, that infallibility which the divine Redeemer willed his Church to enjoy in defining doctrine concerning faith or morals. Therefore, such definitions of the Roman Pontiff are of themselves, and not by the consent of the Church, irreformable. So then, should anyone, which God forbid, have the temerity to reject this definition of ours: let him be anathema. (PA 4)

The distinction is clear: while the *subject* of infallibility is the Roman Pontiff, the charism of infallibility does not inhere in his person. It inheres, rather, in his *office* as "shepherd and teacher of all Christians" (PA 4). In other words, while the pope can speak as a private person or theologian, as Benedict XVI expressly did in his three-part work *Jesus of Nazareth*, or simply to the faithful of the local church of Rome as its bishop, it is only in his capacity as Supreme Pontiff, speaking *ex cathedra*, from the chair of St. Peter as the head of the Universal Church, that he can define a doctrine. Regarding such doctrine, the following qualification applies: it is *only* when he "defines a doctrine concerning faith or morals to be held by the whole Church, [that he] possesses, by the divine assistance promised to him in Blessed Peter, that infallibility which the divine Redeemer willed his Church to enjoy in defining doctrine" (PA 4). The *object* of infallibility flows from this.

3. The Object of Infallibility: As Bishop Vincent Gasser of Brixin, who explained this chapter of *Pastor Aeternus* on behalf of the *Deputatio*, stated, "Absolute infallibility belongs only to God, and the first and essential truth who can never deceive nor be deceived in any way. All other infallibility has limits and conditions by which it is judged to be present. This is true also of the infallibility of the Roman Pontiff."[33] The first of these "limits and conditions" was named above. Infallibility is conditioned by, and limited to, the pope's office as successor of St. Peter and Supreme Pontiff of the Catholic Church. Only his *ex cathedra* statements are infallible. Infallibility is also conditioned by its *object*: only those truths that belong to the Catholic faith itself, in which all the Church's faithful are united. As *Pastor Aeternus* explicitly stated,

> For the Holy Ghost was promised to the successors of Peter not so that they might...make known some new doctrine, but that, by his assistance, they might religiously guard and faithfully expound the revelation or Deposit of Faith transmitted by the Apostles. (PA 4)[34]

Thus, when he defines an article of faith or morals *ex cathedra*, the Roman Pontiff is declaring nothing other than the faith of the Church. This raises a question: How is the Roman Pontiff to discern this faith? Moreover, how is it that the faithful may recognize that what he is declaring to them is nothing other than the faith that they have received from the apostles? In other words, are there any demonstrable conditions that the Holy Father must meet before speaking *ex cathedra*? This question concerns the *act* of infallibility itself.

4. The Act of Infallibility: The importance of an *act* of papal infallibility is self-evident. It means that a judgment has been rendered that explicitly puts an end to freedom of opinion on a question, decisively defines that a specific dogma belongs to the normative faith of the Church, and expressly calls upon all the Church's faithful to receive it with the assent of faith. Now, such a judgment raises its own serious question: How can the faithful be confident that what a pope has defined is truly a matter of the Church's faith and not simply his own private opinion—in which he may err? In other words, are there any demonstrable conditions that the pope must meet before he speaks *ex cathedra*, in order that his statements may be received by the Church with the requisite act of faith?

The importance of this question was not lost on the council, and the bishops were of a number of minds on it. On the one hand, there were those bishops who shared the concern voiced by Maret. The unlimited sovereignty advocated by the extreme ultramontanists, with its concomitant charism of unqualified infallibility, divorced the pope from the Church and opened the door to an arbitrariness of rule contrary to the nature of primacy as such.[35] This danger appeared all the more real, given that the council had yet to consider the very nature of the Church itself—and its own proper infallibility—that papal primacy had been established by the Lord to serve. To counter this danger, these bishops argued for the inclusion of a clause that called for the consultation and consent of the entire episcopate prior to any act of papal exercise of infallibility.

In opposition, the broader ultramontanist majority refused the imposition of any such condition upon the Holy Father. To their collective nose, this reeked of Gallicanism—all the more so as its principle proponents were, like Maret, members of the French episcopate, and threatened to compromise the pope's freedom to act in the defense of the faith. It was precisely with this concern of the majority in mind that the *Deputatio* added to the canon of "On the infallible teaching authority of the Roman Pontiff" that *ex cathedra* judgments of the Roman Pontiff are "irreformable" of themselves "and not by the consent of the Church" (PA 4).

The council was divided. Reconciling the bishops to a common mind, though difficult, did not prove impossible. For those seeking to discern this mind almost 130 years after its formation, however, an appreciation of history is necessary.

As was noted above, the general unpopularity of ultramontanism during the first decades of the nineteenth century was due, in part, to the persistence of Gallicanism, particularly among the theologians and bishops who had been educated in Sulpician seminaries. The spirit of Gallicanism was expressed by the "Four Gallican Articles,"[36] of which the fourth is important for this discussion. It stated that no judgment of the Roman Pontiff can be considered irreformable until it has received the consent of the

Church. Although this article, together with the other three, was rescinded by the King of France in 1693,[37] its spirit endured.

While it would be incorrect to brand Maret and the other bishops of the minority Gallicans, it would not be incorrect to say that their theological convictions had been influenced by Gallican sentiments. The *Deputatio* feared that such convictions could lead to another, broader "outbreak" of Gallicanism, hence its rejection of any juridical dependence of papal definitions upon a judgment by the episcopate. To admit such dependence would amount to a denial of the juridical primacy and infallibility magisterium of the Roman Pontiff, attributing it uniquely to the magisterium of the whole episcopate.[38]

Does not this still leave open the door to arbitrariness of rule and, thereby, obviate any real significance for the Church's reception of *ex cathedra* definitions? According to Bishop Gasser of the *Deputatio*, no. Infallibility is not a matter of the pope receiving direct, divine inspiration. Therefore, it is necessary for the pope to consult the Church before defining any article of faith *ex cathedra*. Among the appropriate means for doing so, councils take pride of place, but use may also to be made of the College of Cardinals, bishops, and theologians. The necessity of such consultation should not, though, be understood as a condition for validity, much less the manner in which it should take place be fixed. If either were the case, this could compromise the ability of the pope to fulfill his Petrine charge to "confirm his brothers" in times of need. The means should be adaptable to the circumstances, not the other way around. The council must trust that the necessary means will be used.[39]

Gasser was calling for an act of faith. He did not calm every fear. This is obvious from the fact that two bishops voted *non placet* (no) when *Pastor Aeternus* was voted upon on July 18, 1870, while some bishops, like Bravard, left Rome before that proverbial moment of truth.[40] Not everyone was of the same mind. Yet, the crucial question is whether *Pastor Aeternus* adequately reflected the mind of the clear majority of the assembled bishops, who, in keeping with their episcopal charge as shepherds and teachers of Christ's flock, truly believed that it reflected the Church's faith. It did enough for Maret to declare, "The minority has triumphed in its defeat!" It now remains to consider, in the aftermath of the council, whether and in what manner the Church itself was able to perceive this.

IV. THE RECEPTION OF PAPAL PRIMACY

On May 14, 1872, the German episcopate received a letter from Otto von Bismarck, chancellor of the German Empire, in which he stated his opinion that the teachings of *Pastor Aeternus* had obviated the authority of the bishops and made them "the agents of a foreign sovereign, of a sovereign, indeed, who through his infallibility is more perfectly absolute than any absolute monarch in the world."[41] Given the situation in Germany at the time, Bismarck's opinion had to be taken seriously. The bishops drafted their reply.

> No doubt the decisions of the Council mean that the Pope's power of ecclesiastical jurisdiction is *potestas suprema, ordinaria et immediata*, a supreme power of government given to the Pope by Jesus Christ the Son of God, in the person of St. Peter, a power which extends directly over the whole Church and so over each diocese and over all the faithful, in order to preserve unity of faith, discipline and government in the Church, and is in no way a mere attribution of certain reserved rights.
>
> But this is not at all a new doctrine. It is a truth recognized in the Catholic faith and a principle known in canon law, a doctrine recently explained and confirmed by the Vatican Council, in agreement with the findings of earlier ecumenical councils, against the errors of Gallicans, Jansenists and Febronians. According to this teaching of the Catholic Church, the Pope is Bishop of Rome but not bishop of another diocese or another town; he is not bishop of Breslau [or] bishop of Cologne, etc. But as Bishop of Rome he is at the same time Pope, that is, the pastor and supreme head of the universal Church, head of all the bishops and the faithful, and his papal

power should be respected and listened to everywhere and always, not only in particular and exceptional cases. In this position the Pope has to watch over each bishop in the fulfillment of the whole range of his episcopal charge. If a bishop is prevented, or if some need has made itself felt, the Pope has the right and the duty, in his capacity as Pope and not as bishop of the diocese, to order whatever is necessary for the administration of that diocese....

The decisions of the Vatican Council do not offer the shadow of a pretext to claim that the Pope has by them become an absolute sovereign and, in virtue of his infallibility, a sovereign more perfectly absolute than any absolute monarch in the world....

In the exercise of papal power, therefore, absolutely nothing has changed. It follows that the opinion that the Pope's position in relation to the episcopate has been changed by the Vatican Council is completely without foundation.[42]

The bishops' reply offered the chancellor no ambiguity into which he could read his own prejudices and fears. How would Pius IX read it?

Venerable Brothers, greetings and apostolic blessing.

The admirable firmness of soul which in the fight for the defense of truth, of justice and of the rights of the Church, fears neither the wrath of the powerful, nor their threats, nor the loss of goods, nor even exile, prison and death, and which has been the glory of Christ in centuries past, has ever since remained her special character and the evident proof that in this Church alone may be found that true and noble liberty whose name is heard everywhere today, but which in truth is to be met nowhere else.

You have again upheld the glory of the Church, venerable Brothers, when you undertook to expound the true meaning of the decrees of the Vatican Council so artificially distorted in a circular which has been made

public, and thus prevented the faithful from developing wrong ideas and ensuring that an odious falsification
should not provide an opportunity for preventing the
free choice of a new pontiff.

Your corporate declaration is marked by clarity and
exactness so that it leaves nothing to be desired, that it
has been a great source of joy to us and that there is no
need for us to add anything to it. But the lies asserted
in some periodicals require of us a more solemn tes-
timonial of our approval for, in order to maintain the
assertions in the said circular which you have refuted,
they have had the impudence to refuse to accept your
explanations, on the pretext that your interpretation of
the conciliar decrees is only a weakened interpretation
in no way corresponding to the intentions of the apostolic See.

We condemn in the most formal manner this lying
and slanderous supposition. Your declaration gives the
pure Catholic doctrine, and therefore that of the Holy
Council and the Holy See, perfectly grounded and
clearly developed by evident and irrefutable arguments
in such a way as to demonstrate to every man of good
faith that, in the decrees under attack, there is absolutely
nothing which is new or which changes anything in the
relations which have existed until now, or which could
provide a pretext for further oppression of the Church
or for hindering the election of a new pontiff.[43]

As if this was not praise enough, Pius went so far as to confirm
it with the fullness of his apostolic authority.[44] In this light, how
then was it possible that in within barely two generations, a
catechism making the following assertions could have received an
imprimatur?

Pope: successor of God, pastor of all the faithful and the
one sent to ensure the common good of the universal
Church and the good of each of the churches.
Q. What is a bishop?

> A. A bishop is a priest specially consecrated in order to occupy among us the place of Our Holy Father the Pope.[45]

This is the nightmare of the council's minority come true. How was this possible? Two reasons: the first is theological and the second a matter of popular opinion.

A. A Matter of Theology

One may say that *Pastor Aeternus* was subjected to three basic schools of interpretation.[46] The first was that of extreme ultramontanism. It took its cue from the extreme ultramontanists who were active both before and during Vatican I. It held that the infallibility of the pope is the source of the infallibility of the Church. The pope is *the* teacher of the Church. The rest of the faithful, including the bishops, are primarily hearers and heeders. There is no consultation with, or the collaboration of, the episcopate in the development of Church teaching or in the definition of a dogma. For that matter, there is no consultation with, or the collaboration of, the episcopate in the Church's governance—aside from the bishops' responsibility to implement the Holy Father's directives within the particular churches he had assigned them.

The dangers of this interpretation are obvious. With regard to primatial jurisdiction, because the Roman Pontiff is the Church's *Supreme* Pontiff, the rights and privileges of bishops as the pontiffs of their local churches are conceived as having been granted to them by the Holy Father, rather than belonging to them by virtue of the fact that they are bishops. In other words, the pope is the only *real* bishop in the Church.

The perceived danger to infallibility was directly related to this vision of the primacy. It disregarded the collegial character of the Church's magisterium. The Holy Father was *the* font from which truth and certitude flow. This, in turn, blurred the lines between an infallible *ex cathedra* decision and the pope's other doctrinal teachings, leading to what occasionally referred to today as "sweeping" or "galloping" infallibility. It called for one-way communication in the Church and for doctrinal centralization.

Although there were never many advocates for this interpretive school, it was very influential and, as evidenced by the catechism cited above, it set the tone for how many Catholics would hear the teachings of Vatican I. This influence was an indirect result of the second, "middle way" school of interpretation advocated by the broad majority at Vatican I. Although it had rejected extreme ultramontanism during the council, because it adhered strictly to the text of *Pastor Aeternus*, it unintentionally provided the room needed for lopsided understanding of papal primacy to develop after the council. After all, there was no *second* Constitution on the Church to provide the context within which *Pastor Aeternus* was to be properly understood. Thus, while the "middle way" may not have been theologically allied with extreme ultramontanism, its way of reading *Pastor Aeternus* permitted extreme ultramontanism's practical effects to carry the day during the postconciliar period—not because the text itself advocated them, but because it did not explicitly contradict them.

The third school of interpretation corresponded to the concerns voiced by the conciliar minority. It more strongly reflected the traditions of the first millennium, like the Vatican I minority did. According to this interpretation, the Church is first and foremost a communion of churches that are led by the bishops in communion with the pope. The pope is first and foremost the head of this body of bishops, and the church of Rome, which the pope leads as its proper bishop, is the center of Church unity. Together with the pope, the bishops are not only responsible for their local churches, but also for the unity of the Universal Church.

This interpretation thoroughly rejected extreme ultramontanism. Infallibility was understood as having been given to the Church as a whole, and is exercised by the bishops in communion with the pope only for the sake of the unity of the Church and in relation to the entire Church. The primary place for issuing infallible decrees is an ecumenical council. In a council, this communion is clearly seen and its testimony to the faith of the Church clearly heard. However, the charism of infallibility may be invoked in another way: through an *ex cathedra* judgment by the Roman Pontiff. Should he act in this way, it is—as it must be—evident that he is not acting in his own name and according to his own opinion, but in the name and according to the mind of the Church, as head of the body of bishops by reason of his office as successor of Peter. This relationship finds expression in the fact that, before declaring anything *ex cathedra*, he makes sure of the cooperation of the bishops, who, as successors of the apostles, are also witnesses and teachers of the Church's faith.

There can be little doubt that this interpretive school reflected not simply the mind of the minority, but also the very meaning of the text itself as explained by the *Deputatio* and accepted by the majority of bishops. Yet, because the text of *Pastor Aeternus* did not *explicitly* affirm this mind, it was vulnerable to interpretations that were not as faithful to the council as their supporters believed. Pius himself did not help matters. Five years before he praised the German bishops' response to Bismarck, which so clearly reflected the contributions of the minority, Pius personally urged Maret to repudiate *On the General Council and Religious Peace*.[47] Pius did not appear so divided, though, when he considered what was being written by his extreme ultramontanist supporters. They wrote much of what they wanted.

In the end, it was the first interpretive school that, in one way or another, was the more popularly held and advocated within the postconciliar Church, so much so that catechisms like the one cited above were considered to faithfully represent authentic Catholic teaching:

> Pope: successor of God, pastor of all the faithful and the one sent to ensure the common good of the universal Church and the good of each of the churches.
> Q. What is a bishop?
> A. A bishop is a priest specially consecrated in order to occupy among us the place of Our Holy Father the Pope.

B. A Matter of Public Opinion

However popular the theological opinions of the "middle way" may have been during the council and however strategic the extreme ultramontanists were in using the former's hermeneutical limitations to their own advantage after the council had

effectively ended,[48] the speed with which ultramontane interpretations of *Pastor Aeternus* were accepted by the Church was due to
more than the theological acumen of its supporters. In the wake of
the collapse of Europe's monarchies and their concomitant ecclesial self-interests, the Holy See's ability to directly appoint bishops
sympathetic to its understanding of *Pastor Aeternus* increased, as
did its freedom to disseminate papal judgments and exhortations.
Yet, these factors alone do not account for the relatively quick
reception of these interpretations of Vatican I. To this must be
added a factor alluded to near the beginning of this chapter: the
manner in which the *person* of the Roman Pontiff had become an
aspect of Catholic identity.

By the time Vatican I opened, Pius IX was becoming increasingly popular. He was seen by many Catholics in Europe and North
America as a living symbol of their own experiences of prejudice,
rejection, and suffering. When Piedmontese troops breached the
Porta Pia in the early hours of September 20, 1870, seizing the last
vestige of the Papal States, this image was sealed in their religious
imagination. The Supreme Pontiff had become the "prisoner of
the Vatican." Ironically, it was this image of the pontiff as prisoner
that would give Pius and his successors the freedom to become
a moral and spiritual force with which to be reckoned. The only
authority the pope now had to lean upon was that inherent in
his role as St. Peter's successor, the visible center of the Church's
unity, and the Catholic world was more than ready to embrace
him in precisely that way—and embrace him they did.

The development of the railroad enabled pilgrims from
throughout Europe the means with which to descend upon Rome,
and the general setting of European affairs following the tumultuous events of 1870–71 permitted them to do so safely. Often their
journeys included the opportunity to be blessed by the pope himself. Photography enabled them to take the pope home with them,
and the Holy See to distribute his image abroad. The pope was no
longer an unknown figure in a distant city. He benevolently smiled
down upon his flock from the walls of parish houses and private
homes all over the world. His words could be read in pamphlets
and in the well-thumbed pages of missals. The advent of the radio
enabled people to hear these words from his own lips. When this
trend is seen within the wider context of the rising tide of late

nineteenth- and early twentieth-century Catholic devotionalism, it is not difficult to see how the Holy Father was able so quickly to be seen by millions of people throughout the world as *their* Holy Father.

At Vatican I, ultramontanism had finally found its day, its voice, and a very receptive audience. Dogmatically speaking, the minority may have triumphed in its defeat, but it would take ninety-two years before the triumph Maret had claimed for it would enjoy its own day, and its supporters be given the opportunity to speak to a Church ready to listen.

CHAPTER 2

PAPAL PRIMACY AT THE SECOND VATICAN COUNCIL

The salient point of this Council is not, therefore, a decision of one article or another of the fundamental doctrine of the Church which has repeatedly been taught by the Fathers and by ancient and modern theologians, and which is presented to be well known and familiar to all. For this a Council was not necessary. But from the renewed, serene and tranquil adherence to all the teaching of the Church in its entirety and preciseness, as it still shines forth in the acts of the Council of Trent and First Vatican Council, the Christian, Catholic and apostolic spirit of the whole world expects a step forward toward a doctrinal penetration and a formation of consciences in faithful and perfect conformity to the authentic doctrine which, however, should be studied and expounded through the methods of research and through the literary forms of modern thought. The substance of the ancient doctrine of the Deposit of the Faith is one thing, and the way in which it is presented is another. And it is the latter that must be taken into great consideration with patience if necessary, everything being measured in the forms and proportions of a magisterium which is predominantly pastoral in character.[1]

I. INTRODUCTION

For many, perhaps most of the bishops assembled for the opening of the Second Vatican Council, it was not until they had heard Pope John XXIII's speech that the significance of the event they were about to shape finally struck them. Among these bishops was Thomas Manning, a Franciscan friar and the prelate nullius of Coroico, Bolivia. In 2000, Bishop Manning recalled his experiences of the Council: "When word got to us in the missions that we were going to have a Council, we all wondered 'Why?' Things were going well," recalled Bishop Manning, "and since the last Council declared the pope infallible, we never thought we'd have another Council. But, there we were. And the pope wanted to know what we thought should be discussed. Being in the missions, I mentioned a few things that would make our life easier, like permission to decide annulments on our own and ordain a few of the older Aymara. They were married, but they were natural leaders, and the native people didn't take well to celibate white-men telling them how to live."

I asked about his experience of the first session. "That was something! We were told we could bring a theological expert with us. So I invited a friar-friend to accompany me to Rome. He'd been in Bolivia a long time, and I thought he'd enjoy a little vacation— take in some sights, maybe see the pope. Well, on the flight home, I told him that I was sorry, but I had to find a real theologian to go with me next time. This was serious."

II. ON THE EVE OF A NEW PENTECOST

On January 25, 1959, Pope John XXIII gathered with cardinals in the Basilica of St. Paul Outside the Walls to celebrate the Feast of the Conversion of St. Paul and the close of the Octave of Christian Unity. In his address, the Holy Father stated that the occasion prompted him "to open our mind to you, confident of your kindness and understanding, regarding certain outstanding points of apostolic activity which have been suggested to us by these three months of presence in and contact with Roman ecclesiastical circles." He noted the societal changes taking place in and around Rome, and how these changes were echoed in the wider world "to whose spiritual governance he is made responsible through the divine mission entrusted to him in the succession of the supreme apostolate!" These changes were not superficial. They revealed a fundamental reorientation of people's lives, which were increasingly concerned more with "the pursuit of so-called earthly goods" than with the grace of Christ. Therefore,

> Venerable brothers and our beloved sons! We announce to you, indeed trembling a little with emotion, but at the same time with humble resolution of intention, the name and the proposal of a twofold celebration: a diocesan synod for the city, and an ecumenical Council for the Universal Church.[2]

The pope noted later the cardinals' reaction, and not without the dry humor for which he was known: "Humanly we could have expected that the cardinals, after hearing our allocution, might have crowded around to express approval and good wishes. Instead there was a devout and impressive silence."[3] It is not difficult to appreciate just how "devout" that silence may have been given the ecclesial climate of the day.

A. Catholicism between the Councils

On that January evening, the Catholic Church presented the world with a face brimming with confidence. In the decades following Vatican I, it had achieved a détente with Europe's secular regimes and began to assert itself again in the public square. It was experiencing a period of marked growth outside the cultural West, particularly in Africa and Asia. For all these achievements, the true source of its confidence was the belief that it was *the* Church that Christ had established upon the Rock of St. Peter, whose successor, the Roman Pontiff, still led it.

Manning had asked, "Why a Council?" In short, it was because this confidence had come at a high price, one the Catholic Church was paying for at the expense of its doctrinal heritage and the health of its ecclesial life, and in doing so supported the extreme ultramontanist ecclesiology that had been in ascendency since the unintended and premature closure of Vatican I.[4]

Although the bishops of Vatican I had no intention of separating the pope from the Church or from themselves as the Church's pastors, the Council's premature closure provided an opportunity for its extreme ultramontanist interpreters to do precisely that. The result was a misdevelopment of theological thinking on the nature of the Church and of the primacy that served its unity. Most theologians fell in line with this vision, and, supporting what they perceived to be the Church's authentic Tradition, began to drive this view of the papacy toward even further conclusions, among which was an ecclesiology in which the Roman Pontiff was conceived of as the source of all authority within the Church, including that of bishops. Why not? After all, the pope was the "successor of God," was he not?

Regarding Catholic ecclesial life, the price was oppressive suspicion toward anyone who did not conform to the mind of papal Rome, particularly as understood by powerful members of the Roman Curia. This atmosphere was particularly prevalent during the last years of the pontificate of Pius XII, when, in an effort to address developments in such disparate fields as genetics and liturgical reform, the pope increasingly ceded administrative oversight of the Church to the Curia. As progressive as Pius XII's mind may have been on these and other issues, the extent to which he permitted the Curia to direct the life of the Church made its cardinal prefects confident that they had the reins of the Church firmly in hand. John XXIII's intention to convoke a council was a shock to that system.

Stunned, once these cardinals had recovered, they sought to steer the Council in a safer direction. Yet, Pope John remained firm in his intention. The Council was to be a new Pentecost for a Church and, indeed, for a world, at the turning of what he firmly believed to be a new era in their shared history.

B. The Mind of the Holy Father

John XXIII was not the first pope to consider calling another Council. Both Pius XI and Pius XII explored the idea of completing the unfinished agenda of Vatican I. The efforts under Pius

XII were more thorough. However, several factors, not the least of which was the devastation of Europe following World War II, ended this exploration. It is not clear whether Cardinal Roncalli was aware of these projects prior to his election as pope. Regardless, the Council he himself would name the *Second* Vatican Council was very much his idea.

1. A New Council for a New World: The timing and the character of this Council bore the stamp of the Holy Father's understanding of history. He read in the signs of the times an epochal turning of events. A new world was emerging from the death and destruction of two world wars. The outbreak of a new "Cold War" between oppressive socialisms and libertine democracies, the rise of liberation movements in developing nations, rapid advances in the sciences, and a growth in material wealth that outpaced the imagination of previous generations signaled the advent of a new age to a man who had spent much of his life studying the effects that a reform-minded Council (in his case, Trent) could have upon history. To John XXIII, convoking a Council at precisely this moment made perfect sense. For however much the Church may not be "of the world," it was most certainly "in the world." Therefore, it was to the world, not as an adversary but as a mother that the Church had to speak.

It did not matter whether Rome's cardinals were ready. It did not matter whether many bishops or members of the theological community, or even many of the faithful were ready. For John XXIII, the world was ready and the Spirit was calling the Church to respond. Therefore, he determined that this Council *could* not simply pick up where the previous one had left off. To speak to a new world, the Council would have to be something new: the *Second* Vatican Council.

2. A New Council for a Renewed Church: The Council's newness was evident from the outset. Unlike previous councils, which had been called to condemn errors, define doctrines, and address specific areas for reform, Vatican II would speak with a magisterium entirely pastoral in character and give the Catholic Church's doctrinal inheritance a voice capable of speaking to the joys and the hopes, the griefs and the anxieties of the people of this new age (see *Gaudium et Spes* 1). As the Holy Father himself stated in his opening allocution to the Council, "The Twenty-first

Ecumenical Council…wishes to transmit the doctrine, pure and integral, without any attenuation or distortion, which throughout twenty centuries…has become the common patrimony of men [*sic*]. It is a patrimony not well received by all, but always a rich treasure available to men of good will."

To fulfill this charge, however, the pope reminded the assembled bishops that the "substance of the ancient doctrine of the deposit of the faith is one thing, and the way in which it is presented is another." Therefore, he exhorted them to respond to the expectation of the "whole world" and take "a step forward toward a doctrinal penetration and a formation of consciences in faithful and perfect conformity to the authentic doctrine, which, however, should be studied and expounded through the methods of research and through the literary forms of modern thought."[5]

The pope wanted the Council to call the Church to a renewed sense of evangelical witness, ecumenical engagement, and social transformation. To accomplish this, it needed to recover elements of its heritage capable of nourishing and ensuring the Church's fidelity to the gospel. Thus, the Council began to assume a character of definitive importance, unfolding gradually in the light not simply of the Holy Father's own reflections, but of the responses that its announcement had elicited from the Church, from the broader Christian community, and indeed from the wider world to which he desired it to speak with the power of a new Pentecost.

Among the responses offered during the Council's preparatory period was one from Augustine Bea, SJ, whom the pope would task with heading the new Secretariat for Promoting Christian Unity. Bea mentioned the following as deserving consideration:

> …[the] doctrine concerning the church, especially the position of bishops. In my opinion bishops must be involved to a greater extent in government both of the universal church and more specifically in their own diocese. It should not be possible for an order to be given or a decision taken on a question concerning a diocese without consulting the local ordinary. Such centralization is certainly not a blessing for the church.[6]

Bea also proposed the question of "the royal rule of Christ" over the Church, and the Holy Spirit as "the principle that guides and enlightens the mystical body of Christ." Among the implications of his vision, one emerges clearly: the need to understand the primacy as standing in necessary relationship both to the mystery of the Church and to the body of bishops that serves that mystery.[7] This understanding would emerge during the Council under the heading of *collegiality*, and it would be the means by which Vatican II would receive the teachings of Vatican I, and, in return, offer the Church the doctrinally richer vision of a primacy-in-collegiality at the service of a Church conceived of as a *communion* of churches. This was the unfinished work of Vatican I.

III. PRIMACY-IN-COLLEGIALITY AT THE SERVICE OF COMMUNION

If Vatican II was to be a gathering of pastors capable of transmitting "the doctrine, pure and integral, without any attenuation or distortion," then it could not, as Pope John stated, simply discuss "one article or another of the fundamental doctrine of the Church."[8] These doctrines would have to be presented with due regard to how they related to one another. This applied as well to Vatican I's doctrines of papal primacy. They had to be presented with due regard for the Church's teaching on the bishops, who with the pope "govern the house of the living God" (*Lumen Gentium* [LG] 18), and what is more, presented in the light of the mystery of the Church the pope and his brother bishops served. This had been the intention of Vatican I. By fulfilling it, Vatican II would stand fully in continuity with the Council that preceded it. The result of this Council's effort to meet this tremendous task is found in its Dogmatic Constitution on the Church, *Lumen Gentium*.

Vatican II's teaching on papal primacy is best understood by following the Council's own line of reasoning, as found in the text of *Lumen Gentium*. This entails a twofold consideration, first of the Council's presentation of the mystery of the Church, which the Council understood not as a perfect society, but as a *communion* in and with the Lord, and second of the Council's explicit teaching on the primacy, which it rooted within the context of *collegiality*.

A. The Church as Communion

Just as the Council did not emerge from John XXIII's mind fully formed in every detail, neither did *Lumen Gentium* and its ecclesiology of *communion* emerge from the Council as a proverbial "done deal." Its teachings on the nature of the Church and its ministry emerged through spirited discussion and debate, particularly concerning the preparatory document *De Ecclesiae*, which the Council took up toward the end of the opening session, November 30, 1962.

The substance of *De Ecclesiae* was captured by one of its notable supporters, Giuseppe Cardinal Siri: "The schema gives an excellent exposition of the truth about the visible Church that has been juridically established by the Lord himself, and this in the light of the Mystical Body of Christ." The reaction of the majority of bishops was captured equally well by Bishop Emiel-Jozef De Smedt, who criticized the schema as too triumphal, clerical, and juridical. The bishops wanted a richer vision of the Church, one that appreciated the Church as mystery, valued diversity as an essential aspect of its unity, and acknowledged the significance of the Eucharist for its life. In a word, the Council decided to begin anew.[9]

During its second session, the Council adopted a new schema as the basis of discussion. This schema was eventually accepted by the Council on November 21, 1964, as *Lumen Gentium*. The Council unfolded its vision of the Church in this Constitution's first three chapters, in which it spoke of the Church as communion in light of (1) its sacramental identity, (2) its life as the people of God, and (3) the dynamic of its being a Church of churches.

1. The Communion of the Church as Sacrament of Salvation

Christ is the Light of nations. Because this is so, this Sacred Synod gathered together in the Holy Spirit eagerly desires, by proclaiming the Gospel to every creature (Mark 16:15), to bring the light of Christ to all men, a light brightly visible on the countenance of the Church. Since the Church is in Christ like a sacrament or as a sign and instrument both of a very closely knit union with God and of the unity of the whole human race, it desires now to unfold more fully to the faithful of the Church and to the whole world its own inner nature and universal mission. This it intends to do following faithfully the teaching of previous councils. The present-day conditions of the world add greater urgency to this work of the Church so that all men, joined more closely today by various social, technical and cultural ties, might also attain fuller unity in Christ. (LG 1)

The break with the recent past was clear: the Church is fundamentally not a juridical reality, but a living reality rooted in the saving mystery of God. Thus, *Lumen Gentium* began not with the rigid categories of social hierarchy, but with dynamic imagery from the Scriptures. The Church is God's sheepfold, vineyard, and temple. It is Christ's bride and body, united to him through baptism and "the breaking of the Eucharistic bread" and filled with "the riches of His glory" (LG 7). This way of speaking was not a rejection of the Church's hierarchical character. Rather, it was a recognition that the language of hierarchy has limits, limits that the richer imagery of Scripture is able to transcend. This enabled the Council to speak of the Church fundamentally as a *mystery*.

It is important to note that the Council did not apply the term *mystery* to the Church as if the Church were something secret or abstruse. Rather, it applied the term in a manner that reflected its biblical and patristic roots, that is, as *sacrament*. Because the Church is rooted in the mystery of God who desires to save all humanity, the Church is the sacrament of this desire.[10] As to how the Church is this "universal sacrament of salvation" (LG 48), the Council indicated two ways: (1) the preaching of God's kingdom and (2) the celebration of the Eucharist.

The proclamation of the kingdom is integral to the Church's identity. Christ inaugurated the Church by his preaching of the kingdom and entrusted the Church with this proclamation when, after his resurrection, "He poured out on His disciples the Spirit promised by the Father" (LG 5). Thus, the Church is the effective means for realizing God's kingdom.

From this source the Church, equipped with the gifts of its Founder and faithfully guarding His precepts of charity, humility and self-sacrifice, receives the mission to proclaim and to spread among all peoples the Kingdom of Christ and of God and to be, on earth, the initial budding forth of that kingdom. While it slowly grows, the Church strains toward the completed Kingdom and, with all its strength, hopes and desires to be united in glory with its King. (LG 5)

The Eucharist is integral to this proclamation. As the sacramental presence of God's kingdom in the world,

the Church, or, in other words, the kingdom of Christ now present in mystery, grows visibly through the power of God in the world. This inauguration and this growth are both symbolized by the blood and water which flowed from the open side of a crucified Jesus, and are foretold in the words of the Lord referring to His death on the Cross: "And I, if I be lifted up from the earth, will draw all things to myself (Jn 12, 32)." As often as the sacrifice of the cross in which Christ our Passover was sacrificed, is celebrated on the altar, the work of our redemption is carried on, and, in the sacrament of the eucharistic bread, the unity of all believers who form one body in Christ (see 1 Cor 10, 17) is both expressed and brought about. All men are called to this union with Christ, who is the light of the world, from whom we go forth, through whom we live, and toward whom our whole life strains. (LG 3)

All people are called to this union with Christ. For through this union, all people enter into communion with God and with one another, and so advance together toward the full realization of the kingdom and "all the fullness of God" (LG 7).

This understanding of the Church as the sacrament of salvation had two effects on the Council. First, it enabled the Council to overcome any dichotomy between the visible and invisible aspects of the Church: "As the assumed nature inseparably united to Him,

serves the divine Word as a living organ of salvation, so, in a similar way, does the visible social structure of the Church serve the
Spirit of Christ, who vivifies it, in the building up of the body"
(LG 8). Second, it allowed the Council to see other Christians
not as schismatics and heretics, but as separated brothers and
sisters. This vision did not imply a compromise of the Council's
understanding of the ecclesial identity of the Catholic Church. It
was a realization that the mystery of the Church is truly *mystery*.
Its presence is not the exclusive property of any one ecclesial
body. This engendered a commitment to seek unity with all who
are in Christ.

> This is the one Church of Christ which in the Creed
> is professed as one, holy, catholic and apostolic....This
> Church constituted and organized in the world as a
> society, subsists in the Catholic Church, which is gov-
> erned by the successor of Peter and by the Bishops
> in communion with him, although many elements of
> sanctification and of truth are found outside of its vis-
> ible structure. These elements, as gifts belonging to the
> Church of Christ, are forces impelling toward catholic
> unity. (LG 8)

To participate in the Church is to share in the saving love God
offered the world in and through Jesus Christ. What is more,
to participate in the Church is to be impelled by Christ to be
visibly in communion with all those who bear his name and, with
them, to share this love with all people. How the Church lives
this dynamic was addressed by the Council in the next chapter of
Lumen Gentium: the Church as the *people of God*.

2. The Communion of the Church as the People of God:
Having considered the mystery of the Church in its totality, from
creation to heavenly consummation, the Council here discussed
this mystery in view of the time between Christ's ascension and
second coming.[11] It did this by way of two questions: (1) *what* is
the Church; and (2) *how* is the Church?[12] These questions were
not addressed to the life of this people strictly *ad intra*, for the
Church's inner life is directly oriented toward its proclamation of
the kingdom. Thus, it must be asked, *what* and *how* is the Church

both *ad intra* and *ad extra,* in other words, in relation to the life of the world?

a. The People of God **ad intra***:* Considered *ad intra,* the Church is the people of God, formed by the "new covenant, the new testament, that is to say" that Christ instituted in his blood. It is a communion of "Jew and gentile" established as one new people "making them one, not according to the flesh but in the Spirit" (LG 9). This vision enabled the Council to go beyond the more juridical view of the Church as having been founded by Christ at a specific point in history in order to see it unfolding within the entirety of God's plan of salvation as revealed in the Scriptures. This led to the rediscovery of the essential continuity between Israel and the Church, of the historical dimensions of revelation, and of a redemption whose final stage must be sought in eschatology.[13]

This continuity, this *communion* of the Church with Israel, also enabled the Council to speak of the Church as a priestly people: "The baptized, by regeneration and the anointing of the Holy Spirit, are consecrated as a spiritual house and a holy priesthood, in order that through all those works which are those of the Christian man they may offer spiritual sacrifices and proclaim the power of Him who has called them out of darkness into His marvelous light" (LG 10, citing 1 Pet 2:4–10). As a further consequence of this anointing, the Church as a whole "cannot err in matters of belief."

> That discernment in matters of faith [*sensus fidei*] is aroused and sustained by the Spirit of truth. It is exercised under the guidance of the sacred teaching authority, in faithful and respectful obedience to which the people of God accepts that which is not just the word of men but truly the word of God. (see 1 Th 2,13) Through it, the people of God adheres unwaveringly to the faith given once and for all to the saints, (Ju 3) penetrates it more deeply with right thinking, and applies it more fully in its life. (LG 12)[14]

In order for one to share fully in this life, it is not enough for one to be visibly numbered among the Church's members. One must also possess the "Spirit of Christ," "persevere in charity," and remain in communion with the Church in body and heart (LG 14). This leads to the question of *how* is the Church: *How* is this people Church with one another? The answer is that the Church is fundamentally a community of equals; it is one body in Christ.[15]

By virtue of their incorporation into Christ through baptism and the "breaking of the bread," all the members of the Church are equally members of Christ's Body. Through the variety of gifts bestowed upon them by the Spirit, they renew and build up the Church (LG 12). This dynamic of *being* Church is manifested in several ways, but preeminently in the "breaking of the bread," for it is in the celebration of the Eucharist that "the common priesthood of the faithful and the ministerial or hierarchical priesthood" come together both to "manifest in a concrete way that unity of the people of God which is suitably signified and wondrously brought about by this most august sacrament" (LG 10, 11).

b. The People of God **ad extra:** As was the case with Israel, God established the Church to further his saving will: "God gathered together as one all those who in faith look upon Jesus as the author of salvation and the source of unity and peace, and established them as the Church that for each and all it may be the visible sacrament of this saving unity" (LG 9). In other words, what the Church is *ad intra* is the necessary, integral basis for what it is *ad extra*: the effective, eschatological witness to what God intends for all people.

> So it is that that messianic people, although it does not actually include all men, and at times may look like a small flock, is nonetheless a lasting and sure seed of unity, hope and salvation for the whole human race. Established by Christ as a communion of life, charity and truth, it is also used by Him as an instrument for the redemption of all, and is sent forth into the whole world as the light of the world and the salt of the earth (see Mt 5, 13–16). (LG 9)

The stark division between the *city of God* and the *city of the world* (*civitas Dei* and the *civitas mundi*) that had characterized the Tridentine Church's relationship *to* the world had to be overcome. It was this recognition of the Church as the people of God, the sacrament of that saving communion into which God desires to draw all people, that enabled the Council to do so. It affirmed that the Church's proper place is *within* the world, to speak its hope to the world.[16] Thus, the Council spoke to the Catholic faithful and catechumens, that they may not fail in the grace they have received (LG 14), to all baptized believers, that the unity Christ wills for his Church may be restored (LG 15), and to "those who have not yet received the Gospel," both those who "sincerely seek God and moved by grace strive by their deeds to do His will as it is known to them through the dictates of conscience," and "those who, without blame on their part, have not yet arrived at an explicit knowledge of God and with His grace strive to live a good life." (LG 16).

"All men are called to belong to the new people of God" (LG 13), and the Church is the effective means by which this call is both offered and answered. It was this vision of the Church that formed the Council's understanding of the ultimate and all-embracing meaning of the prayer and work of the Church: the whole world is to be brought into the people of God and be offered to the Father in Christ its head.[17]

> In this way the Church both prays and labors in order that the entire world may become the People of God, the Body of the Lord and the Temple of the Holy Spirit, and that in Christ, the Head of all, all honor and glory may be rendered to the Creator and Father of the Universe. (LG 17)

3. The Communion of the Church as a Church of Churches: While the Council had stated clearly that there is only one people of God, "which takes its citizens from every race" (LG 13), it also stated with equal clarity that this one people, the one Church, is itself a communion of local or particular churches. These churches are "fashioned after the model of the universal Church, in and from which churches comes into being the one and only Catholic Church" (LG 23).

This vision of the Church as a communion of *churches* has rightly been described as a Copernican revolution in Catholic ecclesiology. Following the Council of Trent, Catholic theology had preferred to speak of the Church as a visible society centered upon Rome as the source of life of every local church, or *diocese*. Now, this new Council was saying that the Church should not be conceived in such a way, as if it were a kind of transnational corporation with its headquarters in Rome and branch offices throughout the world. Rather, the Church should be understood as arising from below, because in every local church, the reality of what we call "the Church" is realized: the communion of believers in all the holy things given to them by Christ.[18]

It is no exaggeration to say that, when compared with Vatican I, this was *the* great, new insight of Vatican II. This Council represented the movement from an ecclesiology that started from the idea of a Universal Church divided into portions called dioceses, to an ecclesiology that understood the Church as the communion of local churches. In order to understand this insight, it is necessary first to ask what Vatican II meant when it spoke about the *local church*.

a. The Local Church as Wholly Church: A word on terminology is in order. The Council was not entirely consistent in its use of the term *local church*. The term could refer to a single diocese or several dioceses in the same region or nation, for example, the American Church, or even to dioceses of the same rite, for example, the Maronite Church. In the strict sense, though, it primarily referred to a diocese,[19] and it was in the third chapter of *Lumen Gentium* that the Council offered its most mature description of the local church.

> This Church of Christ is truly present in all legitimate local congregations of the faithful which, united with their pastors, are themselves called churches in the New Testament. For in their locality these are the new People called by God, in the Holy Spirit and in much fullness. (1 Th 1, 5) In them the faithful are gathered together by the preaching of the Gospel of Christ, and the mystery of the Lord's Supper is celebrated, that by the food and blood of the Lord's body the whole brotherhood may be joined together. In any community of the altar, under the sacred ministry of the bishop, there is exhibited a symbol of that charity and "unity of the mystical Body,

without which there can be no salvation." In these communities, though frequently small and poor, or living in the Diaspora, Christ is present, and in virtue of His presence there is brought together one, holy, catholic and apostolic Church. For "the partaking of the body and blood of Christ does nothing other than make us be transformed into that which we consume." (LG 26)

Three elements emerge from this passage that are fundamental to the identity of the local church. These are (1) its communion with the churches of the New Testament, (2) the presence of Christ in its midst, and (3) its sacramental nature.

The first of these elements is of primary importance. The local church is not simply a territorial gathering of the faithful. It is, in *this* locality, the Church that arose at Jerusalem on Pentecost, when God revealed that all God had intended since gathering Israel to himself was fulfilled. In the saving passion of Jesus Christ, God has renewed humanity and called it into communion with himself as the new people of God. Wherever this communion is present, God's people is present as well. Thus, whether in Jerusalem or Rome, Mexico City, Manila, or New York, wherever the communion of God is found, there exists God's people that bears the whole salvation that God, in Jesus Christ, has destined for all humankind and that God made arise, in the Spirit of the Lord, in the apostolic community at the Pentecost.[20]

This leads to the second element: the presence of Christ. For it is Christ who gathers this new people of God, unites them in the new covenant in his blood, and establishes them as God's Church (see LG 9). It was with this in mind that the Council affirmed that every local church is truly "the Church" because it is *that* locality, in the preaching of the gospel and the celebration of the Eucharist, that Christ is present, gathering and establishing God's people. For this reason the Council did not present the local church as simply a *part* of a whole that alone possesses the fullness of what it means to be Church. Rather, it presented the local church as wholly Church because the local church, in all its members, is in communion with Christ.[21]

The sacramentality of the local church flows from this. Because the local church is the people of God in its own locality, it is the presence of the saving unity to which God calls all people. It does not matter whether this church is small or poor or dispersed. Its identity is not grounded in the "natural" order, but in the order of faith: as a *sacrament*.[22] In this light, one can say that the one Church of Christ is truly and wholly present in every local church, and what is more, that the existence of the Church of Christ resides at this level of the local church. Adhering to its pastor, that is, its bishop, and gathered by him in the Spirit, the local church is the Church's fundamental and active reality in the world.

With this in mind, one may consider how the "one unique catholic Church" arises from the communion of the local churches.

b. The Whole Church as a Church of Churches: Although each local church is *wholly* Church, no one of them can be considered to be the *whole* Church. If each local church is the sacramental presence of the communion of God, then no local church can exist *except* in communion with other local churches, for in each of them is present one and the same reality: the Body of Christ, the people of God, the sacrament of the kingdom. As the Church's principle of both identity and difference, the Spirit recognizes the Spirit and continually urges every local church to establish communion with all the churches—and, indeed, with all people.

This dynamic of mutual recognition leads the churches to another act, that of mutual reception. This entails a lived commitment on the part of the churches to profess the one faith, proclaim the one gospel, celebrate the one Eucharist, and announce together the kingdom of God, whose people they are: "This characteristic of universality which adorns the people of God is a gift from the Lord Himself. By reason of it, the Catholic Church strives constantly and with due effect to bring all humanity and all its possessions back to its source In Christ, with Him as its head and united in His Spirit" (LG 13).

It is in this sense that the Church arises from the communion of local churches, that is, as an existential mystery. Insofar as they come to be through the grace of the triune God, are served by the apostolic ministry and are nourished by the Eucharist, local churches are genuine churches. Formed after the image of the Universal Church, endowed with all the Lord wills his people to possess, they are local realizations of all that the Church is, and it is in them and from their communion that the one, holy, catholic, and apostolic Church comes to exist.[23]

Keeping in mind the observation made by the 1985 Synod of Bishops that "the ecclesiology of communion is the central and fundamental idea of the Council's documents,[24] the proper context for the Council's teaching on the primacy of the Roman Pontiff can now be properly considered: that of *collegiality*.

B. Primacy-in-Collegiality at the Service of Communion

It was with the vision of the Church as communion before them that the Council took up the next topic left unaddressed by Vatican I: the Church's hierarchical constitution, particularly with regard to the episcopate.[25]

This Sacred Council, following closely in the footsteps of the First Vatican Council, with that Council teaches and declares that Jesus Christ, the eternal Shepherd, established His holy Church, having sent forth the apostles as He Himself had been sent by the Father; (see Jn 20, 21) and He willed that their successors, namely the bishops, should be shepherds in His Church even to the consummation of the world. And in order that the episcopate itself might be one and undivided, He placed Blessed Peter over the other apostles, and instituted in him a permanent and visible source and foundation of unity of faith and communion. And all this teaching about the institution, the perpetuity, the meaning and reason for the sacred primacy of the Roman Pontiff and of his infallible magisterium, this Sacred Council again proposes to be firmly believed by all the faithful. Continuing in that same undertaking, this Council is resolved to declare and proclaim before all men the doctrine concerning bishops, the successors of the apostles, who together with the successor of Peter, the Vicar of Christ, the visible Head of the whole Church, govern the house of the living God. (LG 18)

This teaching occasioned one of the Council's most protracted and intense debates. The markedly ultramontanist majority of Vatican I had become Vatican II's clear minority. Fully conscious of their new position, they fought vigorously to ensure that nothing of what they *interpreted* Vatican I to have taught would be compromised. For all the drama this struggle engendered, the vision of primacy adopted by Vatican II was considered by the Council's overwhelming majority to be faithful to *Pastor Aeternus*.[26] This was the vision of the primacy rooted in the collegial unity of the episcopate in the service of a Church of churches.

The Council's vision may be explicated in three steps: (1) the bishops' succession to the apostles as a *college*, (2) the sacramental nature and ecclesial significance of this succession, and (3) the manner in which these combine to root the primacy of the Roman Pontiff firmly within the College of Bishops for the fulfillment of his *missio canonica* (canonical mission) as the "perpetual and visible principle and foundation" for the unity of faith and communion of both the episcopate and the entire people of God (LG 23, see also PA intro.).

1. Successors of the Apostles: The Council began to unfold its understanding of collegiality by recalling how the Lord had "appointed twelve to be with him...whom he would send to preach the Kingdom of God."

> The Lord Jesus, after praying to the Father, calling to Himself those whom He desired, appointed twelve to be with Him, and whom He would send to preach the Kingdom of God; and these apostles He formed after the manner of a college or a stable group, over which He placed Peter chosen from among them. He sent them first to the children of Israel and then to all nations, so that as sharers in His power they might make all peoples His disciples, and sanctify and govern them, and thus spread His Church, and by ministering to it under the guidance of the Lord, direct it all days even to the consummation of the world....And the apostles, by preaching the Gospel everywhere, and it being accepted by their hearers under the influence of the Holy Spirit, gather together the universal Church, which the Lord

established on the apostles and built upon blessed Peter, their chief, Christ Jesus Himself being the supreme cornerstone. (LG 19)

This established, the Council then turned its attention toward apostolic succession, which it presented as a succession in mission on behalf of the gospel. "That divine mission, entrusted by Christ to the apostles, will last until the end of the world, since the Gospel they are to teach is for all time the source of all life for the Church." Therefore, the apostles "appointed as rulers in this society, took care to appoint successors," to whom they handed on "the duty of confirming and finishing the work begun by themselves, recommending to them that they attend to the whole flock in which the Holy Spirit placed them to shepherd the Church of God" (LG 20). It was in these successors that the apostolic succession of bishops was born.

> Among those various ministries which, according to tradition, were exercised in the Church from the earliest times, the chief place belongs to the office of those who, appointed to the episcopate, by a succession running from the beginning, are passers-on of the apostolic seed. Thus, as St. Irenaeus testifies, through those who were appointed bishops by the apostles, and through their successors down in our own time, the apostolic tradition is manifested and preserved. (LG 20)

As successors of the apostles, the bishops preside "in place of God over the flock, whose shepherds they are, as teachers for doctrine, priests for sacred worship, and ministers for governing." Their office belongs to the Church's divine institution, and so is permanent. "Therefore, the Sacred Council teaches that bishops by divine institution have succeeded to the place of the apostles, as shepherds of the Church, and he who hears them, hears Christ, and he who rejects them, rejects Christ and Him who sent Christ" (LG 20).

In his analysis of the first aspect of this teaching, that is, that the College of Apostles is the origin of the College of Bishops, Karl Rahner, whose service as a Council *peritus* involved him in the drafting of this section of *Lumen Gentium*, identified five points as fundamental: (1) the Apostolic College originated from a call by the historical Jesus, and was intended by him to be a permanent body; (2) the apostles' collegial relationship was under Peter, who had been chosen from among them by Christ for this role; (3) for the fulfillment of their mission the apostles were granted a share in Christ's power; (4) this mission was guided and effected by the Holy Spirit; (5) this mission led to the gathering of the Universal Church. Fundamental as these points were, they raise several questions: What were the contours of the collegial relationship shared between Peter and the apostles? When precisely did the Lord confer on the apostles their mission beyond Israel? What does it mean to say that the Lord "founded" the Church upon the apostles and "built" it upon Peter? According to Rahner, the text offers no clear-cut answers.[27]

Such was also the case with regard to the Council's presentation of apostolic succession. Not the least among these questions was how to imagine that apostolic succession came about: as an explicit declaration of Jesus, as a consequence of the revealed, permanent, theological essence of the Church, or as an irreformable decision of the Apostolic Church?[28] These questions are further complicated by the broad consensus among scholars that the understanding of apostolic succession described in *Lumen Gentium* does not directly correspond either to the New Testament testimony concerning local church structures or to what we presently know about the hierarchical constitution of the early local churches.[29] This begs the further question: Why did the Council not make a clearer statement regarding both the constitution of the apostles as a college and the manner in which the College of Bishops arose as the apostles' legitimate successors?

Rahner offered two explanations for the apparent incompleteness of this teaching by Vatican II. First, that the bishops are considered the apostles' true successors was not a matter of debate at the Council; neither as well was the notion that the bishops succeed the apostles as a *college*—a relatively new idea that, although it caused a stir among the minority, was acceptable to the clear majority of the Council. Therefore, simply stating this to be the case was considered sufficient. In other words, it served the Council's purpose.

This leads directly to Rahner's second explanation: the purpose behind this teaching. The teaching that the College of Bishops succeeds the College of Apostles was to serve as the doctrinal basis for what it was about to say concerning the bishops, the successors of the apostles, who along with the Roman Pontiff govern the house of the living God (see LG 18). The bishops' succession to the apostles is as firm and enduring a part of the Church's divinely established constitution as is the pope's succession to the apostle Peter, and together, in collegial unity, they continue the apostles' common charge (*munus*) to teach, sanctify, and govern the people of God, in fidelity to the Lord and to the mission he gave them on behalf of his Father's kingdom.

On this basis the Council declared, "Just as in the Gospel, the Lord so disposing, St. Peter and the other apostles constitute one apostolic college, so in a similar way the Roman Pontiff, the successor of Peter, and the bishops, the successors of the apostles, are joined together." Thus, just as the Roman Pontiff has, by "virtue of his office, that is as Vicar of Christ and pastor of the whole Church, …full, supreme and universal power over the Church," so too,

> the order of bishops, which succeeds to the college of apostles and gives this apostolic body continued existence, is also the subject of supreme and full power over the universal Church, provided we understand this body together with its head the Roman Pontiff and never without this head. (LG 22)

Someone is constituted a member of the College of Bishops "in virtue of sacramental consecration [i.e., episcopal ordination] and hierarchical communion with the head and members of the body" (LG 22). In this light, the sacramentality of episcopacy and its ecclesial consequences can be considered.

2. The Sacrament of Episcopacy and the Church of Churches: The Council declared episcopal ministry to be fundamentally sacramental in nature.

> For the discharging of such great duties, the apostles were enriched by Christ with a special outpouring of the Holy Spirit coming upon them, (see Ac 1, 8; 2, 4; Jn

20, 22–23) and they passed on this spiritual gift to their helpers by the imposition of hands, (see 1 Tm 4, 12; 2 Tm 1, 6–7) and it has been transmitted down to us in Episcopal consecration. And the Sacred Council teaches that by Episcopal consecration the fullness of the sacrament of Orders is conferred, that fullness of power, namely, which both in the Church's liturgical practice and in the language of the Fathers of the Church is called the high priesthood, the supreme power of the sacred ministry. But Episcopal consecration, together with the office of sanctifying [*cum munera sanctificandi*], also confers the office of teaching and of governing [*munera quoque confert docenti et regendi*], which, however, of its very nature, can be exercised only in hierarchical communion with the head and the members of the college. For from the tradition, which is expressed especially in liturgical rites and in the practice of both the Church of the East and of the West, it is clear that, by means of the imposition of hands and the words of consecration, the grace of the Holy Spirit is so conferred, and the sacred character so impressed, that bishops in an eminent and visible way sustain the roles of Christ Himself as Teacher, Shepherd and High Priest, and that they act in His person. Therefore it pertains to the bishops to admit newly elected members into the Episcopal body by means of the sacrament of Orders. (LG 21)

That the Council chose to argue on the basis of the New Testament and the writings of the Church fathers revealed its intent to demonstrate that its teaching on the episcopacy was firmly grounded in both Scripture and Tradition, and so was faithful to Christ's will for the divine constitution of the Church. This demonstration was particularly important, as the Council's teaching broke from a theology of episcopacy that placed bishops in a dependent relationship to the Roman Pontiff for the power to exercise their office, the most recent and developed exponent of which was Pope Pius XII's 1943 encyclical *Mystici Corporis Christi*.

    a. A Significant Shift: *Mystici Corporis Christi* synthesized the centralized view of the Church that had become increasingly common since the close of the Council of Trent. Speaking about episcopacy in the light of a bishop's place within the "individual Christian communities" (i.e., dioceses), which "makeup the one Catholic Church," Pius XII stated,

> They, too, are ruled by Jesus Christ through the voice of their respective Bishops. Consequently, Bishops must be considered as the more illustrious members of the Universal Church, for they are united by a very special bond to the divine Head of the whole Body and so are rightly called "principal parts of the members of the Lord"; moreover, as far as his own diocese is concerned, each one as a true Shepherd feeds the flock entrusted to him and rules it in the name of Christ. Yet in exercising this office they are not altogether independent, but are subordinate to the lawful authority of the Roman Pontiff, although enjoying the ordinary power of jurisdiction which they receive directly from the same Supreme Pontiff. Therefore, Bishops should be revered by the faithful as divinely appointed successors of the Apostles, and to them, even more than to the highest civil authorities should be applied the words: "Touch not my anointed ones!" For Bishops have been anointed with the chrism of the Holy Spirit. (*Mystici Corporis Christi* 42)

While there are some similarities between these passages from *Lumen Gentium* and *Mystici Corporis Christi*, for example, that a bishop is a shepherd who "feeds" and "rules" the people of God entrusted to him "in the name of Christ," their understanding of what belongs to the essence of episcopacy is not among them.

Pius XII's understanding of the episcopal office (*munus*) made use of the traditional distinction between the power of orders (*potestas ordinis*) and the power of jurisdiction (*potestas jurisdictionis*), that is, the power to feed the flock and the power to rule it. Whereas the former is conferred by episcopal consecration (the sacramental quality of which may be said to be implicitly affirmed, otherwise it would be impossible for Pius to speak of any *potestas ordinis*), the latter is exclusively and ultimately conferred by a canonical mission (*missio canonica*) from the Roman Pontiff, thereby making a bishop exclusively and ultimately dependant upon pope as the possessor of preeminent powers for the ability to fulfill his office (*munus*).[30]

In *Lumen Gentium*, this distinction between the powers disappeared. Instead the Council distinguished between *munus* and *potestas*. Through episcopal ordination, the Holy Spirit confers a sacred *potestas* upon a bishop for the fulfillment of a threefold *munus*: to teach, sanctify, and govern the people of God entrusted to his care. All that a bishop needs (in the sense of *potestas*) to fulfill his office is given him by the Spirit. Thus, in no way can bishops be considered vicars of the Roman Pontiff among the people of God. By the Spirit's power and in Christ's own name, they are the visible principle and foundation of the unity of the churches they serve (see LG 23). This does not imply that a bishop is altogether independent in the exercise of his office. While he possesses all he needs to fulfill his office by virtue of episcopal ordination, he may do so only in "hierarchical communion" with the head and members of the College, according to the canonical mission (*missio canonica*) he received upon admission into the College.[31] For it is precisely as a *college* that the bishops succeed the apostles in their charge to sanctify, govern, spread, and nourish the Church "under the guidance of the Lord...even to the consummation of the world" (LG 19).

This break with the recent past was necessary on two counts. The first of these concerned the priority of sacraments within the Church. Whatever is founded upon a sacrament must have priority within the Church, for the Church comes about by faith and the sacraments, and all its essential marks are to be found within the osmosis of faith and sacraments. To deny this would be to forsake the Church's own constitution, to which Vatican II explicitly appealed. For neither the election nor the enthronement of a pope has ever been considered a sacrament. As Pope Benedict XVI demonstrated, when a pope resigns, he simply ceases to be pope.[32]

The second count concerned the relationship between episcopacy and the Council's ecclesiology of communion. All hierarchical power in the Church comes from the sacrament of episcopal ordination, not from anything distinct from the sacrament and having its source in the pope. If the bishops are the visible principle and foundation of unity in the local churches they shepherd, it is because everything they put into operation when exercising their office comes to them from the sacrament. Otherwise, the Catholic Church, whose constituent principles belong only to the sacramental order, that is, to the order of the Spirit, could not have the local churches as the point of departure for its existence.

With this in mind, the Council's understanding of how the bishops fulfill their *munus* can be more clearly considered, both individually within the churches entrusted to their care and collectively as a college for the care of that communion of churches in and from which the one and only Catholic Church comes into being.

b. Collegiality at the Service of Communion: In the light of its teaching on episcopacy as sacrament, the Council was able to speak about the bishops' exercise of their common *munus* in renewed terms. With regard to the service bishops render the churches entrusted to their care, the Council affirmed that they are vicars, not of the pope, but of Christ. For it is from Christ that they receive the power to fulfill their office, and it is "personally...in Christ's name" that they exercise it as "proper, ordinary and immediate" within their churches (LG 27). In Christ's name, the bishops also bear witness to the Gospel and are "stewards of the mysteries of God" (LG 21). This is supremely evident in the Eucharist, by which the Church "continuously lives and grows."

In any community of the altar, under the sacred ministry of the bishop, there is made manifest the symbol of that charity and "unity of the mystical Body, without which there can be no salvation." In these communities, although frequently small and poor, or dispersed, Christ is present by whose power the one, holy, catholic, and apostolic Church is gathered together. For participation in the body and blood of Christ has no other effect than to make us pass over into what we are consuming (LG 26).

As vicars of Christ, the bishops are the "visible principle and foundation of unity" of their churches (LG 23). By virtue of the sacrament of episcopacy, they gather the people of God in their proper locales to be what Christ has established them to be: the *communion* of God, the living proclamation of the kingdom, and the sacrament of humanity's salvation. This service to the local church, which opens it to express effectively its catholicity in communion with other local churches, in its turn, opens every bishop to exercise effectively his office (*munus*) for the welfare of the whole people of God.

Inasmuch as the "task of proclaiming the Gospel everywhere on earth pertains to the body of pastors, to all of whom in common Christ gave His command, thereby imposing upon them a common duty," the bishops "are obliged to enter into a community of work among themselves and with the successor of Peter." This occurs, in the spirit of collegiality, when bishops support each other in their individual labors and work for a common pastoral cause (LG 23). In a preeminent way, it occurs when the Roman Pontiff calls the bishops to act as the College and, in communion with him, exercise the Church's supreme magisterium (LG 22), even to speak with the charism of infallibility (LG 25). Such an act may be exercised solemnly in a council or by the bishops dispersed throughout the world "with the pope" at his behest, or after having presented the fruit of their common efforts to him, with his fiat. However the College expresses and exercises its common *munus*,

> insofar as it is composed of many, expresses the variety and universality of the People of God, but insofar as it is assembled under one head, it expresses the unity of the flock of Christ. In it, the bishops, faithfully recognizing the primacy and pre-eminence of their head, exercise their own authority for the good of their own faithful, and indeed of the whole Church, the Holy Spirit supporting its organic structure and harmony with moderation. (LG 22)

The Council's teachings that the bishops succeed the apostles as a college and that their office is conferred sacramentally place the bishops at the heart of *Lumen Gentium*'s ecclesiology of communion, in both its vertical and horizontal dimensions. The succession of the College secures vertical communion (across time), which guarantees that the local church committed to the bishop shares the identity of the Apostolic Church. It also secures horizontal communion (across space), which guarantees the identity of each local church with every other local church throughout the world. This horizontal communion enables the local church, working out its faith and obedience to the gospel in its own situation, to recognize itself in the other local churches that are working out the same faith and the same obedience in their own particular situations.[33]

Through their place within this dynamic of communion, the bishops "constitute the necessary guarantee" of a local church's identity as wholly Church and, moreover, of the whole Church as a people called from "every people and nation"—in every place and for all time—into communion in and with the saving mystery of the triune God. If this is true for the bishops, insofar as they are members of the episcopal College, then it is true in a particular and, one may say, preeminent way for the College's head, the Bishop of Rome.

3. Primacy-in-Collegiality: In light of *Lumen Gentium*, the Church's hierarchical constitution no longer stands forth like a pyramid, with power flowing from the pope down to the bishops. Rather, through its teachings on communion, collegiality, and the sacramentality of the episcopal office, Vatican II restored the primacy to its traditional context, and as a result changed its emphasis completely: the papacy is rooted in the episcopate. For the Bishop of Rome, as for all the bishops, everything derives from one and the same sacrament, one and the same mission to build and to keep the Church in communion, and one and the same power for the sake of this mission. This power is operative in different ways, according to the office that each bishop has within the College. In the case of the Bishop of Rome, it extends to a special degree, yet always remains within—never above, much less apart from—the sacramental grace of the episcopate.[34]

In this light, one may no longer say with complete accuracy that the pope is *the* Vicar of Christ. Rather, he is Vicar of Christ in collegial fellowship with all Christ's true vicars, with whom he governs the house of the living God (LG 18). The implications of this change are evident in the way Vatican II handled the Bishop of Rome's primacy of jurisdiction and magisterium—*the* subjects defined at Vatican I. It also enables the Church to consider a new way of speaking about the Roman Pontiff's headship of the College: the pope as *corporate personality*.

a. Primatial Jurisdiction: In accord with its reaffirmation of Vatican I, Vatican II explicitly stated in *Lumen Gentium* that in "virtue of his office, that is as Vicar of Christ and pastor of the whole Church, the Roman Pontiff has full, supreme and universal power over the Church. And he is always free to exercise this power" (LG 22). Further, the Council repeated this teaching, albeit in a more expanded form, in its Decree on the Pastoral Office of Bishops, *Christus Dominus* (CD).

> In this Church of Christ the Roman pontiff, as the successor of Peter, to whom Christ entrusted the feeding of His sheep and lambs, enjoys supreme, full, immediate, and universal authority over the care of souls by divine institution. Therefore, as pastor of all the faithful, he is sent to provide for the common good of the universal Church and for the good of the individual churches. Hence, he holds a primacy of ordinary power over all the churches. (CD 2)

What is new in these words? Considered in themselves, they say nothing new. They largely repeat what was taught by Vatican I. Considered in the light of Vatican II's teachings on collegiality and the sacramentality of the episcopate, however, they say a great deal that is new. In counterdistinction to the theology of episcopacy expressed in *Mystici Corporis Christi*, they say that the power of jurisdiction held by the Bishop of Rome, by virtue of his office as Vicar of Christ and shepherd of the Church of churches, is not of a different *kind* than that held by every bishop in his respective church, by virtue of his office as the visible foundation and principle of unity for the people of God entrusted to his care. Rather, it is of a different *degree*; it is that which is proper to the Bishop of Rome by virtue of his office as head of the College of Bishops.

This may be new, but it is by no means novel. This understanding of the primatial jurisdiction of the Roman Pontiff as *episcopal* in nature is rooted in the Church's own Tradition, which holds sacraments to be foundational for the Church's constitution. It is episcopal ordination, not papal election, that confers the apostolic office (*munus*) to sanctify, teach, and *govern* the people of God in the name of Christ. What is more, this understanding is also firmly rooted in teachings of Vatican I. In a very real sense, then, by way of its teaching on episcopacy as sacrament, Vatican II stated publicly what Bishop Zinelli of the *Deputatio* at Vatican I had said only privately: the power of jurisdiction exercised by the Roman Pontiff as part and parcel of his primatial ministry belongs to him *as a bishop*, nothing less and *nothing more.*[35]

Thus, the *power* inherent to the primatial jurisdiction of the Roman Pontiff, for the care of the Universal Church, is the same *power* inherent to the proper jurisdiction of a bishop, for the care of a local church. It is *episcopal* power.

> In virtue of this power [of jurisdiction], bishops have the sacred right and the duty before the Lord to make laws for their subjects, to pass judgment on them and to moderate everything pertaining to the ordering of worship and the apostolate.
>
> The pastoral office or the habitual and daily care of their sheep is entrusted to them completely; nor are they to be regarded as vicars of the Roman Pontiffs, for they exercise an authority that is proper to them, and are quite correctly called "prelates," heads of the people whom they govern. Their power, therefore, is not destroyed by the supreme and universal power, but on the contrary it is affirmed, strengthened and vindicated by it, since the Holy Spirit unfailingly preserves the form of government established by Christ the Lord in His Church. (LG 27, citing PA 3)[36]

This in no way compromises the Roman Pontiff's ability, as defined by Vatican I, to exercise jurisdiction "over all and each of the churches and over all and each of the pastors and faithful," in accord with his primatial office (PA 3). As Vatican II taught, the "proper, ordinary and immediate" jurisdiction of a bishop within his church "is ultimately regulated by the supreme authority of the Church, and can be circumscribed by certain limits, for the advantage of the Church or of the faithful" (LG 27). To say this does not, in its turn, imply that the primatial jurisdiction of the Roman Pontiff is limitless. It, too, is to be exercised "for the advantage of the Church or of the faithful."

While this leaves the Roman Pontiff a great deal of discretion in identifying precisely what constitutes this good, it does acknowledge that whatever the prerogatives acceded to the papacy, they may not be interpreted as obstructing, diminishing, or replacing the legitimate authority of the bishops throughout the world. The proper jurisdiction of local bishops belongs to the divine constitution of the Church. Not to honor it as such would be to act *non aedificationem, sed ad destructionem Ecclesiae*—a clear violation of the purpose of the primacy.

The Catholic Tradition has consistently taught that the purpose of the primacy provides the most fundamental limitation on the pope.[37] While there may be some who wish to define the juridical limits to the Bishop of Rome's primatial jurisdiction in order to explicitly safeguard the legitimate unity-in-diversity inherent to the catholicity of the Church as a communion of churches, others choose to affirm an article of faith of which they could be more certain: that the more one considers the difficulty of the risk that the primacy carries from not being juridically limited, the more sure one may be that ultimately, everything comes back to the indefectibility of the Church. The Catholic Tradition is certain that, if the Bishop of Rome goes beyond the limits imposed on his action by his specific office—the maintenance of the Church and the episcopal college in communion—clergy and laity would react appropriately.

Easier said than done? Certainly. That the clergy and laity will know how to react assumes, of course, that they understand the nature and mission of the primacy, and further that they will be of one mind about it. This is something with which theologians have wrestled since the close of the Council. It will be taken up again more fully in the concluding section of this chapter. Suffice it to say here, the answer has been—and, indeed remains—difficult to discern.

There is one further aspect of Vatican II's teaching that touches upon the issue of primatial jurisdiction and that deserves to be treated here, albeit briefly. Although this aspect is certainly consistent with the Great Tradition of the first millennium of the (so-called) undivided Church, in light of the history of Catholic theology since the Great Schism it may be said to be genuinely new. It is an aspect of an ancient truth reappearing in a new situation: the supreme magisterial authority of the College of Bishops.

The Council was clear: the Roman Pontiff is not the only one who may exercise "full, supreme and universal power over the Church." In communion with him as its head, the College of Bishops also exercises "supreme and full power over the universal Church," for the good of the churches and all their faithful (LG 22). This power may likewise be exercised "over all and each of the churches and over all and each of the pastors and faithful" (PA 3),[38] for it is inherent to the office of teaching (*munus regendi*) that belongs to the College, in head and members, by virtue of episcopal ordination and the apostolic succession it affects.

Vatican II presents us with only one supreme authority in the Church: the College and its head. This authority can operate in two ways: through a collegial act, that is, the College in union with its head, or through a personal act of the pope as head of the College. Thus, every primatial act is essentially collegial.[39] This includes acts of primatial jurisdiction, whether they pertain to churches individually or to their communion. This is so because the papacy, by its very nature, is rooted in the episcopate. For the Bishop of Rome, as for all the bishops, everything derives from one and the same sacrament (episcopacy), from one and the same mission of building and keeping the Church in communion, and from one and the same power given for the sake of this mission. This power may be exercised by the College in communion with its head or in a singular way by the Bishop of Rome as head of the College. Yet, even in this latter instance, the *solicitudo universalis* that the Roman Pontiff exercises always remains within the sacramental grace of the episcopate.[40] It always belongs to him *as a bishop*, nothing less and *nothing more*.

b. Primatial Magisterium: When the Council turned its attention to the issue of the Roman Pontiff's primatial magisterium, it began as one would expect it to have begun: by speaking about the bishops' *munus docendi*, their office as teachers of the faith: "Among the principal duties of bishops the preaching of the Gospel occupies an eminent place" (LG 25).

For the bishops are heralds of the faith who bring new disciples to Christ. They are authentic teachers, that is, teachers endowed with the authority of Christ, who speak to the people entrusted to them the faith to be believed and put into practice; they illustrate this faith in the light of the Holy Spirit, drawing out of the treasury of revelation things old and new (see Matt 13:52);

they make this faith bear fruit and they vigilantly ward off errors that are threatening to the flock (see 2 Tim 4:1–4; LG 27).

This office (*munus docendi*) may be exercised in an ordinary manner by individual bishops within and among the churches entrusted to their care, by the College of Bishops as an expression of their *solicitudo universalis*, or, in a like manner, by the Bishop of Rome as head of the College. Yet, the exercise of the charge to teach in Christ's name is always an exercise of one and the same power, which is conferred upon the College in head and members by one and the same sacrament and for the sake of one and the same mission: to build and to keep the Church in communion, in order that it may effectively proclaim the saving works of God.[41] This is also the case when, in accord with this same *munus docendi*, the charism of infallibility is invoked.

> And this infallibility with which the Divine Redeemer willed His Church to be endowed in defining doctrine of faith and morals, extends as far as the deposit of Revelation extends, which must be religiously guarded and faithfully expounded. And this is the infallibility which the Roman Pontiff, the head of the college of bishops, enjoys in virtue of his office, when, as the supreme shepherd and teacher of all the faithful, who confirms his brethren in their faith, (see Lk 22, 32) by a definitive act he proclaims a doctrine of faith or morals. (cf. PA 4) And therefore his definitions, of themselves, and not from the consent of the Church, are justly styled irreformable, since they are pronounced with the assistance of the Holy Spirit, promised to him in blessed Peter, and therefore they need no approval of others, nor do they allow an appeal to any other judgment. For then the Roman Pontiff is not pronouncing judgment as a private person, but as the supreme teacher of the universal Church, in whom the charism of infallibility of the Church itself is individually present, he is expounding or defending a doctrine of Catholic faith. (cf. commentary by Bishop Gasser, Mansi 52, 1213 AC) The infallibility promised to the Church resides also in the body of Bishops, when that body exercises the supreme magisterium with the

successor of Peter. To these definitions the assent of the Church can never be wanting, on account of the activity of that same Holy Spirit, by which the whole flock of Christ is preserved and progresses in unity of faith [cf. commentary by Bishop Gasser, Mansi 52, 1214 A]. (LG 25)

Nothing of Vatican I has been lost. In fact, Vatican I has been affirmed in a way that reaches beyond the letter of *Pastor Aeternus* and into the context within which its definitions were intended to be read, that is, the divine constitution of the Church, particularly with respect to the collegial relationship the pope has with his brother bishops. As was the case regarding Vatican II's treatment of primatial jurisdiction, this has made all the difference.

The distortions of the extreme ultramontanism that characterized the period after Vatican I have been confronted and corrected. The charism of infallibility may not be interpreted as belonging exclusively to the pope, or as passing through him to the Church. It belongs properly to the people of God as a gift of the Spirit who unites them to Christ. The pope's exercise of this charism is only a particular instance of that which belongs to the whole Church, and, what is more, it is exercised by him only in virtue of his being the Bishop of Rome *and* head of the College of Bishops, in which the Church's supreme authority to sanctify, govern, and *teach* the house of the living God in the name of God's Son resides.

From this perspective, one clearly sees that the one who speaks in this manner is a bishop of the Church, enabled from his presidency of the See of Peter and Paul to rely, in exceptional circumstances, upon the help of the Holy Spirit, not as inspiration or revelation but as assistance. This prevents him from falling into error when, for the benefit of all the churches and the communion of their faithful, he makes a solemn judgment on the truth of the Gospel as it bears upon faith and morals. The Spirit guarantees that such truth genuinely lies within revelation and belongs to the faith of the Church. For what the Roman Pontiff speaks in such instances is nothing other than the faith of the people of God, which they receive as their own.

The manner in which the Council spoke about this reception is fundamental to a proper understanding of the role played by papal teaching, particularly infallibly defined teaching, within the life of the Church, and it is so on two counts: (1) it clarifies the ground of such teachings' validity; (2) it reveals such teachings as part of the broader dynamic whereby "the whole flock of Christ is preserved in the unity of faith and makes progress."

The Council's use of the explanations offered at Vatican I regarding the *ex esse* clause in *Pastor Aeternus* had the effect of clarifying the clause's proper meaning: definitions *ex cathedra* do not derive their validity from subsequent juridical verification by a higher authority distinct from that of the Bishop of Rome.[42] These definitions are valid by virtue of their expressed object: a truth of the faith, which the authority inherent to Roman Pontiff's office as successor of Peter and head of the College of Bishops serves.

This leads to the second of the counts listed above: the place of papal teaching, including infallible teaching, within the dynamic of the Church's progress in faith. Because the people of God is called to make progress in its faith, no infallible definition, including one made by a pope, can be received as a dead letter. Rather, it is received by the Church in such a way as to set into motion a process of clarification by critical reflection that furthers the knowledge of the faith—that is, it is received through a dynamic process of reception.

Reception does not create truth, nor does it legitimize the pronouncement of a definition. Rather, it permits the Church to recognize the faith of the Apostolic Church within the definition, and to clarify the full meaning of this faith for its life and mission in Christ. In other words, an infallible judgment gives to the Church a sense of the truth, declaring the content of that truth in the way the circumstances surrounding its pronouncement require. It silences neither the desire nor the need to deepen the grasp of this truth. The Councils of Nicaea and Ephesus called for the Council of Chalcedon, just as Vatican I called for Vatican II. What Vatican II will call for is something that will be known only in the light of what the Church shall grasp as being of the essence of its faith through the living of this faith. In this process, papal teachings—including infallible teachings—play a necessary, but by no means exclusive, part.

In his capacity as head of the College of Bishops and Supreme Pontiff of the Catholic Church, the Roman Pontiff speaks with precisely the same authority as he acts: that of a bishop, nothing less and *nothing more*. For him to attempt to speak otherwise would be for him to act as something other than—indeed, more than—a pope. His primacy is rooted in the sacramental *munus* of the College, for the service of the communion of the Church of churches. A more contemporary way of describing this is offered by the concept of *corporate personality*.

c. The Pope as Corporate Personality: The concept of corporate personality captures well the significant dialectical tension that exists between the College and its head. The phenomenon of corporate personality occurs when the life of a group becomes so concentrated on one of its members that the group's own understanding of itself becomes embodied in this particular individual. In essence, the group recognizes itself in him.

This recognition occurs in several ways.[43] First, the Roman Pontiff, as head of the College, is clearly situated within the College, never above it. Second, his authority is derived not by juridical fiat from the members of the College, but by his place among them as their head and by his share in the office conferred upon them by episcopal ordination. Third, his role as head of the College requires that he both support the dignity of each member's *missio canonica* and maintain their relationships with one another for the welfare of the communion of the Church and the spread of the gospel. Without this dynamic interaction between the Bishop of Rome and his brother bishops, the College would be unable to recognize itself in him.

In this light, it is impossible to conceive of the pope apart from the College, even when he is exercising his right to speak *ex cathedra*. When the pope speaks "alone," his position demands that, as head of the College, he truly be in communion with his brother bishops. For with them as true vicars and legates of Christ, he discerns the truth of the gospel for which they are together responsible, and what is more, maintains the entire communion of the people of God, in all their churches, in one mind and heart in the Lord.

One should not slavishly apply the concept of corporate personality to the collegial fellowship that exists between the Bishop of Rome and his brother bishops, of course. Its value lies in the analogy it offers: the basic identity between the representative individual and the group in the interplay of dynamic communion helps us to understand better how impossible it is to consider the Bishop of Rome except in connection with the College. If it were otherwise, he would be a head without a body—as much a monster as a body without a head. The one is inseparable from the body he represents. In the Roman Pontiff, the bishops recognize themselves. His contribution to the communion of the College and to the Church of churches they shepherd includes a responsibility that is not shared exactly by any of the others. When he speaks on his own, he is still the one through whom all the others express themselves, and his power is still that of the entire College.

The tension involved in this relationship embraces much more than the proverbial here and now, that is, the horizontal aspect of communion. It also involves communion's vertical aspect. It embraces the entire story of the Church. When the pope speaks, his brother bishops open themselves to recognize and receive the voice of the people of God, the *sensus fidei* of the bishops and of all the faithful of every age. It is the pope's particular responsibility to voice the faith of the Church as it has been passed on by the apostolic succession in all the churches. Though spoken by one person, it is the voice of the body of bishops, in all its fullness.[44]

As universal primate, the Roman Pontiff does not exercise his office in isolation, but in communion with the bishops. This sharing of authority requires considerable forbearance and flexibility both for the pope and his brother bishops and for the entire people of God. The words of Cardinal Suenens are appropriate here: "Collegiality is an art that must be learned in common or not at all."[45] This ancient teaching has engendered considerable debate since the close of Vatican II. This has truly been a time of reception, with all its attendant and difficult questions.

IV. THE RECEPTION OF PRIMACY-IN-COLLEGIALITY

On one level, it may seem odd to speak of the Church's reception of the Council's teachings on papal primacy. After all, the Council adhered closely to Pope John's mandate. It proclaimed no new doctrines. Instead, it strove to take a pastoral step forward "toward a doctrinal penetration and a formation in consciences in faithful and perfect conformity to the authentic doctrine."[46] Thus, what the Council spoke, particularly with regard to the primacy, was nothing other than the deposit of the Church's faith. Seen in this light, it is difficult to speak of the Catholic Church receiving what it already possessed.

On a deeper level, one may speak of the Church's reception of the Council as a *re-reception*. This is particularly the case with regard to the Council's teaching on primacy-in-collegiality in the service of the communion of the Church of churches. Collegiality, the sacramentality of the episcopate, the mystery of the Church as the communion of the people of God: these ancient truths guided the Council. Ultimately, they permitted the Council to conceive of the primacy in a way that would have seemed impossible a few years before. For those raised on catechisms hailing the pope as the successor of God, this vision would have been new indeed. It needed to be received anew. In many respects, the struggle to do this has only just begun.

A. Struggle for the Primacy

While there were those who rejected the Council's teaching on primacy-in-collegiality as a betrayal of Vatican I, they proved to be few. Overall, its reception was widespread, as was observed by the late Rev. Lukas Vischer, an ecumenical observer at Vatican II. He noted that the Council's teaching on collegiality "produced a new consciousness of the Church's mission in every locality."

> The role of the individual bishops and consequently of the local Church was enhanced as the Council sketched a new picture of the bishop and his church. Far more than in earlier times, the individual churches are today conscious of being responsible for the witness of the Church in their localities....The consequence of all this has been a deeper understanding and more vital manifestation of the universality of the Church. The vision of a *communion ecclesiarum* has in fact been realized concretely to some extent. The witness of the Church is

heard through a multiplicity of voices, and the independence of the national and local churches has been manifested in a far greater measure than in earlier times. The universality of the ecclesial community finds expression today not only through its central authority but also through the witness of its parts.[47]

Concomitant with this, collegiality also produced a new consciousness of the pope's mission to serve the unity of the communion of churches. Vischer pointed to three areas where this was most evident in the first decades after the Council, and which can still be seen today.[48] First, the Roman Pontiff has increasingly been seen as the spokesman for the Church. In various ways, it has always been the case that the pope embodied in his person the unity of the Church. Whereas preconciliar popes chose to do so from behind the Vatican walls, recent popes have striven to do so by being as close as possible to the people of God. Although their personal pastoral styles are certainly different, there can be no doubt that people felt Popes John XXIII, John Paul II, and now Francis to be *their* popes— and this whether they are Catholic or not.

This leads to Vischer's second area: that since the Council, the papacy has acquired a greater effectiveness in relation to the churches of other confessional traditions. Whereas preconciliar popes avoided close, fraternal contacts with other Christians, the popes of our postconciliar period have not only received representatives of other churches, they have also been received by them. There is no doubt that the ecclesiological basis for this was the Council's teaching that the one Church of Christ *subsists in*, not *is*, the Catholic Church. In this light, the Bishop of Rome as Peter's successor must be a *pontifex maximus* (great bridge builder), reaching out to Christians of other traditions and to work with them to restore the visible communion of all who are in Christ. Arguably, the most striking example of this was John Paul II's appeal to Christian leaders to search with him for "a way of exercising the primacy which, while in no way renouncing what is essential to its mission, is nonetheless open to a new situation" (*Ut Unum Sint* 95).

The third impact of collegiality upon the papal office is directly related to what was just stated above. If the Roman *Pontifex* is truly to be one who builds bridges of understanding between churches and peoples, he must be a person of understanding himself. For him to teach in a manner divorced from the living faith experience of the churches is not an option. Thus, to teach in a way that is open to loyal, critical feedback, especially from his brother bishops, is essential. It was for this reason that Pope Paul VI issued his 1965 *motu proprio Apostolica Sollicitudo*, establishing the Synod of Bishops, which would advise him and future popes in their task to teach, sanctify, and govern the Church of churches.

As well-meaning as these efforts by recent popes have undoubtedly been, serious questions have been raised about the extent to which they have made the Council's vision of primacy-in-collegiality their own. While it may be argued that the traveling papacy of the postconciliar period has been genuine expressions of the primatial office to promote the communion of God's people by being present to them in their churches, others have observed that these occasions have tended to obscure the legitimate authority of the bishops in the churches entrusted to their care. Concerns have also been raised that the instruments intended to promote the collegial care of the churches by the Bishop of Rome and his brother bishops have, instead, reduced collegiality to the role of merely supporting the exercise of the primacy.

John Quinn, retired archbishop of San Francisco, gave voice to this concern when he said, "Today's synods seem distant from the ideal set forth in the council decree on bishops: 'Acting on behalf of the whole catholic episcopate, it [the Synod] will show that all the bishops in hierarchical communion participate in the care of the whole church.'" Instead, the "tendency since the council would appear to restrict the synod as much as possible." For Quinn, this has exemplified the "ecclesiology reminiscent of the maximalist position at Vatican I. Offensive not only to Catholic bishops, such behavior surely constitutes an obstacle for ecumenism."[49] While attention has rightly been given to the significantly different way Pope Francis held the recent Synod on the Family, *Amoris Laetitia* was issued in his name, not in the name of the Synod.

The years since the close of the Council has been a time of tension, a genuine struggle to realize a primacy-in-collegiality. Saying this is not a veiled attempt to place white and black hats upon those who participate in this struggle. It is not a question of who is right and who is wrong, of winners and losers. Rather, it is a question of struggling to discern how the Council's vision of a primacy-in-collegiality is to be lived within the Church of churches. Ultimately, this struggle calls for the participation of all God's people, but in a special way, it demands genuine dialogue between all the members of the College, that is, the pope and his brother bishops.

It will be a significant dialogue, particularly with regard to the manner in which it will be conducted. The papacy and the episcopate are both of divine origin, and both share the same communion of faith. In this light, the tension between them can perhaps never be fully and finally resolved to the satisfaction of both parties. If we want this tension to be creative for the churches' communion and not lead to domination, then dialogue and understanding among those whose charge it is to sanctify, teach, and govern the people of God is essential.

What is more, it must be a dialogue that is both attentive to the developments in theology and, perhaps more so in this age of the "global village," sensitive to the lived experience of the entire people of God. It must share accumulated insights with charity, humility, and trust in their mutual search for the truth of the Gospel. This dialogue between the pope and his brother bishops may be the critical test of collegiality, demanding wisdom and courage as well as tact and creativity. When their genuine fraternal dialogue is taken as the accepted climate of opinion in ecclesial governance, then one may well say that collegiality has come of age.

For this age to come, though, a good deal of confusion regarding its consequences for the primacy must be clarified. In this sense, this is a confusion that has its origins in Vatican II itself.

B. Challenge to the Primacy

The Council's majority was not in perfect agreement as to the degree to which the primacy of the Roman Pontiff was contextualized by collegiality. Some bishops, under the influence of the ecclesiology that prevailed prior to the Council, tended to read *Lumen Gentium*'s understanding of the "Church of churches" as not being significantly different from a "Church with dioceses." So they tended to see collegiality primarily as a means by which the pope could more effectively exercise the primacy—and they were not without reason for doing so.

Lumen Gentium is replete with affirmations of the limits of the College's authority and of the full independence of the Holy Father as head of the College. The text of *Lumen Gentium* could have been clearer on the balance of power many bishops sought between the pope and the College. Perhaps this was due to a desire for a greater consensus among the bishops than had been achieved at Vatican I, especially in light to the apparent newness of the Council's teaching. Regardless of the reason(s), there were certain ambiguities the Council decided to live with, for both the sake of unity and room for further theological development.

Not all the bishops were content with such ambiguity. Even among those who had voted for *Lumen Gentium*, there was resistance to the Council's overall view of primacy-in-collegiality. They perceived it as a challenge to Vatican I, not that it denied the primacy but that it so contextualized the primacy as to render its authority practically ineffective.[50] It opened the doors to what some observers have called the "nightmare of shared governance," and this could only have the effect of compromising the freedom of the pope.[51] These bishops were never great in number. In fact, they were nowhere near as large as the minority at Vatican I. Yet, they were influential enough to have a Preliminary Explanatory Note (*Nota explicativia praevia*) attached to the revised *modi* prior to the Council's final vote on *Lumen Gentium* in November of 1964.

The Preliminary Explanatory Note (NEP, after the Latin) was one of a number of procedural surprises that led some of the bishops to recall that time as *settimana nera*—Black Week.[52] The NEP explicitly emphasized the prerogative of the Holy Father "to perform certain actions which are not at all within the competence of the bishops" (no. 3). While Council *periti* such as Yves Congar, OP, held that the difference between the constitution and the NEP attached to its *modi* was one of language, not of substance,[53] there were those who advocated that the NEP was an integral part of *Lumen Gentium*, and served as the interpretive key to the whole of the Council's teaching on collegiality.[54]

Prescinding from any further discussion regarding the proper canonical status of the NEP, as well as other specific examples of this minority's influence, *that* these bishops were able to see collegiality as a challenge to the legitimate primacy of the Roman Pontiff exemplifies how, for all its achievements, *Lumen Gentium* presented the Church with an imperfect and incomplete understanding of Roman primacy-in-collegiality in the service of communion. Clearly, more work needs to be done on this important teaching of the Council. As for the areas within which this should take place, this is the topic of the next chapter: "Papal Primacy beyond the Councils."

CHAPTER 3

PAPAL PRIMACY BEYOND THE COUNCILS

The official teaching of the Church proclaims that Christ intended the Petrine ministry to continue permanently in the Church and that bishops are successors to the Apostles and those who exercised oversight in the early church. It declares that the episcopate needs a head for unity and coordination....It teaches that both Pope and bishops are joined in a single College of Bishops, as both are joined in the one Mystery of the Church. The unfinished task—and an urgent one for Christian unity—is to articulate better, and in accord with the authentic tradition of the Church, how these realities function together without injury to either.[1]

I. INTRODUCTION

In his letter of invitation to the 1977 colloquium *Toward Vatican III: The Work That Needs to be Done*, then president of Notre Dame Theodore Hesburgh, CSC, wrote, "The meeting is not designed to be a call for 'Vatican III'—a title which is intended to be symbolic—but rather to block out the scholarly research in theology and in the social sciences which needs to be done before the Church can come to its next critical turning point."[2] This understanding of Vatican II as a "critical turning point" for the Church was not Hesburgh's alone. Rather, it was and remains reflective of the understanding of the better part of the Catholic theological community.

To one degree or another, all councils have marked significant turning points in the life of the Church. With regard to the christological and trinitarian controversies that rocked the patristic church, the councils marked definitive movements toward coherent and canonically enforceable orthodoxies. With regard to the calls for reform that echoed throughout medieval Christendom, the councils provided benchmarks against which errors and abuses could be judged and amended—at least in theory. Nonetheless, Vatican II was unique, and its uniqueness lies in the fact that, whereas all previous councils had been called to counter some perceived threat to the Church's faith and rightly ordered life, this Council was called in order for the Church to rediscover the richness of its faith and life in the light of "the signs of the times." Vatican II was a critical turning point, an "event,"[3] in the life of the Catholic Church because it sought to occasion the new Pentecost John XXIII hoped it would be, and to do so not simply for its own sake, but for the sake of the life of the world.

In this light, Vatican II truly was a "transitional council."[4] It was a first step on the pilgrim road of discovering anew what the Spirit of the Lord is continually making the Church to be: the sacrament, the living proclamation of God's kingdom in and for our world.

As the experiences of the past fifty-plus years testify, the transition ushered in by Vatican II has not been an easy one for the Catholic Church, and this for reasons far too complicated to unpack here. Yet, one of these reasons deserves mention. It is the struggle for the *mind* of the Council.[5] How is the Church properly to understand what the Council taught? What is more, how is the Church to use this understanding as the means to orient its way along the paths of renewal *ad intra* and mission *ad extra*—at least to the extent that one may still speak of an "inside" and an "outside" of the Church as envisioned by the Council? These and similar questions are difficult to answer.[6] One reason for this is the Council's own documents. The conciliar texts, even those that are doctrinal in character, lack the kind of conceptual precision, unambiguous definitions, technical forms, and unity of literary genre to which the councils of Trent and Vatican I had accustomed us. Vatican II used the language of the Scriptures as no previous council had used it, alternating it with historical expositions, analyses of the contemporary situation, and citations of previous councils (half of them from Trent and Vatican I) and references to papal teaching (half of them to Pius XII). No wonder, that even after fifty years, Vatican II still has the ability to bewilder, as well as to inspire, its students.[7]

As was noted in the previous chapter, this bewildering picture is reflected in the Council's teachings on papal primacy. Long after the Council closed, questions remain regarding (1) the proper understanding of the Bishop of Rome's succession to Peter's primacy, (2) his collegial relationship with his brother bishops, and (3) the ways his ministry serves the unity of a Church of *churches*. Certainly, *Lumen Gentium* addressed these issues, and did so in a manner that broke through the rigid dogmatism of the interconciliar period by reframing discussion of the primacy within a context more resonant with the rich heritage of the Church's deposit of faith, that is, the context of collegiality. Yet, more work needs to be done before the Catholic Church can come to that next critical turning point that Hesburgh mentioned and profess its belief in a primacy that not only its own faithful, but all faithful Christians may be able to receive as their own.

In the service of such a reception, I shall briefly address the questions asked above as a sign of the work that "needs to be done" in order that Catholic doctrine on the primacy may continue to develop "in faithful and perfect conformity to the authentic doctrine which, however, should be studied and expounded through the methods of research and through the literary forms of modern thought."[8] I shall begin with the question of the pope's succession to Peter's primacy.

II. "YOU ARE PETER, AND ON THIS ROCK I WILL BUILD MY CHURCH" (MATT 16:18)

It is impossible to speak of the primacy without recalling the apostle Peter and Jesus's gifting him with the keys to the kingdom.

> Simon Peter answered, "You are the Messiah, the Son of the living God." And Jesus answered him, "Blessed are you, Simon son of Jonah! For flesh and blood has not revealed this to you, but my Father in heaven. And I tell you, you are Peter, and on this rock I will build my church, and the gates of Hades will not prevail against it. I will give you the keys of the kingdom of heaven, and whatever you bind on earth will be bound in heaven, and whatever you loose on earth will be loosed in heaven." (Matt 16:16–19)

This passage was cited by Vatican I in the opening chapter of *Pastor Aeternus*, and followed by other familiar exchanges between the Lord and Peter: "Tend my sheep" (John 21:16), and "Strengthen your brothers" (Luke 22:32). Vatican II did not question this appeal to the Gospels, nor did it question the teachings on the primacy that this appeal, in part, premised. Nevertheless, it did do something new, at least for its time. It kept in mind that when the Lord spoke to Peter, he addressed Peter in the midst of his brothers.

A. A Move That Made the Difference

Vatican II did not reject the traditional connection between the Roman Pontiff and the apostle Peter. As its stated reception of *Pastor Aeternus* and its own appeals to the Gospels bear witness, it accepted this connection—though it did not do so uncritically. The Council was aware of recent advances in scriptural and patristic studies that demonstrated a fuller appreciation of Peter's identity as an apostle, and it made use of them. Thus, the Council stated that the primacy in which the Lord established Peter did not separate him from his brother apostles. Rather, it placed him firmly in their midst. He was head, not of a body simply to be directed by him, but of a *college* whose communion he was to foster, and this not simply for the apostles' own sake, but for the sake of the communion of all his disciples—his Body, his Church. This move made—and for those striving to understand the Council's mind and make it their own, continues to make—all the difference.

Of course, questions regarding this move were raised during the Council—and continue to be raised today. In what sense may the apostles' fellowship be characterized as a *college*? What effect does this have upon our understanding of the primacy that the Lord established in Peter—at least to the extent that we can say that he established such a thing at all? How did Peter exercise this primacy among his brother apostles? How did he exercise within the community of believers? What is more, how does this affect Catholicism's understanding of the primacy of the Roman Pontiff as Peter's successor, on the one hand, and, on the other hand, the authority of the bishops as successors of the apostles? There were, and are, no clear, unambiguous answers to these questions in the conciliar texts. The chief reason for this ambiguity is the term *college* itself.

B. The *College* of Bishops?

The concept of the apostles having formed a college does not emerge with necessity from the biblical witness, nor does the Great Tradition provide any extensive discussion of it. Even during Vatican II, scholars expressed doubts about whether the word *college* was appropriate to describe the fellowship of the apostles among themselves, and the discussion at the Council itself was unable to remove the doubt. When one takes the definitions of *Pastor Aeternus* as the point of departure, though, the relevance of the concept becomes immediately apparent, as it served well to put the Roman primacy, as defined at Vatican I, into a new context.

At first glance, though, it can appear that utility was the chief reason for the Council having spoken about the "College of Apostles." The term has no meaning apart from the ease with which it permitted Vatican II to contextualize the primacy of the Roman Pontiff within the authority proper to all bishops by virtue of their having been admitted into the College of Bishops. Yet, this cannot be all there is to it, for if Scripture, together with Tradition, is truly the supreme rule of the Church's faith (see DV 21), then what it tells us about the relationship between Peter and his brother apostles is of far greater value than mere utility. It must tell us something about the heart of their fellowship and of the authority with which Christ endowed them for the care of God's people, his Church. Further, it must tell us something of fundamental significance about both the fellowship and the authority of those who succeed to the apostles, especially Peter's successor: the Bishop of Rome.

C. Primacy, Collegiality, and the Rule of Faith

This issue was taken up several years ago when Pope Emeritus Benedict XVI was still Cardinal Joseph Ratzinger, Prefect of the Congregation of the Doctrine of the Faith (CDF). In an essay titled "The Primacy of Peter and the Unity of the Church," he noted its inescapability, especially with regard to our Church's commitment to ecumenism. Christians of other ecclesial traditions, who nourish themselves with the same Scriptures and "venerable traditions" that we turn to for our sustenance, demand that we recognize this and engage with them in a faithful, critical study of our commonly revered sources. Thus, with "an especially attentive ear to the witness of the Bible" and a spirit of respectful inquiry "into the faith of the nascent Church," Ratzinger posed three questions: (1) What is the actual meaning of the preeminence of Peter within the New Testament; (2) Can a Petrine succession really be justified on the basis of the New Testament; (3) If this succession may be admitted, "can Rome lay a legitimate claim to being its seat?"[9]

To the eyes of some Catholics, these questions may appear to threaten the boundaries of acceptable doctrine. Their purpose, however, is not to cast doubt upon belief in the Petrine succession or in Rome's claim to be it. Rather, inasmuch as these questions concern doctrines fundamental to our own ecclesial Tradition, their purpose is nothing other than to call us to delve deeper into the deposit of Christian faith and develop a clearer understanding of the authority we claim for the Roman Pontiff. We owe this as much to our sisters and brothers of other ecclesial traditions as to ourselves, for if the primacy of the Roman Pontiff is truly part of this *common* deposit, then it does not belong to Catholics alone, but to all who are in Christ. In this light, questions about the specifically *Petrine* nature of the primacy of the Roman Pontiff must be asked—and answered.

III. "STRENGTHEN YOUR BROTHERS" (LUKE 22:32)

If there was uncertainty concerning the relationship between the primacy that Christ instituted in Peter and the authority with which he endowed all the apostles as members of one college, it should come as no surprise that uncertainty remains concerning the implications of collegiality for the relationship between the episcopal college and its head, the Bishop of Rome. Little wonder that before the ink on *Lumen Gentium* had dried, some people had become especially agitated.

A. The Presence of the Past

The concept of collegiality simply did not sit well with the "new" minority at Vatican II. In addition to its apparent novelty, collegiality did not fit easily into then established canonical categories. It held too many uncertainties, which in this minority's opinion could compromise the definitions of *Pastor Aeternus*. The old uncertainties returned. To those whose understanding of ecclesial governance had been shaped by the triumphalism, clericalism, and legalism that followed in the wake of Vatican I, Vatican II's lack of clarity regarding practical relationships between the power of the Roman Pontiff and that of the College of Bishops promised a troubling, uncertain future. Clear guidance was needed if the "Barque of Peter" was to remain on course. Before the Council had even closed, an effort was made to provide just that kind of guidance. Fifty-plus years after the Council closed, its practical effects remain.

The fundamental point at issue remains the balance of power between the Bishop of Rome, on the one hand, and on the other hand, the College of Bishops, of which he is the head. Archbishop Quinn put it well, in words that ring as true today as they did when he spoke them almost two decades ago:

> The official teaching of the Church proclaims that Christ intended the Petrine ministry to continue permanently in the Church and that bishops are successors to the Apostles and those who exercised oversight in the early

church. It declares that the episcopate needs a head for unity and coordination....It teaches that both Pope and bishops are joined in a single College of Bishops, as both are joined in the one Mystery of the Church. The unfinished task—and an urgent one for Christian unity—is to articulate better, and in accord with the authentic tradition of the Church, how these realities function together without injury to either.[10]

Adding to this urgency is the observation of as many bishops, theologians, and canonists that such injury has been done, and all of it has been to one side of the balance: the side occupied by the College of Bishops. This emerges clearly from any critical and dispassionate study of the principle instruments called for by the Council to embody its teachings on collegiality, namely the Synod of Bishops and Episcopal Conferences.

B. Collegiality in the Service of Primacy?

1. The Synod and the Primacy: In the first chapter of their *Christus Dominus* (CD), the bishops at Vatican II called for the establishment of a Synod of Bishops:

Bishops chosen from various parts of the world, in ways and manners established or to be established by the Roman pontiff, render more effective assistance to the supreme pastor of the Church in a deliberative body which will be called by the proper name of Synod of Bishops. Since it shall be acting in the name of the entire Catholic episcopate, it will at the same time show that all the bishops in hierarchical communion partake of the solicitude for the universal Church. (CD 5)

The Council's majority clearly saw the Synod as an opportunity to establish better communication with the Holy See and to share in the governance of the Church. It did not work out as they had hoped. There are numerous reasons given for this. Some observers, including not a few bishops, have seen in this the hand of the Roman Curia as it strives to maintain its own influence in the day-to-day governance of the Church. Such a possible, practical reason aside, the reason is fundamentally ecclesiological, and it lies within the long shadow of *Pastor Aeternus*.

In accord with the provisions established in *Apostolica Sollicitudo*, the Synod exists in order to advise the Bishop of Rome. It is not able to address the Church directly so as to express, in communion with the Roman Pontiff, the judgment of the entire College on the issues set before it—which in any case were set there by a free decision of the Holy Father. Its conclusions are addressed to the *Supreme* Pontiff alone, and it is for him to decide whether they should be published, and if so, how. In other words, the Synod exists as a resource for the Supreme Pontiff to draw upon in his governance of the Church. There is no possibility for collegial decision-making—that is, unless he permits it to do so.

This line of reasoning should not be at all surprising. There is a fundamental incompatibility between an ecclesiology that understands the Primacy in monarchical terms, such as the title *Supreme* Pontiff unambiguously suggests, and an ecclesiology that sees the primacy as firmly rooted in collegiality, such as that given form by a synodal assembly. Whereas the former conducts its affairs within a closed circle and leans on a court that does not readily put up with the crystallization of opinions that might encroach on its own preserves, the latter strives to be continuously attentive to the *sensus fidelium*, represented corporately in the persons of their churches' bishops, even if the end result is not a firm, clear declaration.[11]

This tension has been on display for decades. While the future, further development of the Synod remains open, as Pope Francis has suggested,[12] one can say with certainty that thus far, the Synod has demonstrated an inability on the part of Catholicism's primatial and collegial institutions to coordinate their efforts toward a common objective, at least in a way that, to borrow from Quinn, does no injury to either of them. Much the same may be said for the relationship between the institutions of the primacy and of Episcopal Conferences.

2. Episcopal Conferences and the Primacy: In chapter 3 of *Christus Dominus*, the Council described the Episcopal Conference as "a council in which the bishops of a given nation or territory jointly exercise their pastoral office to promote the greater good which the Church offers mankind, especially through the forms and methods of the apostolate fittingly adapted to the circumstances of the age" (CD 38). In his 1966 *motu proprio Ecclesiae Sanctae*, Pope Paul VI mandated the establishment of Episcopal Conferences throughout the world.[13] Opinions differ over whether these Conferences have made the "manifold and fruitful assistance, so that this collegiate feeling may be put into practical application" of the spirit of collegiality that the Council had intended them to make (LG 23).

After the Council, Episcopal Conferences exercised wide powers of discretion. Some issued documents that greatly influenced the renewal of ecclesial life in nations and regions of the world. Nevertheless, the source of these powers was debated: Did the Conferences properly derive these powers from the bishops' collegial relationship as successors to the apostles, caring for the welfare of the churches entrusted to their care within a particular region of the world, or were these powers to be understood as having been conferred upon them by the Holy See? In his 1998 *motu proprio Apostolos Suos* (AS), John Paul II expressed his view on the question; it clearly favored the latter interpretation.

> Groupings of particular Churches are related to the Churches of which they are composed, because of the fact that those groupings are based on ties of common traditions of Christian life and because the Church is rooted in human communities united by language, culture and history. These relationships are very different from the relationship of mutual interiority of the universal Church with respect to the particular Churches.
>
> Likewise, the organizations formed by the Bishops of a certain territory (country, region, etc.) and the Bishops who are members of them share a relationship which, although presenting a certain similarity, is really quite different from that which exists between the College of Bishops and the individual Bishops. The binding effect of the acts of the episcopal ministry jointly exercised within Conferences of Bishops and in communion with the Apostolic See derives from the fact that the latter has constituted the former and has entrusted to them, on the basis of the sacred power of the individual Bishops, specific areas of competence. (AS 13)

On the question of the collegiality had among the members of a Conference, the pontiff was equally unambiguous.

> When the Bishops of a territory jointly exercise certain pastoral functions for the good of their faithful, such joint exercise of the episcopal ministry is a concrete application of collegial spirit (*affectus collegialis*), which "is the soul of the collaboration between the Bishops at the regional, national and international levels." Nonetheless, this territorially based exercise of the episcopal ministry never takes on the collegial nature proper to the actions of the order of Bishops as such, which alone holds the supreme power over the whole Church. In fact, the relationship between individual Bishops and the College of Bishops is quite different from their relationship to the bodies set up for the above-mentioned joint exercise of certain pastoral tasks. (AS 12)

Even in the face of such clarity by the pontiff, in the light of the Council's teaching in *Lumen Gentium*, it must be asked whether this received authority truly has the strength implied by a full recognition of collegiality, expressed with the Bishop of Rome and referring to his primatial authority, but not dominated by it.[14] This would seem an instance of choosing a false "either… or" instead of the "both…and" the Council called the Church to embrace, and this because it is difficult to reconcile the two things: the Petrine primacy of the Bishop of Rome and the proper authority of the Church's bishops as successors of the College of Apostles. "Favors" appear to be "granted" because dependence on Rome seems the more certain way.[15]

To put it another way, one may say that a concern for "safety" has caused Catholicism's ecclesial imagination to continue to revolve around a monarchial conception of Roman primacy, and to do so without realizing (or perhaps wanting to realize) that in doing so it has turned the very expressions of collegiality called for by the Council into a means of serving not the unity of the Church of churches, but the authority of the primacy whose office holder is effectively understood not so much as Bishop of Rome and head of the College of Bishops as the Church's one and true Universal Pastor.

The official teaching of the Catholic Church declares that Christ intended the Petrine ministry to continue permanently in the Church and that Church's bishops are successors to the College of Apostles. It declares that the episcopate needs a head, a *primate* for its collegial unity and coordination. It maintains that the Bishop of Rome, as successor of Peter, is this primate, and that as he must be free to serve the unity of the Church, he is not juridically bound by the agreement or consent of the College of Bishops, however much he may be morally bound to seek its agreement and to listen to its advice. The Catholic Church further teaches the sacramentality of the episcopate, that the powers exercised by the Roman Pontiff are rooted in the grace of episcopal ordination, and that the primacy he exercises cannot suppress, ignore, or diminish the authority and dignity that belong to his brother bishops by virtue of that same grace. It teaches that both the Bishop of Rome and his brothers are joined in a single College of Bishops, as both are joined in the one mystery of the Church whose essential unity they exist to serve. Truly, the unfinished task of the Council is to articulate better, and in accord with the authentic Tradition of the Catholic Church, how these realities function together without injury to either.

IV. "TEND MY SHEEP" (JOHN 21:16)

As both Vatican I and II make clear, how one understands the one mystery of the Church is significant for how one understands every aspect of the Church's faith and life, including collegiality and primacy. Thus, if one wishes to discover how primacy and collegiality may function together without injuring one another, one must enter into the postconciliar debate on the Church.

A. *Church* of Churches/Church of *Churches*?

From 1999 through 2001, an informal, open theological debate was conducted between the president of the Pontifical

Council for Promoting Christian Unity, Walter Cardinal Kasper,[16] and the Prefect of the CDF, Cardinal Joseph Ratzinger, on the mystery of the Church, specifically on the relationship between the Church Universal and the local churches in and from which the one unique Catholic Church exists. Observers of this debate called this issue one of the most pressing theological tasks in the Church today.[17] Almost two decades after the debate began, it remains so.

To the casual observer, this may appear as an odd topic for debate. Vatican II discussed at length the Church as both a universal and a local reality. As was noted in the previous chapter, this discussion signified the movement from an ecclesiology that started with the idea of the Universal Church divided into portions called dioceses, to an ecclesiology that understands the Church as the communion of churches in and from which the Universal Church arises. Unfortunately, Vatican II was not as clear on this point as perhaps it should have been. Certainly, *Lumen Gentium* may be read as affirming a more "bottom-up," as opposed to a "top-down," ecclesiology. However, it also may be read as affirming the opposite, as it has been by no less an authority than the former Council expert (*peritus*), Pope Emeritus Benedict XVI.

1. The Church as a "*Church* of Churches": In an article titled "The Origin and Essence of the Church," Ratzinger argued that the "temporal and ontological priorities lie with the universal church; a church that was not catholic would not have an ecclesial reality."[18] Article 23 of *Lumen Gentium* appears to support this claim. It states that the local churches in and from which "there exists the one unique catholic church" are "formed in the likeness of the universal church." When one reads this in the light of chapters 1 and 2 of *Lumen Gentium*, in which the mystery of the Church as a universal, *catholic* phenomenon is discussed at length, it is not difficult for one to see this ontological priority of the universal over the local coming to the fore. This perspective is exemplified by the Council's teaching on the relationship between the Roman Pontiff and the bishops as members of the College.

A person "is constituted a member of the Episcopal body in virtue of sacramental consecration and hierarchical communion with the head and members of the body" (LG 22). It is the prerogative of the head of the college, the Roman Pontiff, to admit a bishop into this communion, and it is in accord with the pontiff's assent that a bishop's canonical mission as a member of the College is determined (LG 24; cf. also no. 27). This applies to bishops exercising ordinary authority over particular churches/dioceses as much as it does to titular bishops, whose pastoral responsibilities vary widely. "A diocese is a portion of the people of God which is entrusted to a bishop to be shepherded by him with the cooperation of the presbytery" (CD 11). Through their episcopal oversight of the dioceses entrusted to their care "as a portion of the universal Church," diocesan bishops make an effective contribution "to the welfare of the whole Mystical Body, which is also the body of the churches" (LG 23), over which the Roman Pontiff, who by virtue of his office as Vicar of Christ and shepherd of the whole Church exercises full, supreme, immediate, and universal power over the Church, which he is able to exercise freely (see LG 22).

To conclude from this that local churches, that is, dioceses, are merely subsets of the Church Universal would be false. In his more lengthy treatment of the issue, Ratzinger himself did not draw this conclusion. The churches in each and every locale are true manifestations of "the one and only Catholic Church" (LG 23), for it is in the churches that the members of Christ's Body are, through the ministry of their bishops, "gathered together by the preaching of the Gospel of Christ, and the mystery of the Lord's Supper," wherein they are "transformed" into what they celebrate (LG 26). To speak of the ontological (and what is more, *temporal*, according to Ratzinger) priority of the universal over the local is not to deny or denigrate the ecclesial reality of local churches. Rather, it is to place this reality within its own proper context: the Church's catholicity, which necessarily embraces every place and every time in order that humanity may find its fulfillment in the One who is Lord of every place and time (LG 1–2). To describe the Church in any other way would be to speak of something other than the one unique *Catholic* Church.[19]

2. The Church as a "Church of *churches*": Such a description of the Church is true, those opposed to such an ecclesiology may reply, but only insofar as one conceives of the Church as an abstract phenomenon, not taking into account the existential reality within which the people of God live their faith. Rather, as Kasper stated in his article "On the Church: A Friendly Reply to Cardinal Ratzinger," "The relationship between the universal church and the local churches cannot be explained in the abstract way of theological deductions, because the church is a concrete historical reality. Under the guidance of God's Spirit, it unfolds in history; to history, therefore, we must turn for sound theology."[20] The result of this turn is, as it was for Kasper, an ecclesiology that conceives of the Church's catholicity in terms of its being a communion of *churches*.

Far from reducing the Church to a group of "disconnected assemblies," this communion ecclesiology, as Kasper asserted, revives the ecclesial vision of the first millennium. It excludes "a one-sided emphasis on the local churches as well as a one-sided emphasis on the universal church," thereby countering, in accord with the intention of Vatican II, the "new conception of the church" that arose in the West during the second millennium. That concept "put the emphasis on universality," and "culminated in attributing all authority to the pope."[21] In contrast, communion ecclesiology conceives of the Universal Church and the local church as fully inhering in one another. What is more, it culminates in an understanding of the primacy that grounds the pope's authority in the sacrament of episcopacy and the collegial relationship he shares with his brother bishops in governing the house of the living God (see LG 18).

In offering the above visions of the Church of *churches*, I do not wish to give the impression that they represent *the* ecclesiological positions within postconciliar Catholic theology. Still less would I claim that they capture fully the positions taken by Ratzinger and Walter in their debate. Rather, I offer them as rough sketches of the respective sides of a divide within the Catholic theological community: between those who would hold the ontological priority of the Universal Church to be almost self-evident[22] and those who, like another conciliar *peritus*, Henri de Lubac, SJ, would assert that a "universal church which would have a separate existence, or which someone imagined as existing outside the particular churches, is a mere abstraction."[23] What is more, these sketches bear witness to that lack of clarity in Vatican II that would permit such prominent theologians to be so divided in their visions of the mystery of the Church. While one may be tempted to dismiss this division as simply a theological dispute—a "mere abstraction" in itself—this division does have very real-world implications, not the least of which is the manner in which one will understand the nature and proper exercise of primacy.

B. Universal Pastor/Bishop of Rome?

How one approaches the mystery of the Church necessarily influences how one understands the primacy of the Roman Pontiff. Within the *Church* of churches, the Holy Father emerges clearly as the Holy *Father*. He is the successor of St. Peter, Prince of the Apostles. He is the Vicar of Christ and Supreme Pontiff, the visible principle and foundation of the unity of the Church and of its pastors, the bishops. As the head of the College of Bishops, it is by his decision that men are "elected" and admitted into it, by his discretion that their places within it are determined, and in accord with his directives that they exercise their ministry, in whatever offices he sees fit to confirm them. In the light of the *Church* of churches, the Roman Pontiff is truly the Universal Pastor of a Universal Church—as many people saw St. Pope John Paul II, for example.

Within the Church of *churches*, things appear differently. The Roman Pontiff is seen as standing at the nexus of that communion of churches from which the one unique Catholic Church arises. Communion with him places Christians within a web of relationships spanning not only space, but time as well. This is both manifested and affected by the bond of communion that all the churches' bishops share with him as the Bishop of Rome, head of their College. In communion with him, they announce the Gospel, teach the apostolic faith, and call people into the saving mystery of the new people of God. It is the primacy instituted in Peter's successor as Bishop of Rome that supports all the bishops in their exercise of this ministry of *episcope*, and, indeed, unites all the churches in this one life, this one mission: the unity of the whole human family as the new people of God.

Of course, these visions of the Roman Pontiff's primatial authority are not mutually exclusive. Certainly, the pope is the Universal Pastor of the Universal Church, and he is so because, as the Bishop of Rome, he succeeds to Peter's place among those who "govern the house of the living God" (LG 18). What is more, it is precisely because he stands at the nexus of the communion of the people of God and their pastors that he is the visible principle and foundation of the Church of churches and of the College of Bishops. Yet, because these visions grant priority to some aspects of papal primacy over others, they influence the way one distinguishes between what is of the essence of the primacy and what is not, between what is truly proper to its exercise and what is merely a reflection of the ages (and manifold personalities) through which it has passed.

What is of the essence of the primacy? How right St. Pope John Paul II was when he said of the effort to answer this question, "This is an immense task, which I cannot refuse and which I cannot carry out by myself" (*Ut Unum Sint* 96). It is a task that must include the contributions of the bishops and take into account the *sensus fidei* of all the Church's faithful. What is more, it must also include, as the late and sainted Holy Father said it must, the contributions and reflections of all those who are in Christ, all those with whom the members of the Catholic Church are in a "real but imperfect" communion.

> Could not the real but imperfect communion existing between us persuade Church leaders and their theologians to engage with me in a patient and fraternal dialogue on this subject, a dialogue in which, leaving useless controversies behind, we could listen to one another, keeping before us only the will of Christ for his Church and allowing ourselves to be deeply moved by his plea "that they may all be one…so that the world may believe that you have sent me" (Jn 17:21)? (*Ut Unim Sint* 96)

It deserves to be noted that for almost fifty years, the Catholic Church has been engaged in just such a "patient and fraternal dialogue" with the leaders and theologians of numerous confessional traditions, including that of the Anglican Communion. It is an important product of this dialogue that we now turn our attention.

DISCERNING THE GIFT

Reading the Papacy through the Lens of the Anglican–Roman Catholic International Commission

Our two communions have been separated for over 400 years. This separation, involving serious doctrinal differences, has been aggravated by theological polemics and mutual intolerance, which have reached into and affected many departments of life. Nevertheless, although our unity has been impaired through separation, it has not been destroyed. Many bonds still unite us: we confess the same faith in the one true God; we have received the same Spirit; we have been baptized with the same baptism; and we preach the same Christ.[1]

In its introduction to *The Final Report*, the first Anglican–Roman Catholic International Commission (ARCIC I) did more than simply recount a litany of historical facts: Anglicans and Catholics have been separated for four centuries, have inherited prejudices from their ecclesial forebears, yet are still able to find common ground in a shared inheritance. It also made a declaration of faith: in spite of our visible separation, Anglicans and Catholics are fundamentally one in Christ, and that this unity calls for ever greater degrees of realization until the day we are able to give common witness to the catholicity of the one Church of Jesus Christ by our mutual sharing in "'the teaching of the apostles and to the communal life, to the breaking of the bread and to the prayers' (Acts 2:42)" (ARCIC 1, II.5).

Such a faith finds an echo in nothing less than the Second Vatican Council's Dogmatic Constitution on the Church, *Lumen Gentium*, which declared,

> The Church recognizes that in many ways *she is linked with those who, being baptized, are honored with the name of Christian*, though they do not profess the faith in its entirety or do not preserve unity of communion with the successor of Peter. For there are many who honor Sacred Scripture, taking it as a norm of belief and a pattern of life, and who show a sincere zeal. They lovingly believe in God the Father Almighty and in Christ, the Son of God and Saviour. They are consecrated by baptism, in which *they are united with Christ*. They also recognize and accept other sacraments within their own Churches or ecclesiastical communities. Many of them rejoice in the episcopate, celebrate the Holy Eucharist and cultivate devotion toward the Virgin Mother of God. They also share with us in prayer and other spiritual benefits. Likewise we can say that in some real way they are joined with us in the Holy Spirit, for to them too He gives His gifts and graces whereby He is operative among them with His sanctifying power. Some indeed He has strengthened to the extent of the shedding of their blood. *In all of Christ's disciples the Spirit arouses the desire to be peacefully united, in the manner determined by Christ, as one flock under one shepherd, and He prompts them to pursue this end.* Mother Church never ceases to pray, hope and work that this may come about. She exhorts her children to purification and renewal so that

the sign of Christ may shine more brightly over the face of the earth. (LG 15; my emphases)

The Council expanded upon this statement in its declaration on ecumenism, *Unitatis Redintegratio* (UR), which gave even greater clarity to this vision:

Even in the beginnings of this one and only Church of God there arose certain rifts, which the Apostle strongly condemned. But in subsequent centuries much more serious dissensions made their appearance and quite large communities came to be separated from full communion with the Catholic Church—for which, often enough, men of both sides were to blame. The children who are born into these Communities and who grow up believing in Christ cannot be accused of the sin involved in the separation, and the Catholic Church embraces upon them as brothers, with respect and affection. *For men who believe in Christ and have been truly baptized are in communion with the Catholic Church even though this communion is imperfect.* The differences that exist in varying degrees between them and the Catholic Church—whether in doctrine and sometimes in discipline, or concerning the structure of the Church—do indeed create many obstacles, sometimes serious ones, to full ecclesiastical communion. The ecumenical movement is striving to overcome these obstacles. But even in spite of them it remains true that *all who have been justified by faith in Baptism are members of Christ's body, and have a right to be called Christian, and so are correctly accepted as brothers by the children of the Catholic Church.*

Moreover, some and even very many of the significant elements and endowments which together go to build up and give life to the Church itself, *can exist outside the visible boundaries of the Catholic Church*: the written word of God; the life of grace; faith, hope and charity, with the other interior gifts of the Holy Spirit, and visible elements too. *All of these, which come from*

Christ and lead back to Christ, belong by right to the one Church of Christ. (UR 3; my emphases)

With regard to the "Communions, national or confessional," within which "Catholic traditions and institutions in part continue to exist," the Council acknowledged that "the Anglican Communion occupies a special place" (UR 13).

It was with this vision firmly in mind that Pope Paul VI joined Archbishop Michael Ramsey in issuing the common declaration that established the Anglican–Roman Catholic International Commission (ARCIC), giving it the mandate that continues to guide its work:

> [His Holiness Pope Paul VI and His Grace Michael Ramsey, Archbishop of Canterbury] affirm their desire that those Christians who belong to these two Communions may be animated by these same sentiments of respect, esteem and fraternal love, and in order to help these develop to the full, they intend to inaugurate between the Roman Catholic Church and the Anglican Communion a serious dialogue which, founded on the Gospels and on the ancient common traditions, may lead to that unity in truth, for which Christ prayed.[2]

It is the agreements reached thus far by ARCIC on the issue of primacy—in particular that of the Bishop of Rome—that shall be taken up in this section. This shall be done in two parts: the first treating the issue of Roman primacy in the agreed statements of ARCIC I, and the second treating it in the agreed statements of ARCIC II. Each part will begin with a treatment of the Commission's understanding of communion, or *koinonia*, a concept the Commission considers to be of fundamental importance to its work. Likewise, each part will conclude with a review of the Commission's own assessment of its achievements. The section as a whole will conclude with a brief statement of the issues that will be addressed in the third and final section. Before embarking on this task, a brief introduction on Anglican attitudes toward papal primacy is in order.

CHAPTER 4

ANGLICANISM AND PAPAL PRIMACY

But this historical fact [that at certain times in history the papacy conspicuously failed to maintain the unity of the episcopate and has thereby been the means of perverting the real meaning of Catholicism] cannot justify a wholesale refusal to consider the Petrine claims. Other organs in the one Body have had their times of failure and self-aggrandizement, and we do not therefore conclude that they must be discarded. Hence it seems possible that in the reunited Church of the future there may be a special place for a "primus-inter-pares" as an organ of unity and authority. Peter will be needed as well as Paul and Apollos, and like them he will be chastened and repentant.[3]

I. INTRODUCTION

Witnessing the election of Joseph Cardinal Ratzinger as Pope Benedict XVI was an extraordinary experience. In addition to the uniqueness of the event itself and the excitement surrounding it, it gave me a front row seat to reactions from across the Christian world to the man whom my fellow Catholics acknowledged as the 265th successor of St. Peter. Among these reactions, three stood out in particular for me—all from Anglicans.

The first came to me courtesy of Sky News. The day before the Inauguration Mass, a visibly upset Englishman was giving the interviewer the full measure of his mind: "Disgraceful." That the archbishop of Canterbury would attend "such a thing" and, what is more, that the prince of Wales would postpone his wedding in order to do so himself was disgraceful. "It's a betrayal of the Reformation," was his verdict. "That's what it is, pure and simple."

The second reaction was from the archbishop of Canterbury, Dr. Rowan Williams. During his homily at celebration of the Lord's Supper in Rome's All Saints Anglican Church, the archbishop spoke of the absolute appropriateness of his having been present that morning at Pope Benedict's Inaugural Mass and of the ecumenical relationship between the Anglican Communion and the Catholic Church that made it so appropriate. From the path of Christian unity, he said, there is no exit. Anglicans and Catholics belong to one another, and do so because together we belong to Christ. On the question of whether Anglican and Roman Catholics should take time out from discussing their historic divisions in order to better attend to tensions threatening unity within their own respective communions, in particular within the Anglican Communion, the archbishop responded that it is precisely in the midst of such tensions and potentially new reasons for division that dialogue between Anglicans and Catholics must not only continue, but also be intensified. Through dialogue with the other, each communion would not only come to a better sense of its own identity as "Church," but also draw closer together through a truer understanding of who they, in virtue of their common baptism, are called to be in Christ: his one Church, in and for the world.

The final reaction came from a young college student. He was a member of The Episcopal Church (USA), and together with the friends seated around him, was thrilling in the day's events. They were excited to be attending a Eucharist presided over by the archbishop of Canterbury, even more so since it followed upon the Inauguration Mass, which they had all attended that morning. "It was so exciting to be there this morning, when the Holy Father said Mass," he said. When he learned that not only was I a Catholic ("Are you an Anglican or a Roman Franciscan?"), but that Anglican/

Catholic dialogue was my field of research, he told me of his hope that within his lifetime Anglicans and Catholics would be one and rejoice together in calling the Holy Father "our pope."

Different reactions, indeed! I recall them because they highlight two points of importance for any discussion of Anglican attitudes toward the issue of papal primacy. On the one hand, they illustrate well the three general attitudes identified by the Anglican theologian J. Robert Wright as basic to any evaluation of Anglicanism's historical approach to the papacy. These are (1) the "anti-papal" polemic, which came into its own during the events of the sixteenth and seventeenth centuries, (2) the "non-papal" attitude, which developed over the course of the next several centuries, and (3) the relatively recent growth of a "positive interest" toward some form of papal leadership in the "one church of the future."[4]

On the other hand, the reactions I encountered remind me that history does not develop in a straight line. It is a dynamic reality, and so students of Anglican history are likely to find all three attitudes present in any historical period, however more pronounced some of them would be than others. This rightly acknowledged, Wright's categories of "anti-papal," "non-papal," and "positive interest" do justice to the general ebb and flow of Anglican attitudes, and so may serve to outline this discussion of the question of whether Anglicans could—or for that matter should—join their Catholic sisters and brothers in calling the Bishop of Rome *our* pope.

II. THE "ANTI-PAPAL" PERIOD

The antipapal polemics of the Church of England's early apologists may be divided into two admittedly broad categories: (1) those for whom the papacy was an institution flawed beyond redemption and (2) those who believed the papacy truly could be reformed, and this without any regard to the personal holiness of the man who exercised the office.[5] Let us begin with a few examples of the former.

A. Extreme Antipapists

Among the extreme antipapal polemics of this period is the anonymously penned *A Body of Divinity; or the Sum and Substance of the Christian Religion*. The work had been attributed to James Ussher, archbishop of Armagh (1625–40), in spite of the fact that he consistently denied its authorship. Whether his denials were because he was not the author or that his see was surrounded by people none too eager to embrace England's "reformed religion," this vision of the *Sum and Substance of the Christian Religion* gave voice to vitriol all too common on both sides of the Reformation divide.

> Who is the Antichrist? He is one who under the colour of being for Christ, and under the title of His Vicere-gent, exalteth himself above and against Christ, oppos-ing himself unto Him in all his offices and ordinances, both in Church and Commonwealth; bearing authority in the Church of God; ruling over that City with seven Hills, which did bear rule over nations and put our Lord to death; a Man of Sin, a harlot, a mother of spiritual fornications to the kings and people of the nations, a child of perdition and a destroyer, establishing himself by lying miracles and false wonders. All which marks together do agree with none but the Pope of Rome.[6]

Such anonymity could not be applied to John Whitgift, a future archbishop of Canterbury, when in his inaugural lecture as Lady Margaret Professor of Divinity at Cambridge in 1563, he spoke on the theme *The Pope Is Antichrist*. Though without any commentary as to the personal holiness of the Roman Pontiffs, William Sancroft, archbishop of Canterbury (1678–89), unequiv-ocally stated the firm resolution of his reformed church when he wrote, "The bishops of this church are really and sincerely irrecon-cilable enemies to the errors, idolatries and tyrannies of the church of Rome." Such sentiment was expressed in the daily prayers offered whenever the clergy of the reformed Church of England met in convocation:

We, who according to the rule of our holy reformation, justly and earnestly repudiate the errors, corruptions and superstitions at that time surrounding us and also the tyranny of the pope, may all hold firmly and constantly the apostolic and truly catholic faith, and may serve Thee duly and intrepidly with a pure worship.[7]

In like manner, the faithful of the Church of England were instructed to pray each week, "From the tyranny of the Bishop of Rome and all his detestable enormities, Good Lord, deliver us."[8]

These Anglican divines had rejected the papacy in such strident terms precisely because they believed that it had not only failed to protect the Church from errors of faith, but had itself propagated such errors, including the error of claiming to possess the kind of divinely established magisterium that could make such propagation possible. It is only in this light that one can appreciate the value these churchmen placed upon the declaration that "the Bishop of Rome hath no jurisdiction in this realm of England."[9]

B. Moderate Antipapists

Of course, not all those who denied the juridical claims of the Bishop of Rome were prepared to brand him with the mark of the antichrist. These moderate antipapists held the papacy itself was not beyond redemption. Should the pope embrace the spirit of reform and recognize his predecessors' claims as contrary to both the plain words of Scripture and the testimony of the fathers of the Church, then reconciliation between England and Rome was possible. One example is John Jewel, bishop of Salisbury (1560–71) and author of the *Apologia Ecclesiae Anglicanae* (1562). As he said in the *Recapitulation* of this polemical work,

As the holy fathers in former times, and as our own predecessors have commonly done, we have restored our churches by a provincial convocation, and have shaken off, as our duty was, the yoke and tyranny of the bishop of Rome, to whom we were not bound: who also had no manner of thing like, neither to Christ, nor to Peter, nor to an apostle, nor to any bishop at all. Finally, we say, that we all agree amongst ourselves touching the whole judgment and chief substance of Christian religion, and with one another, and with one spirit, do worship God, and the Father of our Lord Jesu Christ.

...For you must not think that all these things have come to pass rashly, or at adventure: it hath been God's pleasure, that, against all men's [sic] wills well nigh, the gospel of Jesu Christ should be spread abroad throughout the world at these days. And therefore men, following God's bidding have of their own free will restored unto the doctrine of Christ....Wherefore if the pope will have us be reconciled to him, his duty is first to be reconciled to God.[10]

A less polemical expression of this position was offered by William Laud, future archbishop of Canterbury (1633–45), in his 1622 work *Conference with Fisher the Jesuit*. On the relationship between the church of Rome and the Church of England, Laud wrote,

The Roman Church and the Church of England are but two distinct members of that Catholic Church which is spread over the face of the earth. Therefore, Rome is not the house where the Church dwells; but Rome itself, as well as other patriarchal churches, dwells in the great universal house.[11]

It followed that "the Roman patriarchate, by ecclesial constitutions, might perhaps have a primacy of order; but for principality of power, the patriarchates were as even, as equal, as the Apostles were before them."[12] With reference to the relationship between St. Peter and the other apostles,

A "primacy of order" was never denied [the Apostle Peter] by the Protestants; and a "universal supremacy of power" was never granted him by the primitive Christians...."Christ promised the keys to S. Peter"... but so did he to all the rest of the apostles; and to their successors as much as to his. So it is *tibi et illis*, not *tibi non illis*.[13]

This same line of argument was taken up by John Bramhall, archbishop of Armagh (1661–63). Referencing Cyprian of Carthage's *De unitate ecclesiae*, Bramhall argued that

we dare not rob the rest of the Apostles to clothe St. Peter. We say clearly with St. Cyprian,…"The rest of the Apostles were even the same thing that Peter was, endowed with an equal fellowship both of honour and power; but the beginning cometh from unity, the primacy is given to Peter to signify one Church and one chair." It is well known that St. Cyprian made all the Bishophrics in the world to be one mass, "*Episcopatus unus est Episcoporum multorum concordi numerositate diffusus*"; "whereof every bishop had an entire part,"— "*cujus a singulis in solidum pars tenetur.*" All that he attributeth to St. Peter is the "beginning of unity," this primacy of order, this pre-eminence to be the chief of Bishops, to be Bishop of "the principle Church from whence Sacerdotal unity did spring."…This primacy neither did the ancients nor we deny to St. Peter—of order, of place, of pre-eminence. If this "first movership" would serve his turn, this controversy were at an end for our parts. But this primacy is over lean; the Court of Rome have no gusto to it. They thirst after a visible monarchy on earth, an absolute ecclesial sovereignty, a power to make canons, to dispense with canons, to impose pensions, to dispose dignities, to decide controversies by a single authority. This is what made the breach, not the innocent primacy of St. Peter.[14]

Bramhall's use of St. Cyprian exemplifies the deliberate, methodical reflection employed by England's divines for the reformation of their Church, regardless of how extreme or moderate their views may have been. Whatever scholars today may make of their reading of the fathers and approach to the Scriptures, these Reformers' clear intention was to follow in the footsteps of the

Church's great doctors, in order that they may lead the Church back to the authentic, apostolic faith these saints had proclaimed and defended against the errors of their own age.

Of course, the same thing could be said of the Catholic Reformers with them they argued, from "Fisher the Jesuit" to the pope himself. Actually, the same claim could also be made for the charge Pope Paul VI and Archbishop Ramsey gave ARCIC, albeit with one significant difference: now, Anglicans and Catholics are to return to those same sources *together*.

To return to our moderate antipapists, Laud and Bramhall were one with Jewel in a willingness to accord the Bishop of Rome a primacy "of order, of place, of pre-eminence," but not of some divinely ordained magisterium. They held this position based on their reading of the Gospels and the fathers, as well as of the honored principle of St. Vincent of Lérins: on matters of faith, the Christian faithful are bound to believe only what has been held always, everywhere, and by everybody. Thus in their view it was not the Church of England that had abandoned Catholic faith on this point (among others), but the church of Rome. Whether Rome was hopelessly lost was a matter of debate. That England should continue its course of reform, in clear opposition to the claims of the Roman Pontiff, was, however, beyond question.

III. THE "NON-PAPAL" PERIOD

As the tumultuous events of the sixteenth and seventeenth centuries passed into history, a decidedly "non-papal" attitude began slowly to emerge. This attitude is evidenced by the following comment by William Wake, archbishop of Canterbury (1718–37), in which he contrasted the Anglican position on the necessity of communion with the Roman See with that held by the theologians of the Sorbonne (whose decidedly Gallican take on Roman primacy was itself not without some controversy in Catholic circles):

> As to the pope's authority, I take the difference to be only this; that we may all agree, without troubling ourselves with the reasons, to allow him a primacy of order

in the episcopal college. They [i.e., the Gallicans] would have thought it necessary to hold communion with him, and to allow him a little canonical authority over them, as long as he will allow them to prescribe the bounds of it. We say fairly that we know of no authority he has in our realm. But for actual submission to him; they pay as little mind it as we do.[15]

When one hears Wake say that he and his fellow Anglicans paid "little mind" to the pope of Rome, one should not presume that the passions aroused by England's Reformers had burned out. One had only to scratch the surface of English identity to discover that the spirit of "no popery" was alive and well. Rather, it is to acknowledge that with the passing of time, a new era had begun. For churchmen like Wake, *apologiae* against the "detestable enormities" of the Bishop of Rome were unnecessary, however customary their occasional rehearsals may have become. Mary Tudor was dead; Charles V's armada was sunk; the tumultuous reign of James II was over.[16] The Church of England was firmly established within the realm. It could afford to pay little mind to the Bishop of Rome, and so continue to chart the development of its life according to its own reformed identity. One aspect of this life to so develop was the primacy exercised by the archbishop of Canterbury, first within the Church of England and later, as the realm began to spread over new lands, within the churches of what would become the Anglican Communion.

A. The Archbishop of Canterbury

The Church of England's rejection of papal primacy did not entail a rejection of primacy altogether. The question of the royal supremacy aside, the Church was comprised of two archbishoprics that bore, and still bear, the title *primate*: the archbishop of York is *Primate of England*, and the archbishop of Canterbury is *Primate of All England*. Within their respective metropolitan sees, each archbishop continued to exercise juridical authority. It was, as it remains, their right to confirm the election of diocesan ordinaries within their provinces and to preside at episcopal consecrations, to conduct visitations of these diocesan sees, and to receive canonical appeals.

Within the Church as a whole, the cooperation of both primates remains necessary for certain actions to be considered canonically valid. Over the course of time, it was the archbishop of Canterbury who became the preeminent prelate both within the Church of England and within the worldwide Anglican Communion.

It is not without some irony that this development of Canterbury's primacy began in a way that may have shocked Thomas Cranmer and his more immediate, reformed successors. As the realm eventually grew beyond the boundaries of the British Isles, so too did the jurisdictional boundaries of the See of Canterbury. As a result, the archbishop of Canterbury became a de facto universal primate, exercising a jurisdiction that stretched from North America to the Horn of Africa and on to the far corners of the Orient. Granted, the authority exercised by these archbishops was not the same as that claimed by the popes of Rome. Nevertheless, such an expansive jurisdiction contradicted, on its face at least, what has been considered a central principle of the English Reformation: the location of primacy in a regional or national setting.[17] It should come as no surprise, then, that as these overseas communities began to develop their own identities as local churches, they sought—and were granted—various degrees of independence from Canterbury. This process resulted in the development of the Anglican Communion as we know it today: thirty-nine autonomous national/regional provinces whose communion with Canterbury is an integral part of their identity as Anglicans.

This development of the Anglican Communion naturally raised the question of how its provinces would relate to one another as *Anglicans*, without the colonial overtones this term might otherwise signify. The Lambeth Conference (1867) was the first in a series of bodies established to respond to this question. It was followed by the Anglican Consultative Council (1971) and the Primates' Meeting (1979).[18] Recent years have seen the establishment of a series of commissions intended to assist the provinces in addressing controversial issues affecting their bonds of communion, for example, the admission of women to the episcopate (1998) and both the blessing of same-sex unions and the ordination of people in such unions (2003/4). These were followed by the establishment of a commission charged to develop an *Anglican Covenant* that the provinces could adopt as a means of clarifying the question how they *should* relate to one another as the Anglican Communion (2006–2009/10).[19] Central to all these endeavors has been the role played by the archbishop of Canterbury.

The 1930 Lambeth Conference described the ecclesial identity of the Anglican Communion and the significance of the archbishop of Canterbury in the following terms:

> The Anglican Communion is a fellowship within the One, Holy, Catholic and Apostolic Church, of those duly constituted Dioceses, Provinces or regional Churches in communion with the See of Canterbury… bound together not by a central legislative and executive authority, but by mutual loyalty sustained through the common counsel of the Bishops in conference.[20]

Although Lambeth Conferences do not claim any binding authority upon the Communion's provinces, they are in position to claim a significant degree of moral authority, insofar as they give expression to the mind of the Communion. It was with this authority that the 1930 Lambeth Conference asserted that the Anglican Communion "is part of the Holy Catholic and Apostolic Church. Its center of unity is the See of Canterbury. To be Anglican it is necessary to be in communion with that See."[21] With regard to the nature of the primacy held by that see vis-à-vis the bishops in communion with it, the 1968 Lambeth Conference stated,

> Within the college of bishops it is evident that there must be a president. In the Anglican Communion this position is at present held by the occupant of the historic See of Canterbury, who enjoys a primacy of honor, not of jurisdiction. This primacy is found to involve, in a particular way, that care of all the churches which is shared by all the bishops.[22]

The 1978 Lambeth Conference highlighted the personal aspect of this expression of Canterbury's primacy when it stated that the unity of the Anglican Communion "is personally grounded in the loyal relationship of each of the churches to the Archbishop of Canterbury who is freely recognized as the focus of unity."[23]

The particular emphasis in these resolutions of the 1968 and 1978 Lambeth Conferences upon a primacy in necessary relationship to collegiality is reflective of Anglicanism's general approach to the nature of the episcopal office itself. As the *Alternative Service Book* (1980) of the Church of England describes it,

> A bishop is called to lead in serving and caring for the people of God and to work with them in the oversight of the Church. As a chief pastor he shares with his fellow bishops a special responsibility to maintain and further the unity of the Church, to uphold its discipline, and to guard its faith. He is to promote its mission throughout the world.

In this light, the primacy of honor accorded the archbishop of Canterbury may be seen as flowing from the charge he shares with his fellow bishops, in other words, their common responsibility for the unity, discipline, faith, and mission of the Church throughout the world. His role within the Communion is to foster its bonds of unity by assisting his fellow bishops in their task of apostolic leadership, both within their local churches and in the Church worldwide. This is particularly true with respect to the relationship he has with his fellow primates and their particular task of leading the Communion's provinces.

> A Primate's particular role in *episcope* is to help churches to listen to one another, to grow in love and unity, and to strive together towards the fullness of Christian life and witness. A Primate respects and promotes Christian freedom and spontaneity; does not seek uniformity where diversity is legitimate, or centralize administration to the detriment of local churches.[24]

The nature and scope of the archbishop of Canterbury's primacy was described thoroughly and succinctly by the Inter-Anglican Theological and Doctrinal Commission in its 1997 *Virginia Report*. As this description has lost none of its accuracy over the course of the last two decades, it deserves to be cited in full.

[The] See of Canterbury is an important ingredient of Anglican interdependence, yet each of the Provinces is autonomous. The Archbishop of Canterbury is neither a supreme legislator nor a personification of central administrative power, but as a pastor in the service of unity, offers a ministry of service, care and support to the Communion. The interdependence of the Anglican Communion becomes most clearly visible when the Archbishop of Canterbury exercises his primatial office as an enabler of mission, pastoral care and healing in those situations of need to which he is called. The pastoral service of unity is exercised by invitation. For example, at the request of Provincial leaders, the Archbishop has exercised a pastoral role and mediation in the Sudan and Rwanda.

The Archbishop of Canterbury exercises his ministry in relationship with his fellow primates. In considering how to respond to a request for assistance from a Province, he wisely consults all the appropriate resources in the region, the Province and the local diocese. Here, as elsewhere in the exercise of primacy, subsidiarity is important. So too is the exercise of an *episcope* in which personal, collegial and communal elements are held together.

Together with a ministry of presence and teaching, there is also a certain administrative primacy. Historically this has found its unique expression when the Archbishop calls and presides at the Lambeth Conference, where the relationship of the Archbishop of Canterbury to the Communion, and the bishops to each other, is most clearly seen. It is also visible in his chairmanship of the regular meetings of the Primates, and also exercised within the life of the Anglican Consultative Council where the Archbishop of Canterbury acts as its president and as an active participant in its meetings.

It is nevertheless most often the personal pastoral element in the exercise of this office which has become the most visible evidence of the Archbishop of Canterbury as an instrument of unity. Given the magnitude of this ministry, there must be concern that pastoral and spiritual care, beyond the prayers of the Communion, be made available to the Archbishop.[25]

The story of the office of the archbishop of Canterbury is one of continual development, and certain decisions by some of the Communion's provinces, for example, those concerning the ordination of women to the episcopate and the blessing/marriage of same-sex couples, have raised the question of whether and to what extent it should develop further, in order to serve better the unity of the Communion.

In recent years, this question has been given voice in a number of outlets. In addition to *The Virginia Report*, there was the report *To Lead and Serve: The Report of the Review of the See of Canterbury* (2001), commissioned by then Archbishop George Carey, which offered several recommendations aimed at enabling the archbishop of Canterbury to be more personally available to the provinces of the Communion. This call for a more enhanced role was also made by the authors of *The Windsor Report* (2004), commissioned by then Archbishop Rowan Williams, and more recently by the *Anglican Covenant* (2009/10), which is currently being considered by the provinces—with mixed results.

These and any future documents evidence that the primacy exercised by the archbishop of Canterbury within the worldwide Anglican Communion is still evolving. What is more, this evolution is taking place within the context of what may be called the "Anglican Experience," that is, Anglicans' developing a sense of their ecclesial self-identity regarding both who they are as members of the Body of Christ, with roots in the Reformation, and who they are as members of that Body working to restore its visible unity throughout the world. This later aspect of their experience has placed Anglicans in direct conversation with the Catholic Church, a conversation that, in part, has encouraged in some the further development of a positive interest in the papacy as an instrument for the visible unity of all Christians. Before turning my attention to this interest, I shall offer a word on the Anglican experience of primates.

B. A Primate among Primates

As was noted above, a central principle of the Anglican experience has been locating primacy within regional or national settings. Over the centuries, this principle has been instrumental to the development of the Anglican Communion: a communion of thirty-eight independent churches, or "provinces," each led by its own primate. In some provinces, the primate may be a diocesan ordinary, like the archbishop of Canterbury, and serve the province until retirement from active ministry. In other provinces, such as The Episcopal Church (USA), the primate may be a "presiding bishop" who serves the entire province for a set period of time. Thus, primacy at the provincial level is a flexible institution, adapted to the needs and ethos of each region or nation and governed according to the canonical norms of each individual province.

While this principle was referred to earlier when discussing the historical development of the office of archbishop of Canterbury vis-à-vis the Anglican Communion, it is raised again here in order to emphasize the "collegial" nature of primacy—specifically that of the archbishop of Canterbury—within the Anglican experience.

As has been all but explicitly stated above, the archbishop of Canterbury is not the "Anglican pope." Rather, the archbishop should be understood as a pastor in the service of unity, offering a ministry of service, care, and support to the Anglican Communion in and through the relationship he has with his fellow primates. In a very real sense, the archbishop of Canterbury, as primate of the Anglican Communion, is *primus inter pares*, the "first among equals," who exercises his own universal primacy in a markedly personal manner, respecting the legitimate authority of his fellow primates and the canonical norms proper to each of their province. It is this understanding of primacy, rooted in the traditions of the Reformation and developed in the light of the needs and challenges of the times, that the Anglican Communion brings to the table of ecumenical dialogue, particularly dialogue with Roman Catholicism.

In *The Gospel and the Catholic Church*, a young Michael Ramsey, during whose tenure as archbishop of Canterbury (1961–74) the Anglican–Roman Catholic Theological Commission was established, gave voice to this understanding of primacy in the service of the universal communion of the Church of churches when he wrote,

> [A] Papacy which acted as an organ of the Church's general consciousness and authority in doctrine, and which focused on the unity of the one Episcopate might claim to fulfill the tests of true development. [At] certain times in history the Papacy conspicuously failed to do this and has thereby been the means of perverting the real meaning of Catholicism. But this historical fact cannot justify a wholesale refusal to consider the Petrine claims. Other organs in the one Body have had their times of failure and self-aggrandisement, and we do not therefore conclude that they must be discarded. Hence it seems possible that in the reunited Church of the future there may be a special place for a 'primus-inter-pares' as an organ of unity and authority. Peter will be needed as well as Paul and Apollos, and like them he will be chastened and repentant.[26]

In a real sense, one may say that Peter has already been so chastened, and as a result expressed genuine repentance. One thinks of the famous example of St. Pope John Paul II in his encyclical *Ut Unum Sint* (no. 88) and, more recently, that of Pope Francis, who at an ecumenical celebration of Vespers for the Feast of the Conversion of St. Paul stated,

> As the Bishop of Rome and the Shepherd of the Catholic Church, I want to ask forgiveness and mercy for any behaviour on the part of Catholics towards Christians of other Churches that did not reflect the values of the Gospel. At the same time, I invite all Catholic brothers and sisters to forgive if, today or in the past, they have suffered offences from other Christians. We cannot erase what is past, nor do we wish to allow the weight of past transgressions to continue to pollute our relationships. The mercy of God will renew our relationships.[27]

No, Pope Francis did not single out any particular successors of Peter in his statement, but it is difficult to imagine him excluding any of them—or himself, for that matter—from any list of Catholics whose actions toward Christians of other Churches did not reflect the gospel, including their occasional failures to live up to the Lord's charge to Peter:

> Simon, Simon, listen! Satan has demanded to sift all of you like wheat, but I have prayed for you that your own faith may not fail; and you, when once you have turned back, strengthen your brothers. (Luke 22:31–32)

Today's papacy looks a good deal less like the papacy of a century ago when the ecumenical movement was born, and it is not an exaggeration to say that the Catholic Church's participation in the movement has played a significant role in this development. What the papacy of a hundred years from now will look like is uncertain, but one would be on firm ground in maintaining that it will be the kind of papacy that Catholics, as well as Anglicans within the sphere of their own Communion, have been feeling their way toward in recent decades: that is, one striving to exercise a primacy-in-collegiality that freely acknowledges itself to be a state of continual and dynamic development, and in need of being understood and received anew in every age in order that it may serve the unity of all those who call Christ "Lord."

IV. POSITIVE INTEREST

Since the close of Vatican II, there have been indications that this "non-papal" stance has, for some Anglicans, progressed toward an expressed interest in or desire for a form of primatial leadership by the Bishop of Rome in the one Church of the future. This is not entirely new, of course. As much was acknowledged in the report *Doctrine in the Church of England* (1938), which had been commissioned by the then archbishops of Canterbury and York.

> We are united in holding that the Church of England was right to take the stand which it took in the sixteenth

century and is still bound to resist the claims of the contemporary papacy. The account which we have already given of the nature of spiritual and doctrinal authority supplies in large measure the ground of our conviction on this point. With regard to the Church of the future, *some of us look forward to a reunion of Christendom having its centre in a Primacy such as might be found in a Papacy which had renounced certain of its present claims*; some, on the other hand, look forward to reunion by a more federal type of constitution which would have no need for such a Primacy.[28]

One also should not overlook the significance of the Malines Conversations (1921–27). From the perspective of the Anglicans who participated in these meetings, it was perhaps the first time they had engaged in conversation with Catholics who did not dismiss their ecclesial self-identity out of hand. Important as this history was and remains for furthering the positive development of Anglican attitudes toward Catholicism, in general, and the papacy, in particular, the immediate impact of the Second Vatican Council was without precedent. This may be seen in not only the attitudes, but also in the stated opinions of several leaders with the Anglican Communion. In a series of homilies, Kilmer Meyers, former bishop of California, stated,

> What I therefore wish to say—for your further reflection—is that we Anglican and Protestant Christians ought to re-examine our relationship to the Holy See as the chief spokesman for the Christian community in the world. In doing this I am not suggesting that in any sense we abjectly crawl to the feet of the Pope to ask his forgiveness and acceptance. The Second Vatican Council and indeed Pope Paul have pointed to the division of blame among all Christian communities for the present disunity of the Church. The Roman Catholic Church clearly is accepting its own share of the guilt of disunity. But, brethren, we must acknowledge our own guilt as well and this we have been somewhat less than willing to do. If Rome attempts to renew herself

in full view of the whole world, nothing less is required of us....And we must admit our share in initiating and perpetuating the schism of the 16th century....If the Pope will undertake Christian amplification of his own real image, we Anglicans and Protestants should consider most prayerfully our relationship to him. We should, I for one believe, acknowledge him as the Chief Pastor of the Christian Family and we should joyfully acclaim him as the Holy Father in God of the Universal Church. Such a move on our part, taken now, is far more important than our current consultation on the reunion of several American denominations. The truth is, we need the Pope because in this perilous age we need some one symbolically potent bishop to give expression to the Word of the Lord for our day. We need someone to say, as chief pastor in Christ, that the worldwide community of Christians must exert its massive power to halt war and conflict in the world. We need a chief pastor who will lead us in the fight against poverty and the powerlessness of peoples in the earth. We need a Holy Father. We need a Father who can speak and witness to the whole human race in such words as those contained in John's *Pacem in terris* or Paul's *The Progress of Peoples* and, quite simply, as the presence among us of the Fisherman....We today may no longer even think of the reunion of Christendom without the Papacy. For a long time we have harbored the illusion that reunion would come by first uniting Anglicans, Protestants, and the Orthodox. Pope John has changed all of this...changed it all, I believe, by his faithful listening to the winds of the Holy Spirit. Our response to his response should be to seek ways by which spiritually (if not organically) we may return to a Papacy renewed and reformed. This, in my judgment, would in no way constitute a denial of our Reformation loyalties, for Rome herself (including the Papacy) has accepted the principle of continued reformation in the Church.[29]

Though perhaps not with the same degree of enthusiasm of Bishop Meyers, John Moorman, former bishop of Ripon (UK) and senior Anglican observer at Vatican II, struck a similar note when he stated,

> Whether we like it or not, things can never be the same again. In the ecumenical world Rome has, to some extent, taken the initiative, and the question now being asked is: "What is the rest of Christendom going to do about it? How does this apply to the Anglican Communion?" The Anglican Communion began as a "national" Church—the Church of the English people— and, to some extent, it still preserves that characteristic, although it has spread all over the world. Many would like to continue as such; but the days of "national Churches" are over, and the Anglican Communion will probably have to join up sooner or later with one or other of the main "families" or groups of Christians. There are three such "families"—Roman, Orthodox, and Reformed. Here it is interesting to note that, roughly speaking, of every ten people in the world, six are non-Christian, two are Roman Catholic, one is Orthodox, and one Reformed (that is, Lutheran, Anglican, Calvinist, Methodist, Baptist, etc.). With which of these three "families" should the Anglican Communion eventually find its home?…To a great many Anglicans any idea of union with Rome seems quite out of the question. We have had so many years of bitterness, misunderstanding and fear that the obstacles would seem insuperable. But the Vatican Council has made a big difference. Rome is now very anxious to enter into dialogue and discussions with Anglicans, realizing that, behind our differences, we have much in common….The problem as I see it has nothing to do with subjection or submission. The ultimate position of the Pope in relation to other bishops would depend upon Christian unity, and what sort of Church emerged out of the prayers and labours of Christian people. There is no question here of the Roman Catholic Church absorbing all other Christian Churches, but of the whole Christian world trying to rediscover and restore the one Church which Christ

founded and which in the course of time has become split up through man's sin and folly.[30]

Certainly, neither Meyers nor Moorman was an advocate for an uncritical communion with the Bishop of Rome. For Meyers, it was the work toward a reformed and renewed understanding of the papacy inaugurated by Vatican II that conditioned his own enthusiasm, while for Moorman, it was the papacy's apparent openness to rediscover itself and its place in the Christian world from within the context of "the prayers and labours of the Christian people." In essence, theirs was a qualified hopefulness, one born of their genuine confidence in the integrity of their own Anglican Tradition and its ability to help all Christians "to rediscover and restore the one Church which Christ founded and which in the course of time has become split up through man's sin and folly."

Of course, the manner in which popes have exercised primacy since the Council has itself raised questions in many quarters of the Anglican Communion regarding the primacy the Catholic Church actually claims for its Supreme Pontiff. Such questions concern the teachings of Vatican Councils I and II on infallibility, universal jurisdiction, and collegiality; the place of the Roman Pontiff within a Church that understands itself as a *communion* of churches; the effective openness of the Bishop of Rome to listen to the *sensus fidelium* when considering issues that directly impact the lives of the faithful, especially if their input should differ from his own considered positions; and the degree to which Catholicism is open to rediscover the nature and mission of papal primacy together with its "separated brethren." This last issue is particularly sensitive, in the light of Benedict XVI's decision in 2009 to establish an Anglican Ordinariate within the Catholic Church.[31] Does the Catholic Church truly seek to build communion with Anglicans, within the integrity of their own ecclesial tradition, or to lead Anglicans into communion with itself, on its own terms? That the Catholic Church has disavowed the latter, and that this disavowal has been accepted by Anglican leaders, does not mean that people cease asking questions about the sincerity of the former.[32] It should be noted that these questions continue to be raised by Anglicans (among other of the Catholic Church's dialogue partners), even as they dialogue among themselves about the nature and proper exercise of authority beyond the provincial level within their own Anglican Communion.

There is no ready-made solution to the questions and controversies surrounding the issue of ecclesial authority, especially that of the universal primatial authority traditionally claimed by the Bishops of Rome. As John Hind, retired bishop of Chichester (UK), has noted,

> None of this is of course a peculiarly Anglican problem. In recent years the question of authority has moved to centre stage for most world communions. Anglicans depressed about the difficulties they experience are mildly consoled but not reassured when they contemplate the contrast between the apparent clarity of Roman Catholic positions and the actuality of Roman Catholic life in many parts of the world....Anglicans observe that a professedly infallible magisterium is scarcely more successful than their own principle and practice of dispersed authority in guaranteeing either an unambiguous proclamation of gospel truth or even compliance!...have already indicated that the question of universal primacy is already an internal question for the Churches of the Anglican Communion as well as a matter for ecumenical discussion with Roman Catholics and others. The fact that the question is being asked is of course far from an indication of approval for any particular form of such primacy.[33]

There is a further question being asked, as well, one that has emerged clearly in the light of dialogue. As Stephen Sykes, former bishop of Ely, identified it, it is the need to distinguish between authority and power—a need he saw as most striking within the work of ARCIC itself. He contended in his own response John Paul II's invitation to dialogue on the nature of Rome's claim to Petrine primacy, and agreement upon it, that without such a distinction, Anglicans and Catholics will fail to achieve the kind of consensus on primacy that can, for its part, lead to the full, visible communion that we seek.[34]

Questions remain not only for Anglicans who are simply open

to some form of papal leadership in a visibly reunited Church, but also for Anglicans who, like the young brother I met that evening in All Saints Anglican Church, look forward to the day when we can call the Bishop of Rome "our pope." What is more, if the prejudices of Anglicans who would set their face against any form of papal leadership are ever to be effectively addressed, these questions must be resolved, and resolved in a way that affirms the richness of both our Traditions—Anglican and Catholic—so that together we may give greater witness to the catholicity of the one, holy, and apostolic Church of our Lord. It was in the spirit of just such an affirmation that ARCIC began its work on authority in the Church in 1970, and in 1999, presented their agreement on a universal primacy exercised by the Bishop of Rome as "a gift to be received by all the churches."[35] It is to ARCIC's unfolding of this gift that we shall now turn our attention.

CHAPTER 5

THE PRIMACY IN ARCIC I

Divergences since the sixteenth century have arisen not so much from the substance of [our common] inheritance as from our separate ways of receiving it. They derive from our experience of its value and power, from our interpretation of its meaning and authority, from our formulation of its content, from our theological elaboration of what it implies, and from our understanding of the manner in which the Church should keep and teach the Faith. Further study is needed to distinguish between those differences which are merely apparent, and those which are real and require serious examination.[1]

I. INTRODUCTION

From ARCIC I's first meeting at St. George's House, Windsor Castle (January 9–15, 1970) through its last gathering, also held at St. George's House, eleven years later (January 7–11, 1981), the subject of authority proved to be its major topic of discussion. ARCIC produced two agreed statements on this subject, *Authority in the Church I* and *Authority in the Church II*, plus an *Elucidation*, the purpose of which was to reply to the initial observations made by its members' respective ecclesial authorities of *Authority in the Church I*.[2] This chapter will examine the agreements on universal—and, as part and parcel of this topic, specifically Roman—primacy that were reached in each of these documents.

As ARCIC I emphasized in its introduction to *The Final Report*, it considered the historically divisive issue of universal primacy, as it did all the issues it was charged to consider, in the light of the concept of *koinonia*, that is, communion. This concept opened for the Commission, as it once did for the earliest Christians, "the way to the understanding of the mystery of the Church" (FR, intro., no. 4). There it would be proper to begin this discussion of the achievements of ARCIC I with a presentation of its understanding of *koinonia*, as this was explicated by the Commission in its introduction to *The Final Report* (nos. 4–9).

II. *KOINONIA*

In the introduction to *The Final Report*, the Commission stated explicitly, "The subjects which we were required to consider as a result of the Report of the Joint Preparatory Commission all relate to the true nature of the Church. Fundamental to all our Statements is the concept of *koinonia* (communion)" (no. 4). This emphasis upon the concept of *koinonia* needs to be understood in the light of the Commission's charge to engage in "a serious dialogue which, founded on the Gospels and on the ancient common traditions, may lead to that unity in truth, for which Christ prayed."[3] The Commission had chosen to turn to the primal sources of the Church, in order to guide their common reflection upon, and dialogue toward, the unity of their respective Communions. As "reflection on the experience of *koinonia*" was instrumental to the faithful of the apostolic era in opening "the way to the understanding of the mystery of the Church" (FR, intro., no. 4), so too would it be of fundamental importance to ARCIC, as it sought to unfold this mystery for the faithful of its own day and so contribute to the restoration of their visible unity as the one Church of Christ.

A. *Koinonia*: New Testament Image?

It was with no small irony that at the outset of the presentation of its work, the Commission had to contend with the fact that "*'koinonia'* is never equated with 'Church' in the New Testament" (FR, intro., no. 4). In his study "Koinonia as the Basis of New Testament Ecclesiology?" prepared specifically for ARCIC, Schuyler Brown noted, "Not only is *koinonia* never *equated* with *ekklesia* in the New Testament, we never find the two words related to each other in any way."[4] The images of the Church as "body of Christ," "bride," "temple of God," and "vine" were the more dominant metaphors underlying New Testament ecclesiology.[5] One should not conclude from this, however, that *koinonia* tells us nothing about the way New Testament Christians understood themselves as Church. As Brown went on to explain, "If *koinonia* is never attributed to the Church as such in the New Testament, it is certainly attributed to Christians and may thus have at least an indirect bearing on ecclesiology."[6] ARCIC saw this "indirect bearing" in the emphasis placed by the New Testament writers upon the relationships Christians had with one another and, as the body of Christ, "with Christ the Head" (FR, intro., no. 4). With this clearly in view, the Commission was able to make its case.

Union with God in Christ Jesus through the Spirit is the heart of Christian *koinonia*. Among the various ways the term *koinonia* is used in different New Testament contexts, we concentrate on what signifies a relation between persons resulting from their participation in one and the same reality (cf. 1 John 1:3). The Son of God has taken to himself our human nature, and he has sent upon us his Spirit, who makes us so truly members of the Body of Christ that we too are able to call God "Abba! Father!" (Rom 8:15; Gal 4:6). Moreover, sharing in the same Holy Spirit, whereby we become members of the same Body of Christ and adopted children of the same Father, we are also bound to one another in a completely new relationship. *Koinonia* with one another is entailed by our *koinonia* with God in Christ. This is the mystery of the Church (FR, intro., no. 5).

B. *Koinonia* and Primacy

With regard to the manner in which it applied this understanding of *koinonia* to the issue of universal primacy within the Church, the Commission went on to state that it saw such a primacy as

> a necessary link between all those exercising *episcope* within the *koinonia*. All ministers of the Gospel need to be in communion with one another, for the one Church is a communion of local churches. They also need to be united in the apostolic faith. Primacy, as a focus within the *koinonia*, is an assurance that what they teach and do is in accord with the faith of the apostles. (FR, intro., no. 6)

This understanding of universal primacy in the service of the *koinonia* of the Church itself flowed from the Commission's sacramental understanding of the Church.

> The Church as *koinonia* requires visible expression because it is intended to be the "sacrament" of God's saving work. A sacrament is both a sign and instrument. The *koinonia* is a sign that God's purpose in Christ is being realized in the world by grace. It is also an instrument for the accomplishment of this purpose, inasmuch as it proclaims the truth of the Gospel and witnesses to it by its life, thus entering more deeply into the mystery of the Kingdom. The community thus announces what it is called to become. (FR, intro., no. 7)

In this statement, one can hear an echo of the words Pope Paul VI and Archbishop Ramsey offered in their *Common Declaration*: the mutual efforts of Anglicans and Catholics to restore the visible unity of Church may lead to "a strengthening of peace in the world, the peace that only He can grant who gives 'the peace that passeth all understanding,' together with the blessing of Almighty God, Father, Son and Holy Spirit, that it may abide with all men [*sic*] forever."[7] The *koinonia* of the Church exists not for itself, but for the eschatological *koinonia* of all humanity, a mission it fulfills, for its part, "through the preaching of the Gospel, God's gracious offer of redemption" (FR, intro., no. 8). ARCIC's vision of a universal primacy exercised by the Bishop of Rome within the visibly restored *koinonia* of the Church can only be seen through this lens. Thus, the Commission was able to conclude its introduction:

> Christ's will and prayer are that his disciples should be one. Those who have received the same word of God and have been baptized in the same Spirit cannot, without disobedience, acquiesce in a state of separation. Unity is of the essence of the Church, and since the Church is visible its unity also must be visible. Full visible communion between our two Churches cannot be achieved without mutual recognition of sacraments and ministry, together with the common acceptance of a universal primacy, at one with the episcopal college in the service of the *koinonia*. (FR, intro., no. 9)

III. *AUTHORITY IN THE CHURCH I*

In their preface to *Authority in the Church I*, cochairs Henry McAdoo, Anglican archbishop of Dublin, and Alan Clark, Catholic bishop of East Anglia, recalled how it was "precisely in the problem of papal primacy" that the historical divisions between Anglicans and Catholics "found their unhappy origin." What is more, McAdoo and Clark immediately followed this by noting the significance of the issue of universal primacy, specifically as exercised by the Bishop of Rome: "Hence, however significant our consensus on the doctrine of the eucharist and of the ministry, unresolved questions on the nature and exercise of authority in the Church"—specifically, as the context of this statement indicates, the manner in which such unresolved questions relate to those on the nature and exercise of primatial authority in the Church—"would hinder the growing experience of unity which is the pattern of our present relations."[8]

In other words, there could be no true renewal of visible *koinonia* between Anglicans and Catholics without consensus on the ministry of primatial *episcope* that would serve it. While McAdoo and Clark did not claim that such consensus had been reached by the Commission in its 1976 meeting in Venice, they did assert on behalf of their colleagues that the degree of consensus reached in *Authority in the Church I* had "placed these problems in a proper perspective," and, what is more, argued for a "greater communion between our churches," which would have the potential to make "a profound contribution to the witness of Christianity in our contemporary society" (FR, no. 50).

A. Primacy as Rooted in *Episcope*

After opening with an affirmation of the nature and mission of the Church[9] and of its Christ-centered authority to act and speak in his name,[10] the text of *Authority in the Church I* moved quickly to a discussion of *episcope*, specifically the *episcope* of the ministry of bishop, whose "pastoral authority" was presented as a gift of the Spirit for "preserving and promoting the integrity of the *koinonia* in order to further the Church's response to the Lordship of Christ and its commitment to mission (A-I, no. 5). It was from within this perspective that the Commission approached and examined the issue of universal primacy.

In their exercise of the *episcope* inherent to their pastoral office, bishops preserve and promote the *koinonia* of the local churches they respectively serve by ensuring that Christians gathered in their local communities remain "faithful to the Gospel, celebrating the one eucharist and dedicated to the service of the same Lord" (A-I, no. 8). Integral to this service is the need to make the faithful aware of the larger *koinonia* of which they, in communion with their bishop, are a part.[11] This gave rise to the practices of bishops participating in one another's episcopal ordinations and of their gathering together in councils to discuss matters of either regional or universal import (A-I, nos. 8 and 9). This likewise gave rise to the practice of some bishops exercising *episcope* over their brother bishops both at regional and universal levels (A-I, no. 11). "It is within the context of this historical development that the see of Rome, whose prominence was associated with the death there of Peter and Paul, eventually became the principle centre in matters concerning the Church universal" (A-I, no. 12).

B. Primacy as an Expression of *Episcope*

This developed importance of the Bishop of Rome among the bishops of other churches was "explained by analogy with the position of Peter among the apostles," and, further, "was interpreted as Christ's will for his Church" (A-I, no. 12). It was on the basis of this twofold understanding of the primatial *episcope* of the Bishop of Rome that Vatican I defined his Petrine primacy as being "necessary to the unity of the whole Church," a definition elaborated upon by Vatican II from within the context of collegiality.[12] As a result, the "teaching of these councils shows that communion with the bishop of Rome does not imply submission to an authority which would stifle the distinctive features of the local churches. The purpose of this episcopal function of the bishop of Rome is to promote Christian fellowship in faithfulness to the teaching of the apostles" (A-I, no. 12). To illustrate this point, the Commission recalled that, in the past, some bishops of Rome believed themselves duty bound "to intervene in controversies relating to matters of faith," either by lending the prestige of the Roman See to the confirmation of decrees of ecumenical councils or by entering into the disputes of local or regional churches (A-I, no. 17). Such exercises of primatial *episcope* were manifestations of the "special responsibility" incumbent upon all bishops "for promoting truth and discerning error,"[13] albeit in a universal or world-level manner. The Commission did not use the language of "jurisdiction" and "infallibility" in developing this point. For the moment, its emphasis was upon the primacy as an authentic expression of *episcope*, understood in the light of *koinonia* and collegiality, and with a proper balance maintained between primacy and conciliarity as complementary elements of *episcope* in the service of the *koinonia* of the churches.[14]

C. Primacy, Providence, and the Bishop of Rome

It deserves to be noted that these statements were not made with a blind eye toward history. The Commission acknowledged, both in interpretation and in application, that the ministry of a primatial *episcope* located in the Bishop of Rome has varied over the centuries, particularly with regard to how the primacy of Roman Pontiff stood in relationship to the *episcope* of the entire body of bishops, that is, *conciliarity*. Moreover, the Commission also acknowledged that at various points in history, the primacy and conciliarity have each been emphasized at the other's expense.[15] Neither in theory nor in practice has this balance even been fully realized. With regard to misbalances favoring Roman primacy,

> Sometimes functions assumed by the see of Rome were not necessarily linked to the primacy: sometimes the conduct of the occupant of this see has been unworthy of his office: sometimes the image of this office has been obscured by interpretations placed upon it: and sometimes external pressures have made its proper exercise almost impossible. (A-I, no. 12)

Nevertheless, ARCIC declared, "the primacy, rightly understood, implies that the bishop of Rome exercises his oversight in order to guard and promote the faithfulness of all the churches to Christ and to one another. Communion with him is intended as a safeguard of the catholicity of each local church, and as a sign of the communion of all the churches" (A-I, no. 12). Viewing primacy in this light, the Commission concluded by stating,

> If God's will for the unity in love and truth of the whole Christian community is to be fulfilled, this general pattern of the complementary primatial and conciliar aspects of *episcope* serving the *koinonia* of the churches needs to be realised at the universal level. The only see which makes any claim to universal primacy and which has exercised and still exercises such *episcope* is the see of Rome, the city where Peter and Paul died. It seems appropriate that in any future union a universal primacy such as has been described should be held by that see. (A-I, no. 23)

This conclusion certainly did not imply that ARCIC I's work was at an end. As the Commission stated, although this "consensus is of fundamental importance....it does not wholly resolve all the problems associated with papal primacy" (A-I, no. 24). Among these problems it singled out for further discussion (1) the scriptural basis of the Roman See's claim to universal primacy, (2) the teaching of Vatican I that papal primacy is of "divine right," and this council's further teachings regarding (3) papal infallibility and (4) universal jurisdiction (A-I, no. 24). Nevertheless, the Commission believed that the consensus it had reached in *Authority in the Church I* provided the "solid basis" from which these questions could be addressed.

IV. *ELUCIDATION*

The publication of *Authority in the Church I* went neither unnoticed nor uncommented upon by the theological communities of its respective communions, which was exactly what the Commission had wanted. It published *Authority in the Church I* as an invitation to these communities to offer the kind of commentary that would keep its ongoing dialogue truly responsive to, and respectful of, the theological insights and doctrinal heritage of their respective ecclesial Traditions—in a word, to keep them honest. ARCIC I's own response to this commentary was *Authority in the Church I: Elucidation*, which it issued at the same time as its second agreed statement on authority: *Authority in the Church II.*

A. *Elucidation*: Questions on Primacy

As several of the comments received by the Commission touched upon issues it would treat elsewhere, for example, the relationship between infallibility and indefectibility and its understanding of *koinonia*, it chose not to repeat itself. *Elucidation* was, therefore, a deliberately limited document. The Commission would address only those comments upon which *Authority in the Church I* had a direct bearing and that would not be treated at greater length in *Authority in the Church II.*

With regard to its treatment of universal primacy, the comment took the form of "a recurring question": Was the Commission "suggesting that a universal primacy is a theological necessity simply because one has existed or been claimed" (*Eluc.*, no. 1)? To put the issue more bluntly, in recommending a ministry of universal primacy exercised by the Bishop of Rome, was the Commission canonizing history? This question was necessarily related to another recurring question: How did the Commission understand the authority of the Scriptures in relation to that of Tradition? This is a question that the Commission would address at some length in *Elucidation.* To understand its reply, one needs to keep in mind the "two fundamental principles" that the Commission explicitly took for granted in forming its responses in *Elucidation*: "that Christian faith depends on divine revelation and that the Holy Spirit guides the Church in the understanding and transmission of revealed truth" (*Eluc.*, no. 1).

B. Primacy and History

The Commission addressed the charge that it commended "the primacy of Rome solely on the basis of history" head on:

> According to Christian doctrine the unity in truth of the Christian community demands visible expression. We agree that such visible expression is the will of God and that the maintenance of visible unity at the universal level includes the *episcope* of a universal primate. This is a doctrinal statement. But the way *episcope* is realized concretely in ecclesial life (the balance fluctuating between conciliarity and primacy) will depend upon contingent historical factors and upon development under the guidance of the Holy Spirit.
>
> Though it is possible to conceive a universal primacy located elsewhere than in the city of Rome, the original witness of Peter and Paul and the continuing exercise of a universal *episcope* by the see of Rome present a unique presumption in its favor (cf. Authority II, paras. 6–9). Therefore, while to locate a universal primacy in the see of Rome is an affirmation at a different level from the assertion of the necessity for a universal

primacy, it cannot be dissociated from the providential action of the Holy Spirit. (*Eluc.*, no. 8)

With this, the Commission made clear that its affirmation of an *episcope* of universal primacy was not a blind canonization of history, let alone the history of the papacy. Primacy per se and a universal primacy located in the See of Rome, however this is conceived, are conceptually distinct from one another.[16] The affirmation of the former does not necessarily lead to the affirmation of the latter. Anglican experience, in particular its experience of the evolving role of the archbishop of Canterbury, illustrates this point.[17] What is more, this same experience also affords one the opportunity to discern the workings of the Holy Spirit within, and not in spite of, history.

C. Primacy and Providence

As was noted above, ARCIC I affirmed in *Authority in the Church I* that it is precisely for the sake of the lived reality of its *koinonia* with and in Christ that the Church has been gifted by the Holy Spirit with the ministry of *episcope*, and over the course of time and circumstance, guided the Church in the development of this ministry. That this discernment of the Spirit's guidance in this matter "has often been distorted or destroyed by human failings and other historical factors" is undeniable.[18] The history of the papacy itself witnesses to the presence of such undeniable sinfulness. Yet, this same history also bears witness to the presence of grace, and, in this grace, the hand of the Holy Spirit. If primacy cannot be rejected out of this hand by a simple appeal to history, then neither can its location in the See of Rome likewise be rejected. Instead, by reading history through the lens of faith, it is possible to see the "providential action of the Holy Spirit" as "present[ing] a unique presumption" (*Eluc.*, no. 8) in the Roman See's favor. This was the Commission's reading of history, a reading that it would continually expand upon in the years of dialogue that lay ahead.[19]

This did not, as the Commission never claimed it to, settle all questions regarding either the issue of universal primacy, as such, or such a primacy's exercise by the Bishop of Rome. Yet it did, in the Commission's estimation, provide the proper context from within which common replies to these questions could be reached and, with it, the restoration of full, visible communion in diversity between the Catholic Church and the churches of the Anglican Communion could be restored.[20]

V. *AUTHORITY IN THE CHURCH II*

The Commission had concluded *Authority in the Church I* by noting four difficulties regarding the primatial claims of the Roman See that demanded further consideration: "the interpretation of the Petrine texts, the meaning of the language of 'divine right,' the affirmation of papal infallibility, and the nature of the jurisdiction ascribed to the bishop of Rome as universal primate" (A-II, no. 1). After five years of further study and dialogue, it believed itself "able to present a fresh appraisal of their weight and implications" (A-II, no. 1). This appraisal was published as the appropriately titled, agreed statement *Authority in the Church II.*

A. Petrine Texts

On the subject of the so-called Petrine texts, which had "often been discussed in relation to the importance of the bishop of Rome among the bishops" (A-II, no. 2), the Commission acknowledged that while "explicitly stressing Christ's will to root the Church in the apostolic witness and mandate, the New Testament attributes to Peter a special position among the Twelve" (A-II, no. 3). The question of whether these texts contain Jesus's actual words aside, the Commission stated that "they witness to an early tradition that Peter already held this place during Jesus' ministry" (A-II, no. 3). This place was not Peter's due to his own gifts and character, although he had been the first to confess Jesus as Messiah. It was due, rather, "because of his particular calling by Christ" (A-II, no. 5). What is more, although Peter figured prominently among the Twelve, he is always figured *among* them (see A-II, no. 4).[21] His ministry "is that of an apostle and does not isolate him from the ministry of the other apostles" (A-II, no. 5).

The Commission noted that these considerations "help to clarify the analogy that has been drawn between the role of Peter among the apostles and that of the bishop of Rome among his fellow bishops" (A-II, no. 5). This picturing of the relationship between the Bishop of Rome and Peter, whose successor the bishops of Rome claim to be, as one of analogy is significant. It recognizes that the New Testament "contains no explicit record of a transmission of Peter's leadership" (A-II, no. 6). Nor, for that matter, does it contain any such mention of a transmission of apostolic authority beyond that conferred upon Mathias. Even the fathers of the Church were divided in their interpretation.

> Yet, the church at Rome, the city in which Peter and Paul taught and were martyred, came to be recognized as possessing a unique responsibility among the churches; its bishop was seen to perform a special service in relation to the unity of the churches, and in relation to fidelity to the apostolic inheritance, thus exercising among his fellow bishops functions analogous to those ascribed to Peter, whose successor the bishop of Rome was claimed to be. (A-II, no. 6)[22]

With this in mind, the Commission drew the conclusion that "it is possible to think that a primacy of the bishop of Rome is not contrary to the New Testament and is part of God's purpose regarding the Church's unity and catholicity," even though it must be admitted "that the New Testament texts offer no sufficient basis for this" (A-II, no. 7). At this point, the Commission reached back explicitly to its work in *Authority in the Church I* (see A-II, no. 23), and, with the historical sobriety already exhibited in *Elucidation*, declared,

> If the leadership of the bishop of Rome has been rejected by those who thought it was not faithful to the truth of the Gospel and hence not a true focus of unity, we nevertheless agree that a universal primacy will be needed in a reunited Church and should appropriately be the primacy of the bishop of Rome, as we have specified it....In a reunited Church a ministry modelled on the

role of Peter will be a sign and safeguard of such unity. (A-II, no. 9)

B. Divine Right

At this point, the Commission took up the issue of "divine right" as applied to the Roman primacy. By so doing, the Commission entered into explicit discussion with Vatican Council I. This discussion would occupy the remainder of *Authority in the Church II*. Again referring to the agenda it set in *Authority in the Church I*, the Commission posed two questions to the language of "divine right": "What does the language actually mean? What implications does it have for the ecclesial status of non-Roman Catholic communions"? (A-II, no. 10, citing A-I, no. 24b). Its approach to these questions was threefold: "to clarify the Roman Catholic position on these questions; to suggest a possible Anglican reaction to the Roman Catholic position; and to attempt a statement of consensus" (A-II, no. 10).

The Commission explained the Catholic position on "divine right" as meaning that the primacy of the Bishop of Rome, as "successor in the chair of Peter,...derives from Christ" (A-II, no. 11, citing PA 2).[23] Although there is "no universally accepted interpretation of this language" within the Catholic Tradition, the Commission noted, "All affirm that it means at least that this primacy expresses God's purpose for his Church" (A-II, no. 11). This does not imply that "the universal primacy as a permanent institution was directly founded by Jesus during his life on earth," nor "that the universal primate is a 'source of the Church' as if Christ's salvation had to be channelled through him" (A-II, no. 11). Rather,

> [the Roman Pontiff] is to be the sign of the visible *koinonia* God wills for the Church and an instrument through which unity in diversity is realized. It is to a universal primate thus envisaged within the collegiality of the bishops and the *koinonia* of the whole Church that the qualification *jure divino* can be applied. (A-II, no. 11)

On the implication of this understanding of primacy for the ecclesial status of non-Catholic communions, the Commission stated that the "doctrine that a universal primacy expresses the will of God does not entail the consequence that a Christian community out of communion with the see of Rome does not belong to the Church of God" (A-II, no. 12). In support of this, the Commission appealed to the Catholic Church's continued recognition of Orthodox communions as being proper churches, "in spite of division concerning the primacy" (A-II, no. 12, citing UR 14). What is more, it appealed to the teaching of Vatican II that "the Church of God subsists in the Roman Catholic Church," and is neither "co-extensive" nor "exclusively embodied in that Church" (A-II, no. 12). In conclusion, it offered the following interpretation of this teaching:

> The Second Vatican Council allows it to be said that a church out of communion with the Roman see may lack nothing from the viewpoint of the Roman Catholic Church except that it does not belong to the visible manifestation of full Christian communion which is maintained in the Roman Catholic Church. (A-II, no. 12, citing LG 8 and UR 13)

In terms of an Anglican response to this explication of the "divine right" of Roman primacy, the Commission noted how "from time to time Anglican theologians have affirmed that, in changed circumstances, it might be possible for the churches of the Anglican Communion to recognize the development of the Roman primacy as a gift of divine providence—in other words, as an effect of the guidance of the Holy Spirit in the Church" (A-II, no. 13), provided that such a recognition would not entail "a repudiation of their past history, life and experience—which in effect would be a betrayal of their own integrity" (A-II, no. 14). In light of the clarification offered above regarding Roman Catholic teaching on "divine right," the Commission asked rhetorically,

> Given the above interpretation of the language of divine right in the First Vatican Council, it is reasonable to ask whether a gap really exists between the assertion of a

primacy by divine right (*jure divino*) and the acknowledgment of its emergence by divine providence (*divina providentia*). (A-II, no. 13)

Granting this understanding of the "divine right" of the Roman Pontiff, on the one hand, and, on the other hand, what was said above concerning the ecclesial status of Christian communities other than itself,[24] the Commission asserted that Anglican recognition of a Roman primacy *jure divino* could be given without any repudiation of the integrity of its own tradition—or, for that matter, a similar repudiation on the part of Catholics.[25] "Given such a consensus," the Commission concluded, "the language of divine right used by the First Vatican Council need no longer be seen as a matter of disagreement between us" (A-II, no. 15).

C. Universal Jurisdiction

The Commission defined the term *jurisdiction* as "the authority or power (*potestas*) necessary for the exercise of an office" (A-II, no. 16). With respect to the episcopal office, the jurisdiction exercised by bishops varies according to the specific functions of the *episcope* inherent to their respective offices: diocesan ordinary, metropolitan, or primate. Thus, the degrees of jurisdiction associated with these different levels of *episcope* are not in all respects identical. They differ according to the specific functions that a bishop—diocesan ordinary, metropolitan, or primate—"is required to discharge in relation to his fellow bishops."[26] Turning to *universal* primacy, the Commission stated that "within the universal *koinonia* and the collegiality of the bishops, the universal primate exercises the jurisdiction necessary for the fulfilment of his functions, the chief of which is to serve the faith and unity of the whole Church" (A-II, no. 17).

Having recalled Anglican anxieties concerning how the primatial jurisdiction of the Bishop of Rome was defined by (perhaps more to the point, was interpreted in the light of) Vatican I, the Commission stated that the universal primate should exercise—"and be seen to exercise"—his ministry in "collegial association with his brother bishops" as "a service in and to the Church which is a communion in faith and charity of local churches" (A-II, no.

19).[27] This is particularly true in cases when, in accord with his responsibility for "building up the Church," the universal primate exercises his right "to intervene in the affairs of a diocese and to receive appeals from the decision of a diocesan bishop" (A-II, no. 20). For however acceptable such a degree of jurisdiction could be to Anglicans *in principle*, there remained "specific questions about their *practical* application in a united Church" (A-II, no. 22; my emphasis). Though the Commission noted that there are "moral limits" to the jurisdiction of a universal primate,[28] the absence of any precisely defined *canonical* limits did raise the question as to the point at which a possible intervention by the Roman Pontiff into the affairs of local Anglican churches (or even the Communion as a whole) could be said to violate the integrity of these churches' specifically *Anglican* identity.[29] With this in mind, the Commission stated that "Anglicans are entitled to assurance that acknowledgment of the universal primacy of the bishop of Rome would not involve the suppression of theological, liturgical and other traditions which they value or the imposition of wholly alien traditions," an assurance already alluded to by no less a person than Pope Paul VI (A-II, no. 22).[30] It was the Commission's opinion that "what has been said above provides grounds for such assurance" (A-II, no. 22).

D. Infallibility

It may be going too far to contend that the Commission's discussion of Roman primacy thus far was deliberately intended to lay the groundwork for its examination of papal infallibility. The Commission certainly did not make this claim. That said, its treatment of infallibility does follow nicely upon the consensus it had thus far attained, that is, the need for a universal primacy rooted in collegiality, after the example of Peter among his brother apostles, established by Christ for the service of the *koinonia* of the churches, in which name the primate may speak and act in order to preserve and promote that unity in diversity which is an essential mark of the catholicity of the Church. Whatever the reason for its placement within this agreed statement, infallibility was the final subject examined by the Commission in *Authority in the Church II*, and the Commission concluded its treatment on primacy with this forceful statement: "If any Petrine function and office are exercised in the living Church of which a universal primate is called to serve as a visible focus, then it inheres in his office that he should have both a defined teaching responsibility and appropriate gifts of the Spirit to enable him to discharge it" (A-II, no. 33). How the ARCIC reached this conclusion is the question I shall now address.

ARCIC opened its consideration of infallibility by affirming the common belief of Anglicans and Catholics in the Church's indefectibility.[31] From this context, it then asked "whether there is a special ministerial gift of discerning the truth and of teaching bestowed at crucial times on one person to enable him to speak authoritatively in the name of the Church in order to preserve the people of God in the truth" (A-II, no. 23). Yet, before answering this question directly, ARCIC addressed at significant length the issue of the Church's ability to make a "decisive judgment" on a "matter of essential doctrine" (A-II, no. 24).

On the question of whether the Church could make such a judgment, the Commission left no room to doubt its mind.

> Maintenance in the truth requires that at certain moments the Church can in a matter of essential doctrine make a decisive judgment which becomes part of its permanent witness. Such a judgment makes it clear what the truth is, and strengthens the Church's confidence in proclaiming the Gospel. Obvious examples of such judgments are occasions when general councils define the faith. These judgments, by virtue of their foundation in revelation and their appropriateness to the need of the time, express a renewed unity in the truth to which they summon *the whole Church*. (A-II, no. 24; my emphases)

The reference to the *foundational* quality of revelation makes it clear that, in the Commission's mind, the Church does not have the ability "to add to the content of revelation" by means of such judgments (A-II, no. 27). "We are agreed that doctrinal decisions made by legitimate authority must be consonant with the community's faith as grounded in Scripture and interpreted by the mind of the Church, and that no teaching authority can add new revelation to the original apostolic faith" (A-II, no. 23, citing A-I, nos. 2 and 18). Furthermore, to the extent that these decisions are not so consonant, "neither general councils nor universal primates are invariably preserved from error even in official declarations" (A-II, no. 27, citing *Eluc.*, no.3). It is not the case that, in the Commission's mind, "all the statements of those who speak authoritatively on behalf of the Church should be considered permanent expressions of the truth" (A-II, no. 27). Rather, it is the case that in times "where serious divisions of opinion on crucial issues of pastoral urgency call for a more definitive judgment," such a judgment can be made (A-II, no. 27).

> Any such statement would be intended as an expression of the mind of the Church, understood not only in the context of its time and place but also in light of the Church's whole experience and tradition. All such definitions are provoked by specific historical situations and are always made in terms of the understanding and framework of their age (cf. *Authority I*, para. 15). But in the continuing life of the Church they retain a lasting significance if they are safeguarding the substance of the faith. (A-II, no. 27)

As was noted above, this process of discernment and declaration of the Church's mind is a process that involves "the *whole* Church." As the Commission stated, "The Church in all its members is involved in such a definition which clarifies and enriches their grasp of the truth" (A-II, no. 25). This comes about because their "active reflection upon the definition in its turn clarifies its significance" (A-II, no. 25). This statement is itself significant. It reveals that, in the mind of the Commission, the process whereby the Church speaks its mind on "matters of essential doctrine" is not strictly linear in nature. Rather, it is a dynamic process that involves "reflection upon the definition" by the entire people of God. In short, it is a dynamic that entails a definition's *reception*.

The issue of reception is, as ARCIC itself acknowledged, "inherently difficult" (A-II, no. 31). Within the imagination of Catholic theology, it has the ability to conjure the very specter of Gallicanism that, as I noted in the first chapter of this book, so haunted the ultramontanist fathers of Vatican I. Yet, the members of ARCIC claimed to have reached an understanding of reception that could exorcise this specter from the Roman See's fears and enable Anglicans and Catholics together to find consensus on the contentious issue of *papal* infallibility. The Commission stated,

> Although it is not through reception by the people of God that a definition first acquires authority, the assent of the faithful is *the ultimate indication that the Church's authoritative decision in a matter of faith has been truly preserved from error by the Holy Spirit.* The Holy Spirit who maintains the Church in the truth will bring its members *to receive* the definition as true and *to assimilate* it if what has been declared genuinely expounds the revelation. (A-II, no. 25)[32]

With this clearly in mind, the Commission was able to state that the Church's teaching authority is "a service to which the faithful look for guidance especially in times of uncertainty." Yet, "the assurance of the truthfulness" of its judgments "rests ultimately...upon its fidelity to the Gospel." As the Commission succinctly phrased it, "The Church's teaching is proclaimed because it is true; it is not true simply because it has been proclaimed. The value of such authoritative proclamation lies in the guidance that it gives the faithful" (A-II, no. 27).[33] This applies to the decisive judgments of general councils. It applies to the decisive judgments of a universal primate, as well.[34]

It was at this point that the Commission returned to the question of "whether there is a special ministerial gift of discerning the truth and of teaching bestowed at crucial times on one person to enable him to speak authoritatively in the name of the Church in order to preserve the people of God in the truth" (A-II, no. 23). In paragraph 28, the Commission addressed this question directly. While a judgment of the Church is "normally given through synodal decision," there are times when a universal primate "acting in communion with his fellow bishops may articulate the decision even apart from a synod." Therefore, although responsibility for preserving the Church from fundamental error belongs to the whole Church, it may be exercised on its behalf by a universal primate. The exercise of authority in the Church need not have the effect of stifling the freedom of the Spirit to inspire other agencies and individuals. In fact, there have been times in the history of the Church when both councils and universal primates have protected legitimate positions which have been under attack.

In support of this assertion, the Commission cited how this "service of preserving the Church from error" had been performed in the past by various bishops of Rome, such as Pope Leo I, whose intervention at the Council of Chalcedon "helped to maintain a balanced view of the two natures of Christ." With the figure of Pope Leo—a saint on both Anglican and Roman calendars—before them, the Commission went on to state further that this

> does not mean that other bishops are restricted to a merely consultative role, nor that every statement of the bishop of Rome instantly solves the immediate problem or decides the matter at issue for ever. To be a decisive discernment of the truth, the judgment of the bishop of Rome must satisfy rigorous conditions. He must speak explicitly as the focus within the *koinonia*; without being under duress from external pressures; having sought to discover the mind of his fellow bishops and of the Church as a whole; and with a clear intention to issue a binding decision upon a matter of faith or morals. (A-II, no. 29)

This consensus, as I alluded to earlier, did not eliminate all areas of divergent opinion between Anglicans and Catholics. With reference to the conditions laid down by the bishops of Vatican I for issuing an infallible judgment, the Commission noted, "When it is plain that all these conditions have been fulfilled, Catholics conclude that the judgment is preserved from error and the proposition true." However, if "the definition proposed for assent were not manifestly a legitimate interpretation of biblical faith and in line with orthodox tradition, Anglicans would think it a duty to reserve the reception of the definition for study and discussion" (A-II, no. 29). Two principle examples of such a definition are the Marian dogmas of the immaculate conception and the assumption, however exaggerated the importance of these dogmas may be in the religious imaginations of Anglicans and Catholics alike.[35]

Therefore, in spite of the consensus reached concerning both the need for a universal primacy in a visibly reunited Church and the appropriateness of the Bishop of Rome holding this office, "Anglicans do not accept the guaranteed possession of such a gift of divine assistance in judgment necessarily attached to the office of the bishop of Rome by virtue of which his formal decisions can be known to be wholly assured before their reception by the faithful" (A-II, no. 31). Nevertheless, as noted above, the issue of reception is "inherently difficult"—though not, as illustrated above by the consensus reached on it, impossible to surmount—and so,

> it would be incorrect to suggest that in controversies of faith no conciliar or papal definition possesses a right to attentive sympathy and acceptance until it has been examined by every individual Christian and subjected to the scrutiny of his private judgment. We agree that, without a special charism guarding the judgment of the universal primate, the Church would still possess means of receiving and ascertaining the truth of revelation. This is evident in the acknowledged gifts of grace and truth in churches not in full communion with the Roman see. (A-II, no. 31)

After a brief apologia for why it avoided using the term *infallibility* in the work reviewed above, the Commission was confident in stating the following conclusions to its work in *Authority in the Church II*:

> We have already been able to agree that conciliarity and primacy are complementary. (A-I, no. 23)

> We can now together affirm that the Church needs both a multiple, dispersed authority, with which all God's people are actively involved, and also a universal primate as

servant and focus of visible unity in truth and love. This does not mean that all differences have been eliminated; but if any Petrine function and office are exercised in the living Church of which a universal primate is called to serve as a visible focus, then it inheres in his office that he should have both a defined teaching responsibility and appropriate gifts of the Spirit to enable him to discharge it. (A-II, no. 33)

VI. SELF-EVALUATION OF ARCIC I

In their aforementioned preface to *Authority in the Church I*, McAdoo and Clark offered this brief assessment of the Commission's work in the statement, an assessment that could be said to apply to the entire work of the Commission on this subject:

> The present Statement has, we believe, made a signifi-
> cant contribution to the resolution of these questions.
> Our consensus covers a very wide area; though we
> have not been able to resolve some of the difficulties
> of Anglicans concerning Roman Catholic belief relating
> to the office of the bishop of Rome, we hope and trust
> that our analysis has placed these problems in a proper
> perspective. (FR, no. 50)

How is one to evaluate the significance of this contribution? This is a question that can be approached only after other questions have been answered. How was it that this contribution was reached? What was the nature of the consensus that the Commission claimed to have achieved by means of this process? What were those areas upon which the Commission *could* reach resolution, and what significance do they have for the future of Anglican–Roman Catholic dialogue?

The first of these questions relates to the subject of methodology. This was addressed by the co-chairs in their *Preface to The Final Report*.

Acknowledging the growing convergence of method and outlook of theologians in our two traditions, we emphasized our avoidance of the emotive language of past polemics and our seeking to pursue *together* that restatement of doctrine which new times and conditions are, as we both recognize, regularly calling for. (FR, no. 2, citing A-I, no. 25)[36]

Behind this method, one can clearly see the spirit that animated the 1966 *Common Declaration* of Pope Paul VI and Archbishop Ramsey.

In willing obedience to the command of Christ who bade his disciples love one another, they [Pope Paul VI and Archbishop Ramsey] declare that, with His help, they wish to leave in the hands of the God of mercy all that in the past has been opposed to this precept of charity, and that they make their own the mind of the Apostle which he expressed in these words: 'Forgetting those things which are behind, and reaching forth unto those things which are before, I press on towards the mark for the prize of the high calling of God in Christ Jesus (Phil 3:12–14). (FR, no. 117)

Thus, the Commission entered into its "serious dialogue which, founded on the Gospels and on the ancient common traditions, may lead to that unity in truth, for which Christ prayed" (FR, no. 118). Moreover, it did so with an open mind, ready to listen to what its members had to say as men and women of faith and to embrace the truths this "dialogue in charity" would present to them as necessary for the restoration of their full, visible communion as the one, holy, catholic, and apostolic Church of Jesus Christ.[37]

What was the consensus the Commission claimed to have reached by means of this dialogue? What results did it offer, and what was their significance? In paragraph 24 of *Authority in the Church I*, the Commission gave its answer to the first question.

What we have written here amounts to a consensus on authority in the Church and, in particular, on the basic principles of primacy. This consensus is of fundamental importance. While it does not wholly resolve all the problems associated with papal primacy, it provides us with a solid basis for confronting them. It is when we move from these basic principles to particular claims of papal primacy and to its exercise that problems arise, the gravity of which will be variously judged.

This language clearly differs from that used by the Commission to describe its achievements in *Eucharistic Doctrine* and *Ministry and Ordination*. In *Eucharistic Doctrine*, the Commission spoke of "substantial agreement" consistent with the "variety of theological approaches within both our communions," and of their "hope that, in view of the agreement which we have reached on eucharistic faith, this doctrine will no longer constitute an obstacle to the unity we seek" (*Eucharistic Doctrine*, no. 12).[38] In *Ministry and Ordination*, it concluded, "What we have to say represents the consensus of the Commission on essential matters where it considers that doctrine admits no divergence" (no. 17). Thus, what the Commission meant here by "consensus" is not a "unanimous agreement 'on essential matters where it considers that doctrine admits no divergence'" (*Eluc.*, no. 2). Rather, with reference to paragraph 25 in *The Final Report*, it means "a significant convergence with far-reaching consequences." Thus, the Commission was more modest in its claims regarding its consensus on ecclesial authority and, with it, the contentious issue of universal primacy.

As for the results of this dialogue, the Commission found convergence on the following: (1) the complementarity of primacy and conciliarity as elements of *episcope* in the service of the *koinonia* of the churches (A-I, no. 22); (2) the affirmation that the *episcope* of a universal primate belongs to the doctrinal heritage of the *koinonia* (*Eluc.*, no. 8); (3) the need for a universal primacy exercised by the Bishop of Rome as a sign and safeguard of the unity of the *koinonia* (A-II, no. 9); (4) the affirmation that such a primacy of the Bishop of Rome is "part of God's design for the universal *koinonia*" (A-II, no. 15); (5) the necessity of the Bishop of Rome to exercise this primacy in collegial association with his fellow bishops, after the model of the Apostle Peter (A-II, nos. 5 and 19); (6) an understanding that this service of the *koinonia* should not obviate, but support the legitimate diversity of the people of God in their churches (A-I, nos. 21–23; A-II, nos. 19–21).

The significance of these results was made clear in the above citation of *Authority in the Church I*, no. 24: "While it does not wholly resolve all the problems associated with papal primacy, it provides us with a solid basis for confronting them." Questions remained, particularly with regard to the concrete manner in which the Roman Catholic Church defined Roman primacy in the decrees of Vatican Councils I and II. More work needed to be done. Yet, the Commission expressed its belief that it had provided the foundation upon which answers to these questions could be found, agreement reached, and that consensus "on essential matters where it considers that doctrine admits no divergence" could be reached (*Ministry*, no. 17).

CHAPTER 6

THE PRIMACY IN ARCIC II

In a broken world, and to a divided Church, God's "Yes" in Jesus Christ brings the reality of reconciliation, the call to discipleship, and a foretaste of humanity's final goal when through the Spirit all in Christ utter their "Amen" to the glory of God. The "Yes" of God, embodied in Christ, is received in the proclamation and Tradition of the Gospel, in the sacramental life of the Church and in the ways that *episcope* is exercised. When the churches, through their exercise of authority, display the healing and reconciling power of the Gospel, then the wider world is offered a vision of what God intends for all creation. The aim of the exercise of authority and of its reception is to enable the Church to say "Amen" to God's "Yes" in the Gospel.

—*The Gift of Authority*, no. 50[1]

I. INTRODUCTION

In their preface to *The Gift of Authority* (GA), co-chairs Mark Santer, Anglican bishop of Birmingham, and Cormac Murphy-O'Connor, Catholic bishop of Arundel and Brighton, invited the readers of the Commission's (then) newest agreed statement "to follow the path that led to the Commission's conclusions" (GA, preface). The path, they noted, was not quickly traversed. It lasted five years. However, one would not need five years to understand the Statement's contents and appreciate its achievements. One need only enter into the spirit of the dialogue itself to grasp them: the spirit of patient listening, study, and prayer. This in turn enables the spirited reader to face the conclusions to which the dialogue led its participants, conclusions that together form

> a challenge to our two Churches, not least in regard to the crucial issue of universal primacy. Authority is about how the Church teaches, acts and reaches doctrinal decisions in faithfulness to the Gospel, so real agreement about authority cannot be theoretical. If this statement is to contribute to the reconciliation of the Anglican Communion and the Catholic Church and is accepted, it will require a response in life and in deed. (GA, preface)

The reason behind this call for "a response in life and deed" may appear simply a practical—and seemingly self-evident—necessity. If the object of ecclesial authority is the Church's concrete, lived fidelity to the gospel, then agreement between these Communions on this authority must be accompanied by a response that is itself concrete, that addresses as its proper object the faith that Anglicans and Catholics alike place in the God who has revealed his saving love for all humanity in the flesh and blood of Jesus Christ. Yet, the Commission understood its call to be grounded in something deeper than practical and logical necessity. It was grounded, rather, in the Commission's understanding of the gospel itself. Bishops Santer and Murphy-O'Connor stated this point clearly with their allusion to these words of St. Paul:

> For the Son of God, Jesus Christ, whom we proclaimed among you, Silvanus and Timothy and I, was not "Yes and No"; but in him it is always "Yes." For in him every one of God's promises is a "Yes." For this reason it is through him that we say the "Amen," to the glory of God. (2 Cor 1:19–20)

153

Seen through ARCIC's eyes, authority is indeed a gift to the Church: a gift that stands in necessary relationship to the living faith of the *koinonia* in the gospel of Jesus Christ; a gift which is "at the service of God's 'Yes' to his people and their 'Amen'" (GA, preface). Authority, properly understood and exercised, ensures that the proclamation of God's faithful "Yes" to the covenant, which God made with the patriarchs and fulfilled in the flesh and blood of God's Word incarnate is handed on to each new generation of believers, who in turn offer their "Amen" to it, for the glory of God and the sanctification of the world.[2] This is the backdrop against which the Commission held its third dialogue on authority in the Church. It is only with this backdrop clearly in view that one can understand the Commission's conclusions—including those pertaining to a ministry of universal primacy exercised by the Bishop of Rome within the communion of the churches—and face the challenges these conclusions pose to Anglicans and Catholics alike.

As was done with respect to the achievements of ARCIC I, this presentation of the achievements of ARCIC II shall begin by turning its attention to the concept of *communion*—or *koinonia*, the term again favored by the Commission—which continued its role as the ecclesiological foundation for all the Commission's agreed statements. Only with this clearly in mind can full attention be given to the Commission's presentation of the primacy in *The Gift of Authority*.

II. *KOINONIA*

ARCIC II dedicated four years to delving into "the mystery of communion which is given and made visible in the Church."[3] The result of this dedication was the agreed statement *Church as Communion*. As the Commission noted, "This statement on communion differs from previous ARCIC reports in that it does not focus specifically on doctrinal questions that have been historically divisive" (CC, no. 2). Rather, its aim was to lay "a necessary foundation for further work on vital topics which were broached by our predecessors in the first Anglican–Roman Catholic International

Commission" (CC, preface). As the Commission further elaborated in its *Introduction*,

> Its purpose is to give substance to the affirmation that Anglicans and Roman Catholics are already in a real though as yet imperfect communion and to enable us to recognize the degree of communion that exists both within and between us. Moreover, we believe that within the perspective of communion the outstanding difficulties that remain between us will be more clearly understood and are more likely to be resolved; thus we shall be helped to grow into a more profound communion. (CC, no. 2)[4]

In constructing this foundation, the Commission "paid particular attention to the sacramentality of the Church; that is to the Church as a divine gift, grounded in Christ himself and embodied in human history, through which the grace of Christ is mediated for the salvation of humankind" (CC, preface). By approaching the mystery of the Church in this way, the Commission was able to broaden its horizons, examining the nature of *koinonia* not merely from the vantage of the visible renewal of Christian unity, but with an eye toward the renewal of the entire human family: "To explore the meaning of communion is not only to speak of the Church but also to address the world at the heart of its deepest need, for human beings long for true community in freedom, justice and peace and for the respect of human dignity" (CC, no. 3).

Thus, *koinonia* is understood as a "dynamic reality," thrusting us Christians into deeper relationship with one another and deeper relationship with God (CC, no. 3), not simply for their own sake, but also for the sake of their common mission—a mission that we are unable to fulfill due to "the scandal of our divisions....This is the communion to the study of which this document is devoted" (CC, no. 4).

Given the limits of this book, a thorough examination of *Church as Communion* is not necessary. A brief overview of its central themes more than suffices. These themes are (1) Communion in the Scriptures, (2) Communion: Sacramentality and the Church,

(3) Communion: Apostolicity, Catholicity, and Holiness, and (4) Unity and Ecclesial Communion.[5]

1. Communion in the Scriptures: For the Commission, *communion* is a concept grounded in the Scriptures themselves: "The relationship between God and his creation is the fundamental theme of Holy Scripture" (CC, no. 6). This was revealed in the covenant God formed with Abraham and continually renewed with his offspring, Israel (CC, no. 7). Moreover, it was revealed in a preeminent way in the new covenant that God formed with all humanity in the person of God's Son, Jesus Christ. "It is communion with the Father, through the Son, in the Holy Spirit which constitutes the people of the New Covenant as the Church, 'a people still linked by spiritual ties to the stock of Abraham'" (CC, no. 8, citing *Nostra Aetate* 4).

Although the authors of the New Testament used a variety of images when speaking of the Church, it is the term *communion*, or *koinonia*, that captures the meaning inherent in all of them. *Koinonia* signifies "a relationship based on participation in a shared reality" (CC, no. 12), in this case the reality of God's own life poured out for the life of the world in and through Jesus Christ. This relationship to God in and through Christ places the Christian in a dual relationship: with God and with all those who are likewise with God in and through Christ. Thus, "participation in the life of God through Christ in the Holy Spirit" likewise makes all Christians "one with each other" (CC, no. 13). "This community of the baptized, devoted to the apostolic teaching, fellowship, breaking of bread and prayer (Acts 2:42) finds its necessary expression in a visible human community," whose mission is to be an effective witness to the unity of all humanity with God, through communion in and with Christ (CC, no. 15).

2. Communion: Sacramentality and the Church: Jesus Christ, in his life and ministry, "definitively manifested the restored humanity God intends" (CC, no. 16). As Christ, by "who he was, by what he taught, and by what he accomplished through the Cross and resurrection," became "the sign, the instrument, and the first fruits of God's purpose for the whole of creation" (CC, 16), so too is the communion of all those who have life in him the "visible sign...instrument...and foretaste of the fullness of communion to be consummated when Christ is all in all. It is a 'mystery' or 'sacrament'" (CC, no. 17).

"The Holy Spirit uses the Church as the means through which the Word of God is proclaimed afresh, the sacraments are celebrated, and the people of God receive pastoral oversight, so that the life of the Gospel is manifested in the life of its members" (CC, no. 19). This is not to deny that sin exists within the Church. Rather, it is to affirm that God's promises spoken in Christ to a sinful people will not return to him empty. Thus, the Commission was able to say of the people of God, graced and sinful, "Confessing that their communion signifies God's purpose for the whole human race the members of the Church are called to give themselves in loving witness and service to their fellow human beings" (CC, no. 22), in imitation of Christ, their Lord.

It is precisely here that the members of the one Church of Christ, broken by sin, discover anew the grace of its ecumenical vocation:

> To be united with Christ in the fulfillment of his ministry for the salvation of the world is to share his will that the Church be one, not only for the credibility of the Church's witness and for the effectiveness of its mission, but supremely for the glorification of the Father. God will be truly glorified when all peoples with their rich diversity will be fully united in one communion of love. (CC, no. 23)[6]

3. Communion: Apostolicity, Catholicity, and Holiness: The Commission began its discussion of this topic by stating plainly,

> The Church points to its source and mission when it confesses in the Creed, "We believe in one holy catholic and apostolic Church." It is because the Church is built up by the Spirit upon the foundation of the life, death and resurrection of Christ as these have been witnessed and transmitted by the apostles that the Church is called apostolic. It is also called apostolic because it is equipped for its mission by sharing in the apostolic mandate. (CC, no. 25)

Apostolicity is, thus, fundamental to the Church's communion. By its apostolicity the Church in each age is united with the Church of every age in a communion "which spans time and space, linking the present to past and future generations of Christians" (CC, no. 31). While it is the responsibility of the entire people of God, whole and in each its members, to maintain the Church in its apostolicity (CC, no. 32), this responsibility falls most heavily upon the shoulders of those who exercise the ministry of *episcope*, that is, the Church's bishops. For it is "by means of the communion among those entrusted with the episcopal ministry, the whole Church is made aware of the perceptions and concerns of the local churches: at the same time the local churches are enabled to maintain their place and particular character within the communion of all the churches" (CC, no. 33).

Catholicity flows from precisely such communion—a *koinonia* that is universal both in its scope and in its mission. The Church is catholic because,

> by its nature it is to be scattered throughout the world, from one end of the earth to the other, from one age to the next. The Church is also catholic because its mission is to teach universally and without omission all that has been revealed by God for the salvation and fulfilment of humankind; and also because its vocation is to unite in one eucharistic fellowship men and women of every race, culture and social condition in every generation. Because it is the fruit of the work of Christ upon the cross, destroying all barriers of division, making Jews and Gentiles one holy people, both having access to the one Father by the one Spirit (cf. Eph 2:14–18), the Church is catholic. (CC, no. 34)

Such catholicity is inseparable from the mystery of its holiness, which it possesses not due to its own righteousness, but due to the righteousness of God present in the Church through its communion in the life and mission of God's Son, Jesus Christ.

> The Church is holy because it is "God's special possession," endowed with his Spirit (cf. 1 Pt 2:9–10; Eph 2:21–22),

and it is his special possession since it is there that "the mystery of his will, according to his good pleasure" is realized, "to bring all things in heaven and on earth together under one head, Christ" (Eph 1:9, 10). (CC, no. 38)

The Commission summed up the essential interrelatedness of apostolicity, catholicity, and holiness as part of the Church's *koinonia* when it stated,

> When the Creed speaks of the Church as holy, catholic and apostolic, it does not mean that these attributes are distinct and unrelated. On the contrary, they are so interwoven that there cannot be one without the others. The holiness of the Church reflects the mission of the Spirit of God in Christ, the Holy One of God, made known to all the world through the apostolic teaching. Catholicity is the realization of the Church's proclamation of the fullness of the Gospel to every nation throughout the ages. Apostolicity unites the Church of all generations and in every place with the once-for-all sacrifice and resurrection of Christ, where God's holy love was supremely demonstrated. (CC, no. 41)

4. Unity and Ecclesial Communion: In paragraphs 42–48, the Commission sought to bring into tighter focus the imperative for all Christians to make visible again the baptismal unity they already have in Christ, and to chart the course toward this restoration by pointing out the signposts of ecclesial communion, among which the ministry of *episcope* stands out as one of particular importance.

Looking back to the consensus achieved by ARCIC I, the Commission stated, "For the nurture and growth of this communion, Christ the Lord has provided a ministry of oversight, the fullness of which is entrusted to the episcopate, which has the responsibility of maintaining and expressing the unity of the churches." This ministry of oversight has both collegial and primatial dimensions. It is grounded in the life of the community and is open to the community's participation in the discovery of God's will. It is exercised so that unity and communion are expressed, preserved and fostered at every level— locally, regionally and universally. In the context of the communion of all the churches the episcopal ministry of a universal primate finds its role as the visible focus of unity. (CC, no. 45)[7]

Although this paragraph was the only one in which a ministry of universal primacy was explicitly discussed in *Church as Communion*, its significance for the Commission's future dialogue on it are clear. The Commission would continue in the footsteps of its predecessor and address the issue of a ministry of universal primacy, located in the Bishop of Rome, from within the context of the *koinonia* of the churches. What is more, precisely from within this context it would advance these steps by presenting universal primacy as a "gift" bestowed upon the Church by God in order to serve the Church's mission of announcing the gospel.

III. THE GIFT OF AUTHORITY

The new Commission opened its latest agreed statement on authority with a review of its predecessor's achievements:

- acknowledgment that the Spirit of the Risen Lord maintains the people of God in obedience to the Father's will. By this action of the Holy Spirit, the authority of the Lord is active in the Church (cf. *The Final Report, Authority in the Church I*, no. 3);
- a recognition that because of their baptism and their participation in the *sensus fidelium*, the laity play an integral part in decision-making in the Church (cf. *Authority in the Church: Elucidation*, no. 4);
- the complementarity of primacy and conciliarity as elements of *episcope* within the Church (cf. *Authority in the Church I*, no. 22);

160

- the need for a universal primacy exercised by the Bishop of Rome as a sign and safeguard of unity within a reunited Church (cf. *Authority in the Church II*, no. 9);
- the need for the universal primate to exercise his ministry in collegial association with the other bishops (cf. *Authority in the Church II*, no. 19);
- an understanding of universal primacy and conciliarity that complements and does not supplant the exercise of *episcope* in local churches (cf. *Authority in the Church I*, nos. 21–23; *Authority in the Church II*, no. 19). (GA, no.1)

With regard to the admittedly contentious issue of universal primacy, specifically to its exercise by the Bishop of Rome, this degree of convergence was indeed significant. The Anglican and Catholic members of the previous Commission were able to find a great deal of common ground between their respective ecclesial traditions, ground that the members of the new Commission found solid enough to support the more far-reaching consensus they would achieve in *The Gift of Authority*. This included not only the stated belief that "if this statement about the nature of authority and the manner of its exercise is accepted and acted upon, this issue will no longer be a cause for continued breach of communion between our two churches" (GA, no. 51), but also the vision of a ministry of universal primacy, exercised by the Bishop of Rome, within the communion of the churches that, even now, the Commission believed could be of concrete assistance in preserving and promoting communion between the churches of the Anglican Communion and the Catholic Church (GA, no. 60).

A. Primacy in the Service of Synodality

In the opening of its treatment of universal primacy, the Commission noted that in the course of history the "synodality of the Church," that is, its ability to "walk together," has been served by instruments exercising "conciliar, collegial, and primatial authority." This statement echoes clearly the agreement reached in *Authority in the Church I*, regarding the relationships between

(1) primacy and collegiality and (2) primacy and conciliarity: "A primate exercises his ministry not in isolation but in collegial association with his brother bishops" (no. 21); "primacy and conciliarity are complementary elements of *episcope*.... The *koinonia* of the churches requires that a proper balance be preserved between the two with the responsible participation of the whole people of God" (no. 22); "if God's will for the unity in love and truth of the whole Christian community is to be fulfilled, this general pattern of the complementary primatial and conciliar aspects of *episcope* serving the *koinonia* of the churches needs to be realised at the universal level" (no. 23). Yet, this same statement of *The Gift of Authority* also does something new. It places primacy into a broader, new relationship, one necessarily related to the relationships primacy was already understood to share with both collegiality and conciliarity. This was the very process whereby the Church "walks together" in faith, in other words, *synodality*.

This new relationship raises two questions: (1) What did ARCIC II mean by "synodality," and (2) how did ARCIC II understand primacy's relationship to it? To answer these questions, it is important to understand, first, how ARCIC II appropriated the insights of its predecessor on primacy's relationships to collegiality and conciliarity, and, second, how this appropriation affects the service primacy was understood to render "the synodality of the Church." I shall proceed to do this in line with the sequence of relationships suggested above, addressing in order (1) primacy and conciliarity, (2) primacy and collegiality, and finally (3) primacy and synodality.

1. Primacy and Conciliarity: In *Authority in the Church I*, no. 23, ARCIC I stated that "if God's will for the unity in love and truth of the whole Christian community is to be fulfilled," then a "general pattern of complementary primatial and conciliar aspects of *episcope* serving the *koinonia* of the churches needs to be realised at the universal level." ARCIC I repeated this statement in *Authority in the Church II*, and ARCIC II would do so again in *The Gift of Authority* (A-II, no. 33; GA, no. 46). To understand the relationship between primacy and conciliarity, we must ask two questions: What does ARCIC (I and II) mean by conciliarity? In what sense is conciliarity and primacy considered complementary aspects of *episcope*?

The simple answer to the first question may be found in *Authority in the Church I*, no. 19, where the Commission discussed the purpose and the magisterial authority of ecumenical councils. These councils are a means by which the Church, during "times of crisis or when fundamental questions of the faith are in question" may authoritatively express and assert its common faith and mind (A-I, no. 19). They are a concrete manifestation of the communion of the churches, and of the manifold gifts with which the Spirit has endowed the churches in order that they may remain, as the one Church of Jesus Christ, "under the Lordship of Christ" (A-I, no. 7). In this light, the judgments of ecumenical councils are taken as binding, their Spirit-guided decisions on "fundamental matters of faith" being considered as preserved from error (A-I, no. 19). Simple as this answer may be, there is more to the Commission's understanding of conciliarity than may appear at first reading—at least to Catholics, for whom the term *ecumenical council* often enough conjures images of bishops solemnly gathered around the pope in St. Peter's Basilica.

As ARCIC I noted in *Authority in the Church I*, while bishops bear a special responsibility for the "discharging" of ecumenical councils (A-I, no. 19), "the perception of God's will for his Church does not belong only to the ordained ministry but is shared by all its members" (A-I, no. 6). The *episcope* of the bishops is only one of the gifts by which the Spirit builds up Christ's Body. Thus, ARCIC II was able to say in *The Gift of Authority*, "Those who exercise *episcope* in the Body of Christ must not be separated from the 'symphony' of the whole people of God in which they have their part to play" (GA, no. 30). This has been evidenced by the participation of laypeople and "lesser" clergy in the proceedings of numerous councils (A-I, no. 9). What is more, there have been other councils, local or regional in nature, that have bequeathed legacies to the Church no less authoritative than those of their grander counterparts, such as the councils held during the second century that "determined the limits of the New Testament, and gave to the Church a canon which has remained normative" (A-I, no. 16). Even when the decrees of such "lesser" councils are deliberately more constrained in their intent, ARCIC I stated that they are to be received by the local churches for which they are intended "as expressing the mind of the Church" (A-I, no. 10).

In the Commission's mind, all such councils were (and remain) able to speak with authority not simply because of their membership, size, intention, or even the weight of subject matter, but because their teachings were received by the churches as authentic articulations of the apostolic faith,[8] and remain so even in our own day (A-I, no. 15). In this light, conciliarity appears as a broad concept that describes the formal (and often enough gradual) way the Church discerns the mind of the Lord and, under the Spirit's guidance, commits itself to a more authentic living of the Gospel he proclaimed with his own flesh and blood. In short, conciliarity is a process whereby the communion (*koinonia*) of the Church of churches becomes more truly "one body" in Christ, and so lives more fully its vocation as his Body, given for the life of the world.

> The purpose of *koinonia* is the realisation of the will of Christ: "Father, keep them in thy name, which thou hast given me, that they may be one, even as we are one…so that the world may believe that thou hast sent me (John 17:11,21)." (A-I, no. 11)

It is here that the true complementarity of conciliarity and primacy may be discerned, for it is toward the fulfillment of this same purpose that primacy, specifically Roman primacy, exercises *episcope* within the *koinonia*. "The purpose of [the] episcopal function of the bishop of Rome is to promote Christian fellowship in faithfulness to the teaching of the apostles," and this by both safeguarding and promoting "the faithfulness of all the churches to Christ and one another" (A-I, no. 12). It was for this reason, ARCIC I noted, that the (ostensibly) undivided Church of the first millennium deemed the reception of conciliar decrees by the Bishop of Rome as vital to the integrity of its communion, even to the point that this reception became *the* standard by which not only the canonical validity of these decrees, but also the truth of the faith they proclaimed was measured (A-I, no. 17).[9] It was also for this reason that "the bishop of Rome was also led to intervene in controversies relating to matters of faith—in most cases in response to appeals made to him, but sometimes on his own initiative" (A-I, no. 17). For as the bishop of a church whose prominence is associated with the Church's great pillars St. Peter and St. Paul (A-I, no. 12) said,

> It is his duty to assist the bishops to promote in their churches right teaching, holiness of life, brotherly unity, and the Church's mission to the world. When he perceives a serious deficiency in the life or mission of one of the churches he is bound, if necessary, to call the local bishop's attention to it and to offer assistance. There will also be occasions when he has to assist other bishops to reach a common mind with regard to their shared needs and difficulties. (A-I, no. 11.)[10]

"The authoritative action and proclamation of the people of God to the world…are not simply the responsibilities of each church acting separately, but of all the local churches together" (A-I, no. 8). As ARCIC II noted in *The Gift of Authority*, "The mutual interdependence of all the churches is integral to the reality of the Church as God wills it to be" (GA, no. 37). When the churches gather in council, specifically in ecumenical council, they exercise the *episcope* necessary to affect this unity of faith and life, that is, an *episcope* universal in its scope and in its power to bind. It is this same *episcope* that the Bishop of Rome exercises when, in his capacity as primate of the Universal Church, he calls the churches, in and through the persons of their bishops, to remain faithful to the teachings of the apostles and to the *koinonia* that gives those teachings life. In this light, communion with the Bishop of Rome is indeed "a safeguard of the catholicity of each local church, and…a sign of the communion of all the churches" (A-I, no. 12). For in the singularity of his person, Rome's bishop effectively manifests that which all the churches collectively reveal themselves to be: the unity born of, and inherent to, the diversity of all those numbered among the members of Christ's Body—Christ's one, holy, catholic, and apostolic Church.

2. Primacy and Collegiality: *Collegiality* was the term used by ARCIC I to describe the relationship shared among bishops as members of the episcopal college by virtue of their "succession" to the college of the apostles. With respect to primacy, collegiality marks how the Bishop of Rome as the "successor" of the apostle Peter relates to his brother bishops, either individually or as a body, in the exercise of the *episcope* proper to him as universal primate. While it may be argued that collegiality is a concept more properly Catholic than Anglican,[11] it is clear from the testimony of its three agreed statements on authority that the full membership of ARCIC (I and II) believed collegiality to be a term it could make its own. Bearing in mind what was noted earlier concerning the Petrine texts, that Peter's ministry was that of an apostle and did not isolate him from the ministry of his brothers (A-II, no. 5), collegiality became for both ARCIC I and II not primacy's counterweight, but the proper context within which it is to be approached and the exercise of its *episcope* to be appreciated.

Collegiality was first referred to in *Authority in the Church I*, no. 21, where ARCIC I stated, "A primate exercises his ministry not in isolation but in collegial association with his brother bishops. His intervention in the affairs of a local church should not be made in such a way as to usurp the responsibility of its bishop." However, it was in the preceding paragraph that the commission stated clearly what "collegial association" entailed:

> The bishops are collectively responsible for defending and interpreting the apostolic faith. The primacy accorded to a bishop implies that, after consulting his fellow bishops, he may speak in their name and express their mind. The recognition of his position by the faithful creates an expectation that on occasion he will take an initiative in speaking for the Church. Primatial statements are only one way by which the Holy Spirit keeps the people of God faithful to the truth of the Gospel. (A-I, no. 20)

In light of paragraph 20, it may be said that the commission's understanding of the collegial relationship had between the primate and his episcopal brothers was marked by the following characteristics: it is episcopal, representative, recognizable, and complementary. I shall examine each of these in turn.

That the bishops are "collectively responsible for defending and interpreting the apostolic faith" is entirely consistent with what ARCIC stated earlier in *Authority in the Church I* regarding episcopal ministry. By virtue of their ordination, bishops share in the Spirit's gift of *episcope*, which endows them with the authority necessary to preserve and promote "the integrity of the *koinonia* in order to further the Church's response to the Lordship of Christ and its commitment to mission" (A-I, no. 5). In the exercise of this *episcope*, each bishop is obliged to make the church within which he presides "aware of the universal communion of which it is part" (A-I, no. 8), for "every bishop receives at ordination both responsibility for his local church and the obligation to maintain it in living awareness and practical service to the other churches" (A-I, no. 10). Collegiality thus describes the kind of relationship had between bishops in the fulfillment of their charge. It is a relationship wholly mutual in nature in which they may expect to be supported and corrected, as the need arises, as together they fulfill their vocation to serve the "Church of God" as it exists both in their own local churches and in the communion they share (A-I, no. 10).

It is precisely this relationship among the members of the College of Bishops that provides the primate—the Bishop of Rome—with the root from which his ministry takes shape. If the Roman Pontiff is endowed with the *episcope* needed to fulfill his responsibilities as universal primate, it is because he is first and foremost a bishop, and as such is necessarily related to all those who exercise *episcope* within the churches over which they preside. In this context, the maxim of Gregory the Great proves itself: the honor of the Roman Pontiff is truly the honor of his brothers, for what he is for the Church as Bishop of *Rome* he is because of who he is among his brothers: *Bishop* of Rome, *primus inter pares* within their College.

Collegiality's representative character flows from the discussion of its episcopal character. In their own persons, bishops give expression to the unity that their churches share with one another (A-I, no. 8). They represent to the communion the churches within which they preside, and in turn represent to the faithful of these churches the wider communion within which their communities live.[12] Such representation is especially evident when the bishops exercise their ministry in common. On these occasions, the *episcope* they exercise collectively is of a higher degree than that which they exercise individually within their own dioceses or regions. On these occasions, the bishops act as a body, as a *College*, and do so in the name of the Body they collegially serve, that is, the unity in diversity that is the Body of Christ, the Church.

It is in this same manner that the Bishop of Rome represents the College of Bishops when he exercises the *episcope* proper to him as primate. His ministry *is* their ministry, exercised in a singular way. He acts in their name because he is, primarily, their brother. He knows their mind. He shares in it. As the first among them, he has both the right and the obligation to act according to that mind. This is never more the case when the need arises for the churches to be reminded of who they are as Church, the sacrament of God's presence in and for the world (CC, nos. 16–24). On those occasions, what the Roman Pontiff speaks to the churches is nothing less (and nothing more!) than their own faith. This is the faith in which his own church shares. It is the faith proclaimed by the bishops, as did the apostles before them, and, as the apostle Peter did before him, it is this faith that the Bishop of Rome exhorts the churches to live in fidelity to their Lord.

When the Bishop of Rome exercises this *episcope* as head of the College of Bishops and primate of the communion of the Church of churches that the College both represents and serves, it is vital that he be seen to be doing so. This is collegiality's third characteristic: the collegial nature of the Bishop of Rome's primatial actions must be recognized as such. This is particularly true in cases when the Roman Pontiff is called upon to define solemnly, "from the chair of Peter in the church of Peter and Paul," an article of the Church's faith. As ARCIC II noted,

> Any such definition is pronounced *within* the college of those who exercise *episcope* and not outside that college. Such authoritative teaching is a particular exercise of the calling and responsibility of the body of bishops to teach and affirm the faith. When the faith is articulated in this way, the Bishop of Rome proclaims the faith of the local churches. It is thus the wholly reliable teaching of the whole Church that is operative in the judgement of the universal primate. (GA, no. 47; original emphases)

168

For the Bishop of Rome to do otherwise—to either act without reference to his brother bishops or, much less, to be *seen* to act without such reference—would be for him to risk compromising the churches' ability to receive his teaching as a true articulation of "the authentic faith of the whole Church, that is, the faith proclaimed from the beginning" (GA, no. 47). In this light, this third characteristic of collegiality is more than a matter of sound practicality. It touches the very heart of *episcope* itself, which the Spirit has entrusted to the bishops "for preserving and promoting the integrity of the *koinonia* in order to further the Church's response to the Lordship of Christ and its commitment to mission" (A-I, no. 5). For the Bishop of Rome to act in any other way would be for him to abuse his primatial trust, compromise his ability (even if not his right) to speak in the name of the Church, and so fail in his responsibilities as St. Peter's successor. This has been the case in the past, and may well be the case again in the future (A-I, no. 18). For ARCIC I, however, such "errors of judgment" must be acknowledged and their causes corrected if Roman primacy is to regain its place in a visibly reunited Church.

Finally, there is the matter of a collegial primacy being complementary in character. Much has been said in this regard in the above discussion of primacy's relationship to conciliarity. There is one other aspect of primacy's complementarity that remains to be discussed, and that is the way primatial *episcope* complements the *episcope* exercised by all bishops in the fulfillment of their apostolic charge.

> If primacy is to be a genuine expression of *episcope* it will foster the *koinonia* by helping the bishops in their task of apostolic leadership both in their local church and in the Church universal. Primacy fulfils its purpose by helping the churches to listen to one another, to grow in love and unity, and to strive together towards the fullness of Christian life and witness; it respects and promotes Christian freedom and spontaneity; it does not seek uniformity where diversity is legitimate, or centralise administration to the detriment of the local churches. (A-I, no. 21)

Discerning the Gift

Though universal in its scope, Christian faith is intensely local in character. It is rooted in the experience of the local church. "Each local church is rooted in the witness of the apostles and entrusted with the apostolic mission. Faithful to the Gospel, celebrating the one eucharist and dedicated to the service of the same Lord, it is the Church of Christ" (A-I, no. 8). It is the primate's apostolic charge to foster this realization of "Church" within the local churches. It is also his Petrine charge to foster this life among them, reminding the churches that they are not alone. "The mutual interdependence of all the churches is integral to the reality of the Church as God wills it to be" (GA, no. 37). They are intimately and integrally related to one another, for they are one Body in the Lord whose gospel they proclaim and whose Eucharist they share. This leads to the discussion of primacy and the synodal character of ecclesial life.

3. Primacy and Synodality: ARCIC II defined its use of the term *synodality* in *The Gift of Authority*, no. 34.

> The term *synodality* (derived from *syn-hodos* meaning "common way") indicates the manner in which believers and churches are held together as they [walk together in Christ]. It expresses their vocation as people on the Way (cf. Acts 9.2) to live, work and journey together in Christ who is the Way (cf. Jn 14.6). They, like their predecessors, follow Jesus on the way (cf. Mk 10.52) until he comes again.

In this light, synodality may be seen as the means by which the fullness of the Church's communion—the unity of all humanity in Christ—is achieved. To put it another way, synodality is the means by which the churches realize both their communion as the one Church of Jesus Christ and their Lord's saving will to, under the Spirit's guiding hand, the living sacrament of his undivided Body given in and for the life of the world.

Consistent with the approach ARCIC I took toward conciliarity and collegiality in *Authority in the Church I and II*, in *The Gift of Authority* ARCIC II saw synodality at work first and foremost in the life of the local church. This was supremely the case during celebrations of the Eucharist.

170

In the local church the Eucharist is the fundamental expression of the walking together (synodality) of the people of God. In prayerful dialogue, the [presider] leads the people to make their "Amen" to the eucharistic prayer. In unity of faith with their local bishop, their "Amen" is a living memorial of the Lord's great "Amen" to the will of the Father. (GA, no. 36)

In the Eucharist, all that marks the members of the Church as God's pilgrim people are present. Here the Spirit shapes anew each local church "through the grace of reconciliation and communion in Christ," enabling it to "be faithful to the 'Amen' of Christ and...sent into the world to draw all people to participate in this 'Amen'" (GA, no. 35). The presence of the Spirit maintains the local church in the apostolic Tradition and confirms it in the "saving truth revealed in Christ" (GA, no. 35), as it hears the word proclaimed and receives the bread newly broken. This is principally the ministry of the bishop.[13] By means of this ministry, the people of God are confronted by the mystery of their own faith and the life that flows from it. What is more, in the bishop's person they discern the communion they share with all the churches scattered throughout the world, that is, all those communities of faith in which this same Word and Sacrament are being heard and received and confirmed anew in order that all people may be drawn into the one Church of Christ and join their "Amen" to God to the "Amen" offered on behalf of all humanity by God's beloved Word made flesh, Jesus Christ.

This Church, together with the saving communion it represents, requires a conciliarity that acknowledges the gifts with which the Spirit has endowed it and that is willing to listen to what the Spirit is saying to God's people through these same gifts. It also requires a collegiality willing to give voice to this Word, in order that the churches in which the bishops preside may be confirmed in the gospel that binds them both to one another and to the apostles. The Commission expressed both of these points when it stated,

The mutual interdependence of all the churches is integral to the reality of the Church as God wills it to be.

No local church that participates in the living Tradition can regard itself as self-sufficient. Forms of synodality, then, are needed to manifest the communion of the local churches and to sustain each of them in fidelity to the Gospel. The ministry of the bishop is crucial, for this ministry serves communion within and among local churches. Their communion with each other is expressed through the incorporation of each bishop into a college of bishops. Bishops are, both personally and collegially, at the service of communion and are concerned for synodality in all its expressions. These expressions have included a wide variety of organs, instruments and institutions, notably synods or councils, local, provincial, worldwide, ecumenical. The maintenance of communion requires that at every level there is a capacity to take decisions appropriate to that level. When those decisions raise serious questions for the wider communion of churches, synodality must find a wider expression. (GA, no. 37)

Finally, at the universal level, this communion requires the ministry of a universal primate whose ministry is a service to the "unity in diversity" of all who "walk together" as one Body in Christ. It is only with this firmly in mind that one may consider how ARCIC II envisioned the Bishop of Rome to be endowed with this characteristically "Petrine" ministry—as we shall do now.

B. The "Petrine" Character of Primacy

1. The Apostolic Character of the Primacy: Having already recognized that the "pattern of complementary primatial and conciliar aspects of *episcope* serving the *koinonia* [i.e., the communion] of the churches needs to be realised at the universal level" (GA, no.46, citing A-I, no. 23), ARCIC II now looked to the testimony of Scripture and the Church's living Tradition for guidance regarding how this service of universal primacy may be realized.

Regarding Scripture, the Commission recalled explicitly the discussion of ARCIC I concerning the Petrine texts, "In the pattern found in the New Testament one of the Twelve [i.e., Peter] is chosen by Jesus Christ to strengthen the others so that they will remain faithful to their mission and in harmony with each another" (GA, no. 46, referencing A-II, nos. 2–5). To this, the Commission added a lengthy citation from St. Augustine of Hippo, the most influential of the fathers of Western Christianity. The citation came from a sermon on the Feast of the Martyrdom of the apostles Peter and Paul, copatrons of the local church of Rome, as an expression of the Commission's understanding of "the relationship among Peter, the other apostles and the whole Church."

> After all, it is not just one man that received these keys, but the Church in its unity. So this is the reason for Peter's acknowledged preeminence, that he stood for the Church's universality and unity, when he was told, *To you I am entrusting*, what has in fact been entrusted to all. I mean to show you that it is the Church that has received the keys of the kingdom of heaven. Listen to what the Lord says in another place to all his apostles: *Receive the Holy Spirit*; and straight away, *whose sins you forgive, they will be forgiven them; whose sins you retain, they will be retained* (Jn 20.22–23). This refers to the keys, about which is said, *whatever you bind on earth shall be bound in heaven* (Mt 16.19). But that was said to Peter…Peter at that time stood for the universal Church. (GA, no. 46)[14]

Read in the light of the synodality, this presentation of the Petrine nature of Roman primacy takes on a new significance. It is not only the case that the primacy of the Bishop of Rome cannot be understood apart from the *episcope* of other bishops—just as the primacy of Peter within the community of the Twelve cannot be understood apart from the authority of the other apostles (see A-II, nos. 8–9, 19). It is also the case that his primacy cannot be understood apart from the unity of the one Church of Jesus Christ, which, enlivened and empowered by the Holy Spirit, speaks and acts with the authority of its Lord.

Throughout *The Gift of Authority*, ARCIC II spoke of the many ways in which this is manifested. The authority of the Church is manifested in the life of the individual believer, when he or she offers his or her "Amen" to God's "Yes" in Christ, an "Amen" that can never be offered in isolation from the "Amen" of the Church to all that God has revealed in Christ.[15] It is manifested in the celebration of the Eucharist, when the local community of believers is united in a communion that neither space nor time can circumscribe.[16] It is manifested in the "handing on" of the apostolic Tradition, which is itself "an act of communion whereby the Spirit unites the local church of our day with those that preceded them in the apostolic faith" (GA, no. 16), so that they may be able to receive the word of God—"the uniquely inspired witness to divine revelation" (GA, no. 19), in which the Church possesses "an authoritative record of the apostolic Tradition" (GA, no. 21)—"in many varied circumstances and continually changing times" (GA, no. 16). What is more, it is manifested when the Church exercises the authority

> Jesus bestowed upon his disciples...for mission, to preach and to heal (cf. Lk 9.1–2, 10.1)....In the early Church, the preaching of the Word of God in the power of the Spirit was seen as the defining characteristic of apostolic authority (cf. 1 Cor 1.17, 2.4–5). In the proclamation of Christ crucified, the "Yes" of God to humanity is made a present reality and all are invited to respond with their "Amen." (GA, no. 32)

It is at this point that one begins to see manifested the radically apostolic character of authority in the Church, including that of primatial, "Petrine" authority.

> Thus, the exercise of ministerial authority within the Church, not least by those entrusted with the ministry of *episcope*, has a radically missionary dimension. Authority is exercised within the Church for the sake of those outside it, that the Gospel may be proclaimed "in power and in the Holy Spirit and with full conviction" (1 Thess 1.5). This authority enables the whole Church to embody the Gospel and become the missionary and prophetic servant of the Lord. (GA, no. 32)

2. Primacy as Authority for Mission: Following its citation of St. Augustine in support of its understanding of the Petrine character of universal primacy, the Commission turned its attention to the undeniable fact that this primacy has been exercised by the Bishop of Rome, and accepted by the churches for the welfare of their communion in Christ.

> Historically, the Bishop of Rome has exercised such a ministry either for the benefit of the whole Church, as when Leo contributed to the Council of Chalcedon, or for the benefit of a local church, as when Gregory the Great supported Augustine of Canterbury's mission and ordering of the English church. This gift has been welcomed and the ministry of these Bishops of Rome continues to be celebrated liturgically by Anglicans as well as Roman Catholics. (GA, no. 46)

At this point, one cannot help but recall these words of Archbishop Michael Ramsey:

> But this historical fact [that at certain times in history the Papacy conspicuously failed to maintain the unity of the Episcopate and has thereby been the means of perverting the real meaning of Catholicism] cannot justify a wholesale refusal to consider the Petrine claims. Other organs in the one Body have had their times of failure and self-aggrandisement, and we do not therefore conclude that they must be discarded.[17]

If the conspicuous failures of those who once sat upon Peter's *cathedra* were enough to divide the visible communion of the Church of churches, might the recollection of those moments when Bishops of Rome showed themselves to have truly been "Peter" be enough now for Christians to consider that the primacy claimed by the See of Rome may have something to offer them in their work of restoring their communion and give credence to their profession to be Christ's one, holy, catholic, and apostolic Church (see A-II, no. 13)? The members of ARCIC II believed in this possibility, and this even with respect to that aspect of primacy that has caused no small amount of controversy over the centuries: the nature and exercise of papal teaching magisterium.

C. Primacy and Teaching Magisterium

"Within his wider ministry, the Bishop of Rome offers a specific ministry concerning the discernment of truth, as an expression of universal primacy" (GA, no. 47). These words call to mind the discussion of ARCIC I on papal infallibility in *Authority in the Church II*. The Commission was able to find a degree of common ground on this issue that surprised many of its members (see A-I, no. 25). Nevertheless, the issue remained problematic, specifically when considered in light of the relatively recent papal pronouncements on the immaculate conception and the assumption, not to mention the manner in which papal infallibility was defined by the First Vatican Council in its decree *Pastor Aeternus* (see A-II, nos. 30–31). ARCIC II was perhaps understating the issue a bit when it said that this "particular service has been the source of difficulties and misunderstandings among the churches" (GA, no. 47). Regardless, in *The Gift of Authority*, the Commission believed it had found a way not around, but through these difficulties and misunderstandings to a ground solid enough for them to stand upon and assert, "if this statement about the nature of authority and the manner of its exercise is accepted and acted upon, this issue will no longer be a cause for continued breach of communion between our two churches" (GA, no. 51). This ground is expressed in paragraph 47,[18] and may be broken open under the following headings: (1) Primatial Magisterium as Rooted in the Faith of the People of God; (2) Primatial Magisterium as an Expression of the *Koinonia*; (3) Universal Teaching Magisterium as Intrinsic to the Ministry of Universal Primacy.

1. Primatial Magisterium as Rooted in the Faith of the People of God: "Every solemn definition pronounced from the chair of Peter in the church of Peter and Paul may…express only the faith of the Church." Here ARCIC II affirmed what its predecessor said, namely that "no teaching authority can add new revelation to the original apostolic faith" (A-II, no. 23, citing A-I, nos. 2, 18). Rather, it is the case that, when the Bishop of Rome exercises his Petrine charge to strengthen his brothers,[19] he speaks "authoritatively in the name of the Church in order to preserve the people of God in the truth" (A-II, no. 23), the very truth of the gospel from which Christ has promised that his Church will not stray.[20]

The question here arises: How may the Church be sure of this? This question may well be interpreted as opening the way to a discussion of the process by which the authoritative teachings of those entrusted with *episcope* are received by the entire people of God. Such an interpretation would not be unwarranted. In fact, ARCIC II took up the issue of such a reception by the Church earlier in paragraph 43. However, in paragraph 47, it moved the discussion in another direction: toward that of the collegial relationship shared between the Bishop of Rome and his fellow bishops as members of the episcopal College. By taking this route, the Commission broadened the discussion's horizons, and did so by taking up the context within which reception finds its significance: the synodal nature of the Church.

2. Primatial Magisterium as an Expression of the *Koinonia*: With the opening lines of paragraph 47, the Commission acknowledged that the Bishop of Rome's "specific ministry concerning the discernment of truth…has been the source of difficulties and misunderstandings among the churches." Therefore, the Commission stated clearly that "every solemn definition pronounced from the chair of Peter in the church of Peter and Paul…is pronounced *within* the college of those who exercise *episcope* and not outside that college" (emphases in GA). This is not a matter of mere practicality. It is founded upon the very nature of the *episcope* that the Roman Pontiff precisely as the *Bishop* of Rome shares with other bishops as members of the College: "Such authoritative teaching is a particular exercise of the calling and responsibility of the body of bishops to teach and affirm the faith."

> The duty of maintaining the Church in the truth is one of the essential functions of the episcopal college. It has the power to exercise this ministry because it is bound in succession to the apostles, who were the body authorised and sent by Christ to preach the Gospel to all the nations. The authenticity of the teaching of individual bishops is evident when this teaching is in solidarity with that of the whole episcopal college. The exercise of

this teaching authority requires that what it teaches be faithful to Holy Scripture and consistent with apostolic Tradition. This is expressed by the teaching of the Second Vatican Council, "This teaching office is not above the Word of God, but serves it." (GA, no. 44, citing DV 10)

Thus understood, when the Bishop of Rome solemnly defines a matter of faith, he is speaking not his own mind, but the mind of the entire College of Bishops, of which he is the "first" member. What is more, when the Bishop of Rome does act in this way, it is not with an *episcope* different in *kind* from that of his fellow bishops. It is a difference only in *degree*: it corresponds precisely to the universal character of his Petrine ministry.

Finally, when the Bishop of Rome gives voice to the mind of the College of Bishops on a matter of faith, what he is declaring is nothing less—and nothing more—than the faith of the Church of churches in every locale and, moreover, in every generation. For it is precisely this faith that the College is empowered by the Spirit to preach and to teach, not as a body of impersonal "truths" that they merely "handed on,"[21] but as a living reality in which the bishops themselves, as members of people of God, intimately share.

> Those who exercise *episcope* in the Body of Christ must not be separated from the 'symphony' of the whole people of God in which they have their part to play. They need to be alert to the *sensus fidelium*, in which they share, if they are to be made aware when something is needed for the well-being and mission of the community, or when some element of the Tradition needs to be received in a fresh way. The charism and function of *episcope* are specifically connected to the *ministry of memory*, which constantly renews the Church in hope. Through such ministry the Holy Spirit keeps alive in the Church the memory of what God did and revealed, and the hope of what God will do to bring all things into unity in Christ. In this way, not only from generation to generation, but also from place to place, the one faith is communicated and lived out. This is the ministry exercised by the bishop, and by ordained persons under the

bishop's care, as they proclaim the Word, minister the sacraments, and take their part in administering discipline for the common good. The bishops, the clergy and the other faithful must all recognise and receive what is mediated from God through each other. Thus the *sensus fidelium* of the people of God and the ministry of memory exist together in reciprocal relationship. (GA, no. 30)

How may the Church know that what the Roman Pontiff is declaring at such times is indeed its own faith? Simply put, because the Church recognizes it as such. It is the faith God's people hear in their local communities, in their celebrations of Word and Sacrament. It is the faith they hear in communion with the bishops of their respective churches, when these same bishops exhort them to be the Body of Christ for men and women who have never heard the saving word of the gospel. It is the faith they hear in communion with the faithful throughout the communion of churches, as together they come to realize that they are united in a communion of faith that transcends the boundaries of space and time—the faith of the one, holy, catholic, and apostolic Church of Jesus Christ. It was with this vision of the synodality of the Church before their eyes, this symphony in their ears, that ARCIC II was able to say,

When the faith is articulated in this way, the Bishop of Rome proclaims the faith of the local churches. It is thus the wholly reliable teaching of the whole Church that is operative in the judgement [*sic*] of the universal primate. In solemnly formulating such teaching, the universal primate must discern and declare, with the assured assistance and guidance of the Holy Spirit, in fidelity to Scripture and Tradition, the authentic faith of the whole Church, that is, the faith proclaimed from the beginning. It is this faith, the faith of all the baptised in communion, and this only, that each bishop utters with the body of bishops in council. It is this faith which the Bishop of Rome in certain circumstances has a duty to discern and make explicit. (GA, no. 47)

179

3. Universal Magisterium as Intrinsic to the Ministry of Universal Primacy: Bringing an end to its discussion of the teaching magisterium of a universal primacy exercised by the Roman Pontiff, the Commission stated, "The reception of the primacy of the Bishop of Rome entails the recognition of this specific ministry of the universal primate" (GA, no. 47). This statement stood in continuity with what ARCIC I had stated at the conclusion of *Authority in the Church II*:

> This does not mean that all differences have been eliminated; but if any Petrine function and office are exercised in the living Church of which a universal primate is called to serve as a visible focus, then it inheres in his office that he should have both a defined teaching responsibility and appropriate gifts of the Spirit to enable him to discharge it. (A-II, no. 33)

In like fashion, it was the conclusion that the Commission drew in the light of the discussion that preceded it—and not naïvely so.

Like its predecessor, ARCIC II was well aware of the humanity of those who exercise *episcope* in the Church: "It is clear that only by the grace of God does the exercise of authority in the communion of the Church bear the marks of Christ's own authority. This authority is exercised by fragile Christians for the sake of other fragile Christians" (GA, no. 48). This is no less true of those who exercise the *episcope*, the authority of Peter. Yet, neither is such fragility nor the sin that all too often follows upon it stronger than the promise of Christ to preserve and maintain his Church in the truth. The Church is *indefectible* in its faith, and its solemn, *infallible* magisterial pronouncements are at the service of this indefectibility. It was with faith in God's promises, vouchsafed in Christ, that ARCIC II was able to offer its vision of Roman Primacy as "a gift to be received by all the churches" (GA, no. 47), for the sake of both their communion as the one Church of Jesus Christ and their common mission as the sacrament of his abiding presence in and for the world.

> When the churches, through their exercise of authority,
> display the healing and reconciling power of the Gospel,

then the wider world is offered a vision of what God intends for all creation. The aim of the exercise of authority and of its reception is to enable the Church to say "Amen" to God's "Yes" in the Gospel. (GA, no. 50)

IV. SELF-EVALUATION OF ARCIC II

In *The Gift of Authority*, no. 52, the Commission expressed its view that it had "deepened and extended" its agreement upon the following issues:

- how the authority of Christ is present and active in the Church when the proclamation of God's "Yes" calls forth the "Amen" of all believers (paragraphs 7–18);
- the dynamic interdependence of Scripture and apostolic Tradition and the normative place of Scripture within Tradition (paragraphs 19–23);
- the necessity of constant reception of Scripture and Tradition, and of re-reception in particular circumstances (paragraphs 24–26);
- how the exercise of authority is at the service of personal faith within the life of the Church (paragraphs 23, 29, 49);
- the role of the whole people of God, within which, as teachers of the faith, the bishops have a distinctive voice in forming and expressing the mind of the Church (paragraphs 29–30);
- synodality and its implications for the communion of the whole people of God and of all the local churches as together they seek to follow Christ who is the Way (paragraphs 34–40);
- the essential cooperation of the ministry of *episcope* and the *sensus fidei* of the whole Church in the reception of the Word of God (paragraphs 29, 36, 43);
- the possibility, in certain circumstances, of the Church teaching infallibly at the service of the Church's indefectibility (paragraphs 41–44);

- a universal primacy, exercised collegially in the context of synodality, as integral to *episcope* at the service of universal communion; such a primacy having always been associated with the Bishop and See of Rome (paragraphs 46–48);
- how the ministry of the Bishop of Rome assists the ministry of the whole episcopal body in the context of synodality, promoting the communion of the local churches in their life in Christ and the proclamation of the Gospel (paragraphs 46–48);
- how the Bishop of Rome offers a specific ministry concerning the discernment of truth (paragraph 47).

Compared to the points of convergence that it inherited from ARCIC I, this view of ARCIC II is certainly justified. Yet, the depth and extent of its agreement applied to more than simply individual points of consensus, however many they were. In the view of ARCIC II, they applied as well to the significance of this consensus as a whole: "We believe that if this statement about the nature of authority and the manner of its exercise is accepted and acted upon, this issue will no longer be a cause for continued breach of communion between our two churches" (GA, no. 51).

In these words one is able to hear echoes of the judgments ARCIC I offered regarding the significance of its statements *Eucharistic Doctrine* and *Ministry and Ordination*. The Commission had reached an agreement that, in its judgment, created the ecclesial common ground upon which Anglicans and Catholics could affirm *and advance* their communion in the Lord. In a word, the Commission had not only pointed out the common ground upon which Anglicans and Catholics could stand and declare their brother/sisterhood in Christ, but had also provided them with the theological foundation they would need to build up that unity as an effective proclamation of the "reconciling power of the Gospel" (GA, no. 50).

As experience teaches every faithful Christian, reconciliation with God and neighbor does not come easily. It entails penitence and a purification of memory. What is more, it also entails a living appreciation for the challenge to conversion—the challenge to examine one's life in the light of the gospel and to commit oneself to living what one has learned with greater intentionality and integrity. From the perspective of Catholicism, a great deal has been both learned and lived from the graced experience of the Second Vatican Council. Yet, there is a great deal more that remains to be done. With regard to the issue of Roman primacy, ARCIC II asked a few pointed questions to those areas of our life where development is needed for the sake of the gospel:

> The Second Vatican Council has reminded Roman Catholics of how the gifts of God are present in all the people of God. It has also taught the collegiality of the episcopate in its communion with the Bishop of Rome, head of the college. However, is there at all levels effective participation of clergy as well as lay people in emerging synodal bodies? Has the teaching of the Second Vatican Council regarding the collegiality of bishops been implemented sufficiently? Do the actions of bishops reflect sufficient awareness of the extent of the authority they receive through ordination for governing the local church? Has enough provision been made to ensure consultation between the Bishop of Rome and the local churches prior to the making of important decisions affecting either a local church or the whole Church? How is the variety of theological opinion taken into account when such decisions are made? In supporting the Bishop of Rome in his work of promoting communion among the churches, do the structures and procedures of the Roman Curia adequately respect the exercise of *episcope* at other levels? Above all, how will the Roman Catholic Church address the question of universal primacy as it emerges from "the patient and fraternal dialogue" about the exercise of the office of the Bishop of Rome to which John Paul II has invited "church leaders and their theologians"? (GA, no. 57)

Over the years, I have heard many Catholics give voice to a concern that questions such as these arise from an unspoken desire to "water down" Catholicism, to dilute its distinct spiritual and doctrinal heritage in favor of a more generic, "catch-all" Christianity that, while appealing to many people both inside and outside "the Church," is ultimately incapable of nourishing anyone with the "truth" of the gospel. The experience garnered from these encounters has taught me that it is not enough simply to point out the fact that there are a great many equally concerned, equally devout Catholics whose mind is markedly different their own—including that of a few sainted popes. Rather, what is needed is to demonstrate that the desire that gives rise to such questions is one that seeks for the Catholic Church to be more truly itself, to be more deeply committed to its doctrinal heritage not as a dead letter from the past, but as a living reality capable of drawing us into deeper communion with all people who place their faith, their hope, and their love in Christ Jesus. This is precisely the desire of ARCIC II.

The Commission called upon the Catholic Church to rethink its understanding of the universal primacy of the Roman Pontiff, not with an eye toward repudiating the definitions of *Pastor Aeternus*, but with an eye toward continuing the process of doctrinal development already evident in *Lumen Gentium*. This is the process that sees the insights of the past not as a dead letter, universally applicable in every time and place, but as a living reality capable both of speaking a word of faith and hope in new times and new conditions *and also* of allowing the faith and hope present in the people of these times and conditions to reshape our understanding of the word we have received. With regard to Roman primacy, what ARCIC II is calling forth from the Catholic Church is, in effect, a *re-reception* of its own teaching (see GA, no. 62) in a time when the churches have begun to listen anew to their Lord's prayer for their unity as his Body, and in a condition of desperate need on the part of the world to see realized in its midst the reconciling love of the gospel that we Christians so often read in our churches, but too often fail to live out with one another—most strikingly so precisely *within our churches*.

Within this context, Catholics, together with their brothers and sisters in the Anglican Communion and in all other confessional Traditions, need to consider more deeply—and more personally—these words from ARCIC II:

Jesus prayed to the Father that his followers might be one "so that the world may know that you have sent me and have loved them even as you have loved me" (Jn 17.23). When Christians do not agree about the Gospel itself, the preaching of it in power is impaired. When they are not one in faith they cannot be one in life, and so cannot demonstrate fully that they are faithful to the will of God, which is the reconciliation through Christ of all things to the Father (cf. Col 1.20). As long as the Church does not live as the community of reconciliation God calls it to be, it cannot adequately preach this Gospel or credibly proclaim God's plan to gather his scattered people into unity under Christ as Lord and Saviour (cf. Jn 11.52). Only when all believers are united in the common celebration of the Eucharist (cf. *Church as Communion*, 24) will the God whose purpose it is to bring all things into unity in Christ (cf. Eph 1.10) be truly glorified by the people of God. The challenge and responsibility for those with authority within the Church is so to exercise their ministry that they promote the unity of the whole Church in faith and life in a way that enriches rather than diminishes the legitimate diversity of local churches. (GA, no. 33)

How might Catholicism re-receive its own teachings on the primacy in light of its doctrinal heritage and of the unity it declares this primacy to serve? This is the question that shall be taken up in the next and final section.

OFFERING THE GIFT

Foundations for a Roman Catholic Response to the Anglican–Roman Catholic International Commission

We have come to a shared understanding of authority by seeing it, in faith, as a manifestation of God's "Yes" to his creation, calling forth the "Amen" of his creatures. God is the source of authority, and the proper exercise of authority is always ordered towards the common good and the good of the person. In a broken world, and to a divided Church, God's "Yes" in Jesus Christ brings the reality of reconciliation, the call to discipleship, and a foretaste of humanity's final goal when through the Spirit all in Christ utter their "Amen" to the glory of God. The "Yes" of God, embodied in Christ, is received in the proclamation and Tradition of the Gospel, in the sacramental life of the Church and in the ways that *episcope* is exercised. When the churches, through their exercise of authority, display the healing and reconciling power of the Gospel, then the wider world is offered a vision of what God intends for all creation. The aim of

187

the exercise of authority and of its reception is to enable the Church to say "Amen" to God's "Yes" in the Gospel.

—ARCIC II, *The Gift of Authority*, no. 50

Among the various authorities established to enable us to make this "Amen," ARCIC explicitly and purposefully named the primatial *episcope* of the Bishop of Rome as "a gift to be received by all the churches" (GA, no. 47), including the Catholic Church.

Most Catholics would probably find this appeal more than a bit puzzling. That Anglicans would need to be open to such a "recovery and re-reception…of universal primacy by the Bishop of Rome" would seem self-evident (GA, no. 62). Historically, Anglicans have defined themselves, in part, by their rejection of just such a primacy. But Catholics? Acceptance of the universal primacy of the Bishop of Rome is a defining characteristic of what it means to be a *Roman* Catholic. How are they to receive anew ("re-receive," in the language of ARCIC) what they have never rejected? Is there any real meaning in this call from ARCIC, or is it merely some form of theological sleight of hand?

Speaking to a symposium on Petrine ministry, Cardinal Walter Kasper, former head of the Pontifical Council for Promoting Christian Unity, responded directly to this question, stating that re-reception is "not an *escamotage* (sleight of hand)." It entails the interpreting of a dogma "according to the 'normal' and common rules of dogmatic hermeneutics. According to these rules, dogmas should be abided by in the sense in which the Church once declared them." This demands not "an irrational and fundamentalist compliance with a formula," but "a progressive deepening in the understanding of the truth that was revealed once and for all."[1] In other words, re-reception is a dynamic process whereby we plumb a dogma's meaning within the context of the rich deposit of Christian faith. ARCIC's call for Catholics to re-receive "the exercise of universal primacy by the Bishop of Rome" (GA, no. 62) is then a call for us to become more authentically Catholic— united to one another by the bond of our communion with the Bishop of Rome and united to the entire people of God by the baptismal bond of our communion with Christ.

Seen in this light, it may be said that the Catholic Church has been re-receiving the primacy of the Roman Pontiff throughout its history, including its more recent history. At Vatican I, it sought to answer both rationalism's challenge to the very existence of such a thing as "revealed truth" and, having affirmed its existence, Gallicanism's minimization of the papacy's role in discerning the contours of this truth. At Vatican II, it strove to penetrate the rich deposit of Christian faith so that it could both renew its own life and reinvigorate its proclamation of the gospel to a new and emerging world. This dynamic discernment brought about a renewed understanding of how papal primacy relates to the authority of the Church's bishops, who, as the legitimate successors of the College of Apostles in communion with the successor of St. Peter, "govern the house of the living God" (LG 18). Today, the Catholic Church faces the challenge of discerning how this gift of Petrine primacy relates to the authority of the Church itself as the people of God, with all their many gifts, and its mission of proclaiming the gospel of God's reign to all people today. An integral part of this history has been the almost fifty-year history of the Anglican–Roman Catholic International Commission.

In the following chapters, I shall consider the ways the Catholic Church may respond to challenges ARCIC named at the conclusion of *The Gift of Authority*, so the Petrine primacy of the Bishop of Rome may be received by all Christians as a gift of the Lord enabling them "to say their 'Amen' to God's 'Yes' in the Gospel" with one mind and one voice (GA, no. 50). Throughout these considerations I shall further demonstrate how both ARCIC's challenges and the responses they call forth are entirely consonant with the deposit of Christian faith and, moreover, with the primacy of the Roman Pontiff that we Catholics have been striving and struggling to re-receive since the close of Vatican I.

CHAPTER 7

"YOU ARE PETER...": SUCCESSOR OF ST. PETER AND BISHOP OF ROME

And Jesus answered him, "Blessed are you, Simon son of Jonah! For flesh and blood has not revealed this to you, but my Father in heaven. And I tell you, you are Peter, and on this rock I will build my church, and the gates of Hades will not prevail against it."

—Matthew 16:17–18

Wherefore we teach and declare that, by divine ordinance, the Roman Church possesses a pre-eminence of ordinary power over every other Church, and that this jurisdictional power of the Roman Pontiff is both episcopal and immediate.

—Vatican Council I, *Pastor Aeternus* 3

The New Testament contains no explicit record of a transmission of Peter's leadership; nor is the transmission of apostolic authority in general very clear. Furthermore, the Petrine texts were subjected to differing interpretations as early as the time of the Church Fathers. Yet the church at Rome, the city in which Peter and Paul taught and were martyred, came to be recognized as possessing a unique responsibility among the churches: its bishop was seen to perform a special service in relation to the unity of the churches, and in relation to fidelity to the apostolic inheritance, thus exercising among his fellow bishops functions analogous to those ascribed to Peter, whose successor the bishop of Rome was claimed to be.

—ARCIC I, *Authority in the Church II*, no. 6

A primacy exercised by the Bishop of Rome that enables the Church "to be the authentic catholic *koinonia*" is a gift ARCIC believes "could be offered and received even before our churches are in full communion" (GA, no. 60). What is more, it is a gift that ARCIC believes could also be offered to and received by all the churches as we strive together to answer our Lord's call for unity (see GA, no. 47).

> Such a universal primate will exercise leadership in the world and in both communions, addressing them in a prophetic way. He will promote the common good in ways that are not constrained by sectional interests, and offer a continuing and distinctive teaching ministry, particularly in addressing difficult theological and moral issues. A universal primacy of this style will welcome and protect theological enquiry and other forms of the search for truth, so that their results may enrich and strengthen both human wisdom and the Church's faith. Such a universal primacy might gather the churches in various ways for consultation and discussion (GA, no. 61).

In the mind of the Commission there is no doubt that the gift of such a primacy depends upon the efforts of Anglicans and Catholics alike to address a series of issues within their own respective ecclesial communities that have the potential to threaten the consensus ARCIC has achieved. With respect to the Catholic Church,

> the Second Vatican Council has reminded Roman Catholics of how the gifts of God are present in all the people of God. It has also taught the collegiality of the episcopate in its communion with the Bishop of Rome, head of the college. However, is there at all levels effective participation of clergy as well as lay people in emerging synodal bodies? Has the teaching of the Second Vatican Council regarding the collegiality of bishops been implemented sufficiently? Do the actions of bishops reflect sufficient awareness of the extent of the authority they receive through ordination for governing the local church? Has enough provision been made to ensure consultation between the Bishop of Rome and the local churches prior to the making of important decisions affecting either a local church or the whole Church? How is the variety of theological opinion taken into account when such decisions are made? In supporting the Bishop of Rome in his work of promoting communion among the churches, do the structures and procedures of the Roman Curia adequately respect the exercise of *episcope* at other levels? Above all, how will the Roman Catholic Church address the question of universal primacy as it emerges from "the patient and fraternal dialogue" about the exercise of the office of the Bishop of Rome to which John Paul II has invited "church leaders and their theologians"? (GA, no. 57)

This list is challenging, though not unfamiliar. It includes questions that Catholics have already identified as outstanding in the work of postconciliar renewal. Moreover, it also includes questions long asked by the Catholic Church's ecumenical partners. Therefore, it is appropriate to ask how the Catholic Church will respond to questions about the primacy, not as they shall emerge over the course of a conversation yet to begin, but as they have already emerged from the patient and fraternal dialogue(s) in which it has been engaged since the close of Vatican II.

Any one of these questions is worthy of a book in its own right—some of which are included in the bibliography. What I shall attempt here is more modest: it will be to read Catholicism's still-developing doctrines on papal primacy anew through the lens of ARCIC, in order (1) to identify areas where these doctrines are in need of further development and (2) to demonstrate how ARCIC's consensus enables the Catholic Church—perhaps better said, us who are Catholics—to respond in ways that are both true to our Catholic heritage and open to the "ecumenical aspirations" of all our dialogue partners. What is more, I shall also do this in the conviction that the vision it affords is not solely for our own sake as Catholics, as we strive (and often enough struggle) to re-receive the primacy during this period of postconciliar renewal, nor is it even for the sake of the "ecumenical aspirations" (UUS 95) we share with our sisters and brothers in Christ. The need for new insights and greater consensus concerning how Roman primacy may effectively be a "visible sign and guarantor" (cf. LG 18) of Christian unity—of our "Amen" to Christ—is a call that must be answered for the sake of our common vocation as the people of God: to be the sacramental sign of the saving "Yes" God spoke to all humanity in Jesus Christ (see GA, no. 8).

> I ask not only on behalf of these, but also on behalf of those who will believe in me through their word, that they may all be one. As you, Father, are in me and I am in you, may they also be in us, so that the world may believe that you have sent me (John 17:20–21).

When the primacy we have received from Vatican Councils I and II is read through the lens of ARCIC, three general areas stand out as being in need of development: (1) the primacy's peculiarly *Petrine* character, (2) the relationship between the primacy's own proper authority and episcopal authority, and (3) the manner in which primatial authority of the Bishop of Rome relates to the communion of the Church of churches. Each of these areas will receive a chapter in its own right, beginning here with the first of these, the peculiarly *Petrine* character of the primacy claimed for the Roman Pontiff.

I. INTRODUCTION

> Now when Jesus came into the district of Caesarea Philippi, he asked his disciples, "Who do people say that the Son of Man is?" And they said, "Some say John the Baptist, but others Elijah, and still others Jeremiah or one of the prophets." He said to them, "But who do you say that I am?" Simon Peter answered, "You are the Messiah, the Son of the living God." And Jesus answered him, "Blessed are you, Simon son of Jonah! For flesh and blood has not revealed this to you, but my Father in heaven. And I tell you, you are Peter, and on this rock I will build my church, and the gates of Hades will not prevail against it. I will give you the keys of the kingdom of heaven, and whatever you bind on earth will be bound in heaven, and whatever you loose on earth will be loosed in heaven." (Matt 16:13–19)

All that we Catholics have had to say regarding the primacy of the Roman Pontiff has depended upon our traditional beliefs that the Lord established Peter as *primus*, first, among the apostles and that this primacy has been preserved *de jure divino*, according to the will of God, in the apostolic succession of Rome's bishops. This is particularly evident in the decrees of Vatican Councils I and II.

Not surprisingly, Vatican Councils I and II both assumed these beliefs as foundational for their respective teachings. Obviously, ARCIC could not make this same assumption. The differing ways Anglicans and Catholics have interpreted the same Scriptures and Apostolic Tradition demanded that ARCIC look back to them as to first principles and examine what Catholicism claims to be inherent to the primacy of the Roman Pontiff as successor of St. Peter. Therefore, before offering any response to the questions explicitly raised in *The Gift of Authority*, it is important that we Catholics return to these same principles ourselves and consider how ARCIC's consensus challenges us to develop further our beliefs in the primacy that Lord established in Peter and the authority with which the person who succeeds the apostle in this ministry is entrusted.

This return shall be made in two steps. The first shall review ARCIC's consensus on the scriptural and historical grounds of the primacy. The second shall offer a Catholic response to the questions that arise implicitly from this consensus: (1) How might a continued theological reflection on the Petrine texts renew Catholicism's understanding of the primacy of the Roman Pontiff as a ministry for the unity of all God's people? (2) What would reflection upon the necessary connection Catholicism claims to exist between St. Peter and the See of Rome tell us about the primacy we claim for Rome's bishop as the apostle's successor?

II. ARCIC ON THE PETRINE PRIMACY OF THE ROMAN PONTIFF

A. ARCIC on the Petrine Texts

ARCIC noted that "while explicitly stressing Christ's will to root the Church in the apostolic witness and mandate, the New Testament attributes to Peter a special position among the Twelve" (A-II, no. 3). Whether the Petrine texts contain the actual words that Jesus addressed to Peter, for example, "You are Peter [the Rock], and upon this rock I will build my church" (Matt 16:18), these texts collectively witness to a primitive tradition that Peter held some position of preeminence during the time of Jesus's ministry.

This does not imply that everything attributed to Peter was unique to him. In several instances what is said of him is also said of the entire company of apostles. Moreover, this apostolic authority was not restricted to Peter and the rest of the Twelve. St. Paul, for example, was—and is—honored as an apostle (see A-II, no. 4). Nevertheless, in the eyes of the New Testament writers, Peter held a position of special importance, one freely bestowed upon him by Christ for the sake of his brother apostles' unity in faith and mission. Peter's was the ministry "of an apostle," and so, far from isolating him from his brothers, it rooted him squarely in their midst.

In accordance with the teaching of Jesus that truly to lead is to serve and not to dominate others (Luke 22:24ff), Peter's role in strengthening the brethren (Luke 22:32) is a leadership of service. Peter, then, serves the Church by helping it to overcome threats to its unity (e.g. Acts 11:1–18), even if his weakness may require help or correction, as is clear from his rebuke by Paul (Gal 2:11–14). These considerations help clarify the analogy that has been drawn between the role of Peter among the apostles and that of the bishop of Rome among his fellow bishops. (A-II, no. 5)

B. ARCIC on the Petrine Primacy *cum* Roman Primacy

Although the New Testament "contains no explicit record of a transmission of Peter's leadership," nor is it clear concerning "the transmission of apostolic authority," nevertheless from the time of the early Apostolic Fathers onward, the local church of Rome,

the city in which Peter and Paul taught and were martyred, came to be recognized as possessing a unique responsibility among the churches: its bishop was seen to perform a special service in relation to the unity of the churches, and in relation to fidelity to the apostolic inheritance, thus exercising among his fellow bishops functions analogous to those ascribed to Peter, whose successor the bishop of Rome was claimed to be. (A-II, no. 6)

ARCIC perceived the historical root of this primacy, both of the local church of Rome and, concomitantly, of its bishop, to lie in the emergence of what may be termed "regional primacies" (*Eluc.*, no. 7): "Early in the history of the Church a function of oversight of the other bishops of their regions was assigned to bishops of prominent sees. Concern to keep the churches faithful to the will of Christ was among the considerations which contributed to this development" (A-I, no. 10). "It is within the context of this historical development that the see of Rome," the Commission stated, "whose prominence was associated with the death there of Peter and Paul, eventually became the principal centre in matters concerning the Church universal," and the preeminence of the Bishop of Rome among his brother bishops, "as explained by analogy with the position of Peter among the apostles," interpreted as Christ's will for his Church (A-I, no. 12).

ARCIC did recognize that to speak of the primacy of the Roman Pontiff as being rooted in the will of Christ has proved a dividing line between Anglicans and Roman Catholics. Nevertheless, it asserted, "We believe that the primacy of the bishop of Rome can be affirmed as part of God's design for the universal *koinonia* in terms which are compatible with both our Traditions. Given such a consensus, the language of divine right...need no longer be seen as a matter of disagreement between us" (A-II, no. 15).[2] Thus, the members of ARCIC could say together that

> the purpose of this episcopal function of the bishop of Rome is to promote Christian fellowship in faithfulness to the teaching of the apostles. The theological interpretation of this primacy and the administrative structures through which it has been exercised have varied considerably through the centuries. Neither theory nor practice, however, has ever fully reflected these ideals. Sometimes functions assumed by the see of Rome were not necessarily linked to the primacy: sometimes the conduct of the occupant of this see has been unworthy of his office: sometimes the image of this office has been obscured by interpretations placed upon it: and sometimes external pressures have made its proper exercise almost impossible. Yet the primacy, rightly understood, implies that the bishop of Rome exercises his oversight in order to guard and promote the faithfulness of all the churches to Christ and one another. Communion with him is intended as a safeguard of the catholicity of each local church, and as a sign of the communion of all the churches. (A-I, no. 12)

In this light, we Catholics can address ARCIC's call for us to demonstrate how the doctrines advanced by the Vatican Councils concerning "the role…of the bishop of Rome among his fellow bishops" (A-II, no. 5) are truly "modelled on the role of Peter" (A-II, no. 9), whom, we believe, Christ "set…over the rest of the apostles and instituted in him the permanent principle…and… visible foundation" of the College of Bishops and, indeed, of "the whole multitude of believers" (cf. PA, intro.).

III. A CATHOLIC RESPONSE

Building on the consensus achieved by ARCIC, how might a continued theological reflection on the Petrine texts renew Catholicism's understanding of the primacy of the Bishop of Rome as a ministry for the unity of all God's people?

1. Postconciliar Reflection on the Question: The decades since the close of the Second Vatican Council have not seen a shortage of studies on either the nature of papal primacy or the doctrines that Catholicism holds concerning that primacy. Some of the most far-reaching studies have been those in which Catholic theologians engaged in partnership with colleagues from other confessional traditions. *Peter in the New Testament*, edited by Raymond Brown, PSS, Karl Donfried, and John Reumann,[3] and *Peter and Paul in the Church of Rome: The Ecumenical Potential of a Forgotten Perspective*, by William Farmer and Roch Kereszty, O.Cist., are excellent examples.[4]

There has been no shortage of works by Catholic theologians in their own right, several of whom are noted in the bibliography to this book. The section below takes up the work of one of these theologians, Joseph Ratzinger, then Pope Benedict XVI, and in turn Pope Emeritus. His reflections on the primacy are noteworthy here for two reasons: (1) they are directly applicable to the question raised above, and (2) they have the potential to affect our understanding of the papacy and its significance for ecumenical dialogue for the foreseeable future—not the least effect being the fact that he now bears the title of Pope *Emeritus*.

2. Reflections on the Question by a Future Pope: In "The Primacy of Peter and the Unity of the Church," Ratzinger offered an exegesis of the various images of Peter in the New Testament.

This culminated in a lengthy explication of Jesus's words to Peter in Matthew 16:17–19—arguably the most significant passage of Scripture for the Petrine primacy of the Roman Pontiff.

> Blessed are you, Simon son of Jonah! For flesh and blood has not revealed this to you, but my Father in heaven. And I tell you, you are Peter, and on this rock I will build my church, and the gates of Hades will not prevail against it. I will give you the keys of the kingdom of heaven, and whatever you bind on earth will be bound in heaven, and whatever you loose on earth will be loosed in heaven.

Ratzinger then drew this conclusion about the significance of Jesus's words, which, according to traditional Catholic teaching, established the primacy that the apostle and his successors would possess "for the continual salvation and permanent benefit of the Church" (PA 2).

> This seems to me to be a cardinal point: at the inmost core of the new commission, which robs the forces of destruction of their power, is the grace of forgiveness. It constitutes the Church. The Church is founded upon forgiveness. Peter himself is a personal embodiment of this truth, for he is permitted to be the bearer of the keys after having stumbled, confessed and received the grace of pardon. The Church is by its nature the home of forgiveness, and it is thus that chaos is banished from within her. She is held together by forgiveness, and Peter is the perpetual living reminder of this reality: she is not a communion of the perfect but a communion of sinners who need and seek forgiveness. Behind the talk of authority, God's power appears as mercy and thus as the foundation stone of the Church; in the background we hear the word of the Lord: "It is not the healthy who have need of the physician, but those who are ill; I have not come to call the righteous but sinners" (Mk 2:17).[5]

By forgiveness, Ratzinger had in mind a dynamic reality. It is a reality that draws the baptized believer into ever-deeper bonds of communion with God and God's people by being reconciled ever more deeply to both as a member of the Body of God's reconciling Word made flesh, Jesus Christ. It is within this dynamic that Peter's primacy—and the doctrines Vatican I based upon it—find their renewed significance, as may be seen in both the name Jesus gave Peter and the power of the keys he bestowed upon him.

a. The Rock: A Sign of God's Covenant Fidelity to His People: Ratzinger began his discussion of the apostle's new name by drawing upon the work of Gerhard Schulze-Kadelbach. That Jesus called Simon bar Jonah "Peter"—Rock—is one of the things about which we can be certain.[6] What is more, we can also be certain that the name indicated what Jesus intended Peter to be for his community of believers, his *ecclesia*—that is, his "Church": the firm foundation upon which it could stand and profess its faith. To shed greater light on this point, Ratzinger turned to an insight of Joachim Jeremias, that in the background of Simon's new name "stands the symbolic language of the holy rock." Citing a rabbinical story recounted by Jeremias, Ratzinger continued,

> Yahweh spoke: "How can I create the world, when godless men will arise to vex me?" But when God looked upon Abraham, who was also to be born, he spoke, "Behold, I have found a rock upon which I can build and found the world." He therefore called Abraham a rock: "Look upon the rock from which you have been hewn" (Isa 51:1).[7]

As Abraham, by the grace of faith, was "the rock that holds back chaos, the onrushing primordial flood of destruction, and thus sustains creation," Peter "now becomes by virtue of his Abrahamic faith, which is renewed in Christ, the rock that stands against the impure tide of unbelief and its destruction of man [*sic*]."[8]

In his name, Peter received from the Lord "a promise for a time-transcending gathering of a new people—a gathering that stretches beyond his own lifetime." In his faith, Peter is a rock that shall not be overcome, and this not because of any virtue or merit of his own, but "because God does not abandon his *ecclesia* to the powers of destruction."[9] For Ratzinger, this necessarily entailed that he be endowed with the ability to preserve effectively the Church in its faith. The gift of the keys signifies this.

b. The Power of the Keys: Preserving Unity by the Power of Forgiveness: According to Ratzinger, the keys' true meaning is best understood in light of Jesus's confrontation with the Pharisees in Matthew 23:13, where he condemned them for locking heaven's doors: "Woe to you, scribes and Pharisees, you hypocrites. You lock the kingdom of heaven before human beings. You do not enter yourselves, nor do you allow entrance to those trying to enter." In contrast, Peter stands forth as the one who "opens the door to the Kingdom of Heaven; his is the function of doorkeeper, who has to judge concerning admission and rejection (cf. Rev 3:7)."[10]

This meaning sheds new light on the definitions of *Pastor Aeternus*: "the significance of the reference to the keys clearly approximates the meaning of binding and loosing."[11] They stand for the authority to make doctrinal decisions concerning what is (and what is not) in accord with the Church's faith, and, further, indicate the power to discipline those who refuse to think and live according to this faith. To borrow from John Paul II, this is a strong affirmation of the power and the authority without which the primatial office established by the Lord in the apostle Peter "would be illusory" (UUS 94). This affirmation is not, however, a new way of using Scripture to justify the Roman Pontiff's primatial claims. Rather, it is an affirmation of his Christ-ordained responsibility to ensure that the word of faith that people need to hear is available through Peter.

This reading of the power of the keys comes into clearer focus when we examine it in the light of John 20:23: "If you forgive the sins of any, they are forgiven them; if you retain the sins of any, they are retained." In the light of this passage, it becomes apparent that at its core the power to bind and loose means the authority to forgive sins. It is this authority that, in Peter, Jesus commits to the Church (cf. Matt 18:15–18). Thus understood, everything about Peter's primacy is fundamentally rooted in the grace of forgiveness, through which all people receive the strength to offer their "Amen" to what God accomplished for them in the person of Jesus Christ. It is through such forgiveness, then, that "God's power appears as mercy and thus as the foundation stone of the Church,"[12] and that the specifically *Petrine* primacy of the Roman

Pontiff finds its significance within the communion of God's people: to strengthen the faith-filled "Amen" of the Church's pastors and faithful, in all their churches, "so that they will remain faithful to their mission and in harmony with each other" (GA, no. 46, citing A-II, nos. 2–5).

What would reflection upon the necessary connection we say exists between St. Peter and the See of Rome tell us about the primacy we claim for the Bishop of Rome as the apostle's one true successor?

Shortly after my arrival at St. Anthony Shrine in Boston, Massachusetts, I received a letter accusing me of being part of a conspiracy to destroy the Catholic Church in the city. (For the record, it named the conspiracy's leaders as the shrine's rector and the city's archbishop.) It was an interesting letter. Chief among the reasons for its author's accusation was my having once referred to the Holy Father as "the Bishop of Rome." In an effort to set my doctrine straight, the author informed me that the Holy Father is *not* a bishop. "He is the *Pope*—the Successor of Peter and the Vicar of Christ on earth!"

It would be an easy thing to dismiss the author as an overly zealous Catholic, more Catholic than the pope—including the present Holy Father, who has an affinity for the title of Bishop of Rome. In addition to being uncharitable, though, such a dismissal would be intellectually dishonest. There is plenty of space within the history of Catholicism for the opinion of my would-be instructor in all things Catholic. This space is due not so much to what the Catholic Church has taught about the primacy as to what it has left underdeveloped: the necessary connection between the Petrine primacy and the church of Rome, of which the pope is, in every sense of the word, bishop.

1. The Church of Rome as the Root of Primacy: Vatican I referred to the intrinsic connection between the See of Rome and the primacy of its bishop when it stated that "the Roman Church possesses a pre-eminence of ordinary power over every other Church, and that this jurisdictional power of the Roman Pontiff is both episcopal and immediate" (PA 3). This statement is highly significant. It acknowledges that it is the primacy of the

Roman Church within the Church of churches that both carries and explains the primacy of the Roman Pontiff. In spite of its significance, however, the implications of this progression from the primacy of the Roman Church to that of its pontiff was not taken up by either Vatican I nor Vatican II.[13] This is a silence that ARCIC would have us address. After all, as the noted biblical scholar John P. Meier put it, "A papacy that cannot give a credible historical account of its own origins can hardly hope to be a catalyst for unity among divided Christians."[14]

It is certain that Christianity arrived in Rome before either St. Peter or St. Paul did, and some form of primacy seems to have been accorded its community there. This is evident from Paul's letter to "all God's beloved in Rome, who are called to be saints," in which he spoke of having longed to visit it

> because your faith is proclaimed throughout the world. For God, whom I serve with my spirit by announcing the gospel of his Son, is my witness that without ceasing I remember you always in my prayers, asking that by God's will I may somehow at last succeed in coming to you. For I am longing to see you so that I may share with you some spiritual gift to strengthen you—or rather so that we may be mutually encouraged by each other's faith, both yours and mine. (Rom 1:7–12)

What encouragement Paul received from Rome is a matter of speculation. We do know, however, that Rome received much from Paul, as well as from his brother apostle, Peter. The martyrdom of these pillars of the Church was heard by early Christians as the apostles' preeminent proclamation of the faith. This enhanced the preeminence of Rome's Church, helping to establish it as *the* acknowledged touchstone of faith for "all the beloved of God," wherever they lived out their call to holiness.

To speak of Rome's preeminence is not to say that it was acknowledged to possess "ordinary power" among the churches, to borrow the terminology of Vatican I. Nevertheless, Rome's preeminence came to have great importance within the Church of churches, and its subsequent development reflected this. St. Ignatius of Antioch extolled the Roman Church as "a Church without blemish, which holds the primacy of the community of love, obedient to Christ's Law, bearing the Father's name."[15] Its faith was the measure of orthodoxy. As St. Irenaeus of Lyon declared, "It has the tradition and the faith which comes down to us after having been announced to men [sic] by the Apostles."[16] Moreover, its life of faith was an example of true charity. Its consciousness of its apostolic roots demanded no less an expression of its catholicity.[17] In time, its consciousness would demand no less an exercise of *episcope* on behalf of the wider Church's catholicity by the bishop who led it in Peter's stead.[18]

In the light of this history, it is proper to see the primacy of the Bishop of Rome as arising from that of his see. This was the church that credited its faith to the Church's preeminent missionary, Paul, and its preeminent confessor, Peter, and to which the wider *ecclesia* looked for strength and encouragement in the same faith. As the *episcope* credited to St. Linus, Rome's first recorded bishop,[19] developed into an established and recognized office,[20] it was only natural that the one exercising it would be seen to represent Rome's Petrine strength in a singular way to the communion of churches. This development is witnessed to by the fact that the Roman See became *the* court of appeal for other churches throughout the first millennium and its bishop was honored as the one who presided in love over the Church's great patriarchal sees. Other churches claimed a Petrine heritage, but only one was acknowledged to be the church over which Peter still presided in the person of its bishop: the Church of Rome.[21]

2. The Successor of Peter as Bishop of the Church of Sts. Peter and Paul: In the light of what has already been discussed, this manner of succession should be obvious. As my friend in Boston demonstrated, however, this is not so obvious to everyone—including some Catholics. For the sake of clarity, therefore, let the obvious be stated: the Roman Pontiff succeeds to St. Peter's primacy by virtue of the fact that he is the *Bishop* of Rome.

a. Succeeding St. Peter? The Uniqueness of Peter for the Life of the Church: As has been noted, there is no scriptural evidence that anyone succeeded Peter as an apostle. What is more, there is no evidence from the Apostolic Tradition of any such succession. Instead, this Tradition testifies to something quite different: that Peter and Paul named Linus to be Rome's first *bishop*. Whatever leadership Peter may have provided the Roman Church, it was not what later generations would identify as the *episcope* of a residential bishop.[22] Peter was a unique figure, so much so that we Catholics continue to honor him in the liturgy as our shepherd[23] and our leader in the faith,[24] who from his place in heaven still guides us.[25] In the strict sense, as ARCIC affirmed and Tradition testifies, no one succeeded Peter, for no one could replace him. As if to underscore this, for centuries Rome's bishops referred to themselves as Peter's *vicars*—a title we have not entirely forgotten.[26]

b. Petrine Succession: Re-presenting the Apostle through the Ministry of Episcope: If the Roman Pontiff does not succeed Peter in the strict sense, how may we speak of him as Peter's successor? We may do so in the sense attested to by Tradition and reclaimed by ARCIC: the Roman Pontiff succeeds St. Peter after the fashion of St. Linus, the apostle's first claimed successor: he re-presents Peter to the Church as the visible principle of its unity of faith in Christ.

The Holy Father succeeds to Peter's primacy, not as one who replaces the apostle, but as one who re-presents him through his ministry as the *Bishop* of Rome. He does this every time he initiates people into the people of God entrusted to his care by the apostles Peter and Paul, and so orders the life of this people as the Body of Christ that it may more effectively be the sacrament whereby God draws all humanity to himself. This is a ministry that, by its very nature, reaches out to the world. That we recognize the right and duty of the Bishop of Rome to exercise this ministry universally is testimony to the *episcope* that he exercises locally for it is there, from within the local church of Rome, that he reaches out to confirm, nourish, and foster the communion of all the churches from which arises the one Church of Jesus Christ (see LG 23).

IV. CONCLUSION

Seeing the Petrine primacy of the Roman Pontiff in this light reframes the terms in which the Catholic Church understands him to be the successor of St. Peter. He is the successor not of

Peter's person, as if he were a replacement for the apostle, but of Peter's ministry to confirm the community of Christ's disciples, his *Church*, in the gospel of God's reconciling love for all people, precisely in order that it may be the sacrament of this love for the life of the world. Moreover, he succeeds to this ministry precisely because he is the *Roman* Pontiff, that is, bishop of the local church of Rome, which, to borrow from St. Irenaeus, is founded upon the Tradition and the faith proclaimed by the pillars of the Church themselves, the apostles Peter and Paul.

Such a succession roots the Roman Pontiff's essentially Petrine ministry *within* the Church, not above it, beginning with the local church entrusted to his care and extending out to embrace the broader communion of the Church of churches throughout the world. Seeing his primacy in this light reframes not only the terms in which we understand it per se, but also the terms in which we understand the ways in which he relates both to the entire community of the faithful in all their churches and also those who are, in a certain sense, Peter for those churches—the Church's bishops, successors of apostles who together with the Bishop of Rome as the head of their College "govern the house of the living God" (LG 18).

CHAPTER 8

"STRENGTHEN YOUR BROTHERS...": PRIMACY AND EPISCOPACY

Simon, Simon, listen! Satan has demanded to sift all of you like wheat, but I have prayed for you that your own faith may not fail; and you, when once you have turned back, strengthen your brothers.

—Luke 22:31–32

This Sacred Council, following closely in the footsteps of the First Vatican Council, with that Council teaches and declares that Jesus Christ, the eternal Shepherd, established His holy Church, having sent forth the apostles as He Himself had been sent by the Father; and He willed that their successors, namely the bishops, should be shepherds in His Church even to the consummation of the world. And in order that the episcopate itself might be one and undivided, He placed Blessed Peter over the other apostles, and instituted in him a permanent and visible source and foundation of unity of faith and communion.

—Vatican Council II, *Lumen Gentium* 18

In spite of being strongly rebuked by Christ and his dramatic failure in denying him, in the eyes of the New Testament writers Peter holds a position of special importance. This was not due to his own gifts and character although he had been the first to confess Christ's Messiahship. It was because of his particular calling by Christ (Luke 6:14; John 21:15–17). Yet while the distinctive features of Peter's ministry are stressed, this ministry is that of an apostle and does not isolate him from the ministry of the other apostles. In accordance with the teaching of Jesus that truly to lead is to serve and not to dominate others (Luke 22:24ff), Peter's role in strengthening the brethren (Luke 22:32) is a leadership of service. Peter, then, serves the Church by helping it to overcome threats to its unity (e.g. Acts 11:1–18), even if his weakness may require help or correction, as is clear from his rebuke by Paul (Gal 2:11–14). These considerations help clarify the analogy that has been drawn between the role of Peter among the apostles and that of the bishop of Rome among his fellow bishops.

—ARCIC I, *Authority in the Church II*, no. 5

I. INTRODUCTION

But [Jesus] said to them, "The kings of the Gentiles lord it over them; and those in authority over them are called benefactors. But not so with you; rather the greatest among you must become like the youngest, and the leader like one who serves. For who is greater, the one who is at the table or the one who serves? Is it not the one at the table? But I am among you as one who serves.

You are those who have stood by me in my trials; and I confer on you, just as my Father has conferred on me, a kingdom, so that you may eat and drink at my table in my kingdom, and you will sit on thrones judging the twelve tribes of Israel.

> Simon, Simon, listen! Satan has demanded to sift all of you like wheat, but I have prayed for you that your own faith may not fail; and you, when once you have turned back, strengthen your brothers." (Luke 22:25–32)

The second area in which ARCIC calls for further development is Catholicism's understanding of the relationship between primatial and episcopal authority. This is by no means new territory for Catholics. Fifty-plus years after the close of Vatican II, discerning and explicating a more adequate harmony between primacy (specifically papal primacy) and episcopacy is one of the most pressing tasks of the Church today. To put the issue somewhat bluntly, can papal primacy be conceived in such a way that it does not derogate from the proper authority of the Church's bishops, either as individuals or as a college, *and* can the authority of the bishops be understood in such a way that it does not essentially compromise the fullness of authority that is necessary to an effective ministry of papal primacy?[1]

That would be quite a balancing act, indeed! This chapter will address how ARCIC's consensus on the primacy calls the Catholic Church to discern precisely this balance, principally by calling the Catholic Church to continue to renew its understanding of primacy's essentially *episcopal* nature and of the bond this creates between the Roman Pontiff and his brother bishops as together they "direct the house of the living God" (LG 18). As was the case with the previous chapter, this chapter shall first briefly review ARCIC's understanding of the episcopal nature of the primacy and its attendant call for renewal, before considering how the Catholic Church may respond to this call in a way that is faithful to its ecclesial heritage.

II. ARCIC ON THE EPISCOPAL NATURE OF THE PRIMACY

For ARCIC, the authority with which Jesus endowed his disciples was, above all, authority for mission, that is, to proclaim effectively the gospel of the kingdom of God, vouchsafed for humanity in the "Yes" God spoke, once and for all, in Christ Jesus.

> In the proclamation of Christ crucified, the "Yes" of God to humanity is made a present reality and all are invited to respond with their "Amen." Thus, the exercise of ministerial authority within the Church, *not least by those entrusted with the ministry of* episcope, has a radically missionary dimension. Authority is exercised within the Church for the sake of those outside it, that the Gospel may be proclaimed "in power and in the Holy Spirit and with full conviction" (1 Thess 1.5). This authority enables the whole Church to embody the Gospel and become the missionary and prophetic servant of the Lord. (GA, no. 32; my emphases)

A *sine qua non* of this missionary and prophetic service is the Church's communion (*koinonia*) in and with Christ. Any compromise of this communion, in turn, compromises the effectiveness of the Church's mission.

> When Christians do not agree about the Gospel itself, the preaching of it in power is impaired. When they are not one in faith they cannot be one in life, and so cannot demonstrate fully that they are faithful to the will of God, which is the reconciliation through Christ of all things to the Father (cf. Col 1.20). As long as the Church does not live as the community of reconciliation God calls it to be, it cannot adequately preach this Gospel or credibly proclaim God's plan to gather his scattered people into unity under Christ as Lord and Saviour (cf. Jn 11.52). Only when all believers are united in the common celebration of the Eucharist (cf. *Church as Communion*, 24) will the God whose purpose it is to bring all things into unity in Christ (cf. Eph 1.10) be truly glorified by the people of God. (GA, no. 33)

It is against the backdrop of this mission-driven ecclesiology that the episcopal nature of the primacy comes to the fore, for it is precisely to preserve and promote the Church's communion in service of the gospel that primacy exists, as a necessary and essential expression of the Church's ministry of *episcope*. This is the case with respect to both (1) its universal expression, as exercised by the bishops in their local churches, including the bishop of the local church of Rome, and (2) its singular expression, as exercised by the entire College of Bishops.

A. The Primate as Bishop

"Believers follow Christ in communion with other Christians in their local churches." It is within their local churches that they "share Christian life" and

> are sustained by the means of grace which God pro-
> vides for his people: the Holy Scriptures, expounded
> in preaching, catechesis and creeds; the sacraments;
> the service of the ordained ministry; the life of prayer
> and common worship; the witness of holy persons. The
> believer is incorporated into an "Amen" of faith, older,
> deeper, broader, richer than the individual's "Amen"
> to the Gospel....Every baptised person shares the rich
> experience of the Church which, even when it struggles
> with contemporary questions, continues to proclaim
> what Christ is *for his Body*. Each believer, by the grace
> of the Spirit, together with all believers of all times and
> all places, inherits this faith of the Church in the com-
> munion of saints. (GA, no. 13, emphasis in original)

It was for this reason that ARCIC devoted the time that it did to discussing the significance of episcopal ministry for the communion of each local church—and this necessarily includes the ministry of the Bishop of Rome. First, he is the *Bishop* of Rome. It is for the sake of this local church that he has been endowed by the Spirit with all the authority proper to him as its bishop: to teach the faith, to celebrate the sacraments, and to maintain the church in holiness and truth (see GA, no. 36). He is charged with the ministry of renewing the memory of Rome's Christian community concerning the hope God has given it in Christ (see

GA, no. 30). In this way, he works to preserve and promote the communion of the church of Rome, so that its faithful may offer their "Amen" to the reconciling "Yes" God spoke, once and for all, in Christ Jesus.

Of course, neither this hope nor this "Amen" belong to the church of Rome alone. They belong to all the churches and to the communion they share as the one Church of Jesus Christ (see A-I, no. 8; GA, no. 37). For this reason "every bishop receives at ordination both responsibility for his local church and the obligation to maintain it in living awareness and practical service of the other churches" (A-I, no. 10). In the case of the Bishop of Rome, the concern for the communion of the Church of churches takes on uniquely universal scope: to ensure that his brothers properly exercise the ministry of *episcope* with which they have been entrusted (see A-I, no. 21), in order that the communion, which they pastor together, may be the missionary and prophetic servant the Lord wills it to be.

It is precisely in this light that ARCIC spoke of the universal *episcope* of the Bishop of Rome. When he speaks and acts from the chair of Peter in the church of Sts. Peter and Paul, the Roman Pontiff does so as successor to Peter's ministry of unity (see A-II, no. 12; GA, no. 47), which has its origin in the will of Christ (see A-II, no. 11; GA, no. 46). The difference between the *episcope* of primacy and that proper to a bishop in his local church is one of degree, not kind (cf. *Eluc.*, no. 6). It is the authority inherent to the ministry of *episcope* itself. Thus understood, it is the nature of primatial *episcope* to complement the authority of a local bishop. It is not the latter's rival or origin. This becomes clearer when one considers the manner in which primatial *episcope* stands in relationship to the *episcope* of the College of Bishops.

B. The Primate within the College of Bishops

This topic was treated at length in chapter 6 under the heading "Primacy and Collegiality." Therefore, it is necessary to recall only a few pertinent points here. The first point is straightforward, and concerns the context within which the primatial *episcope* of Roman Pontiff is to be understood: "The bishops are collectively

responsible for defending and interpreting the apostolic faith"
(A-I, no. 20).

The bishops are responsible for defending and interpreting
the faith, not as a collection of individuals engaged in a common
task, but as brothers who share in the same ministry, related to one
another as members of the College of Bishops (cf. GA, no. 37).
Thus, when the bishops exercise their *episcope* for the welfare of
the communion (*koinonia*) of their churches as the one Church of
Jesus Christ, they do so in communion with one another as brothers, laboring as one to preserve and promote "the integrity of the
koinonia in order to further the Church's response to the Lordship
of Christ and its commitment to mission" (A-I, no. 5).

It is with this context clearly in view that ARCIC was able
to say that, in his role as universal primate, the Bishop of Rome
"exercises his ministry not in isolation but in collegial association
with his brother bishops" (A-I, no. 21). For the responsibility of
maintaining the communion of the Church of churches in

> the truth is one of the essential functions of the epis-
> copal college. It has the power to exercise this ministry
> because it is bound in succession to the apostles, who
> were the body authorised and sent by Christ to preach
> the Gospel to all the nations. The authenticity of the
> teaching of individual bishops is evident when this
> teaching is in solidarity with that of the whole episcopal
> college. (GA, no. 44)

The primacy accorded to the Bishop of Rome, as modeled
upon that accorded Peter among the apostles (cf. A-II, no. 9),
"implies that, after consulting his fellow bishops, he may speak in
their name and express their mind. The recognition of his position
by the faithful creates an expectation that on occasion he will take
an initiative in speaking for the Church" (A-I, no. 20).

> Within his wider ministry, the Bishop of Rome offers a
> specific ministry concerning the discernment of truth,
> as an expression of universal primacy. This particular
> service has been the source of difficulties and misunder-
> standings among the churches. Every solemn definition

pronounced from the chair of Peter in the church of Peter and Paul may, however, express only the faith of the Church. Any such definition is pronounced *within* the college of those who exercise *episcope* and not outside that college. Such authoritative teaching is a particular exercise of the calling and responsibility of the body of bishops to teach and affirm the faith. When the faith is articulated in this way, the Bishop of Rome proclaims the faith of the local churches. It is thus the wholly reliable teaching of the whole Church that is operative in the judgement of the universal primate. (GA, no. 47)

It is important to note that when discussing the primacy, ARCIC used the language of doctrine and theology, and not that of canon law. This is understandable. The language of canon law belongs properly to a later stage of dialogue, when Anglicans and Catholics begin to walk together in service of the gospel (see GA, no. 56ff.). This did not, however, prevent ARCIC from asking questions with canonical implications.

The Second Vatican Council has reminded Roman Catholics of how the gifts of God are present in all the people of God. It has also taught the collegiality of the episcopate in its communion with the Bishop of Rome, head of the college. However, is there at all levels effective participation of clergy as well as lay people in emerging synodal bodies? Has the teaching of the Second Vatican Council regarding the collegiality of bishops been implemented sufficiently? Do the actions of bishops reflect sufficient awareness of the extent of the authority they receive through ordination for governing the local church? Has enough provision been made to ensure consultation between the Bishop of Rome and the local churches prior to the making of important decisions affecting either a local church or the whole Church? How is the variety of theological opinion taken into account when such decisions are made? In supporting the Bishop of Rome in his work of promoting communion among the churches, do the structures and procedures of the Roman Curia adequately respect the exercise of *episcope* at other levels? (GA, no. 57)

It is with an eye toward these questions that a Catholic response to ARCIC may be considered.

III. A ROMAN CATHOLIC RESPONSE

"The Second Vatican Council has reminded Roman Catholics of how the gifts of God are present in all the people of God. It has also taught the collegiality of the episcopate in its communion with the Bishop of Rome, head of the college....Has the teaching of the Second Vatican Council regarding the collegiality of bishops been implemented sufficiently?" (GA, no. 57)

1. Acknowledging Our Present: A Time of Contention for the Mind of the Council

In formulating a response to ARCIC's call for renewal—to receive anew (or "re-receive" in ARCIC's terminology) those aspects of our doctrinal heritage that enable us to embrace a renewed vision of the primacy—we must do so with a clear-eyed view of the present situation of our own Catholic Church.

In a word, we Catholics find ourselves in a moment of uneasy transition, a period of struggle (at times contentious) as we strive to understand and follow the mind of Vatican II, that is, the way the bishops understood the event they were shaping—not only by means of the texts they were producing, but also through the process by which they were producing and later seeking to give life to those texts—for the renewal of the Church both *ad intra* and *ad extra*. What is more, this is a struggle complicated by the fact that even former "fathers" and *periti* can occasionally find themselves in fundamental disagreement about the Council's mind, including its mind on the petrine primacy of the Roman Pontiff.

a. *The Councils on Primacy and Episcope: Teaching without Resolution.* Why this struggle? One answer lies in the fact that, despite their consensus on the conciliar texts, the Council's majority was not unanimous in their understanding of the precise meanings of everything the texts contained, principally how to reconcile the definitions of *Pastor Aeternus* with the concept of collegiality newly recovered in *Lumen Gentium*. A brief look at the teachings enumerated in these conciliar documents demonstrates this.

The Council affirmed the divine origin both of the primacy and of the episcopacy within the Church. It rejected any opposition between the two. It also asserted that the College of Bishops needs a head to serve as its principle of unity and of coordination of activity. It taught that the Lord entrusted the primacy personally to St. Peter and his successors so that they might serve the collegial unity of the apostles' successors, the College of Bishops, and of the Church. It proposed as necessary to such personal primacy the freedom to foster the unity of the Church in such a way that this freedom is not legally conditioned by the approval of the bishops. It also affirmed that the primacy is bound to respect and collaborate with the bishops, which is also divinely established by Christ for the well-being of the Church. It taught that both the College of Bishops, as a whole together with their head, and the primate as head of the College, have an obligation and right to care for the unity of the Church as a whole. It affirmed the sacramentality of the episcopacy and thereby the dignity of each individual bishop as a Vicar of Christ in such a way that the primacy does not and cannot diminish that dignity. It stated that the primacy and the episcopacy are bound together by ties of hierarchical communion. Yet in the face of all these teachings, the Council did not explain precisely how they fit and function together.[2]

Even a close examination of the texts, especially those that are doctrinal in character, do not provide the kind of clarity one would reasonably expect to find. They lack the kind of conceptual precision, unambiguous definition of positions, technical forms, and unity of literary genre to which Trent and Vatican I had accustomed us. Passages using the language of the Bible as no previous council had used it alternate with historical expositions, analyses of the then contemporary situation, and, not least, citations of previous councils (half of them from Trent and Vatican I) and references to papal teaching (half of them to Pius XII). Little wonder that, fifty-plus years since the Council closed, we are still struggling to interpret and integrate it into the living faith of our Church.[3]

Among the interpretations made of the Council's teaching regarding the relationship between primacy and collegiality were those that effectively placed collegiality in a supporting role to the primacy, and turned an (at least) opaque eye toward the dignity of the episcopacy. The result is illustrated well by my would-be instructor in all things Catholic: "The Holy Father isn't a *bishop*. He's the *Pope!*" More substantially, it is illustrated by the way the two institutions intended by the Council to embody collegiality developed after its close: Episcopal Conferences and the Synod of Bishops. These were touched upon in chapter 3. They shall now be taken up at greater length.

b. *Collegiality at the Service of Primacy? First Steps toward a Primacy-in-Collegiality Gone Awry.*

i. *Episcopal Conferences and Primacy.* Although gatherings of bishops at regional and national levels have been a part of the Church's life from its earliest centuries, Episcopal Conferences as we now know them have their historical roots in the early nineteenth century.[4] The effectiveness of these Conferences was recognized by the Council, which, in turn, encouraged their spread and further development. Since the Council's close, and in accord with the norms established by Pope Paul VI in his 1966 *motu proprio Ecclesiae Sanctae*, Episcopal Conferences have become the commonplace way for bishops to work together for the "increase of faith" and "maintenance of discipline" in their respective churches (cf. *Christus Dominus* 36), and to make "a manifold and fruitful contribution to the concrete application of the spirit of collegiality" (LG 23).

For many Conferences, this application of the spirit of collegiality took the form of pastoral letters aimed at bringing the faith to bear on contemporary social issues. The result was not without controversy, and not simply with regard to the letters' substance. Questions were raised regarding the letters' authority and, more specifically, to the authority of the Conferences that issued them. Certainly, Vatican II had affirmed that the bishops' *munus pastorale* included the office of teaching. Moreover, the newly promulgated Code of Canon Law declared that "the bishops who are in communion with the head and members of the college, whether individually or joined together in conferences of bishops or in particular councils…are authentic teachers and instructors of the faith for the Christian faithful entrusted to their care" (can. 753). Yet, to what extent could a Conference's action, though made in the spirit of collegiality, be considered a collegial act, and, following this, what degree of "religious submission of mind" were the faithful required to show these actions as "the authentic magisterium of their bishops?" (can. 753).

Such questions were not new. They had been raised at the Council.[5] Among those now asking questions were two former proponents of the collegiality, who, in the wake of the Council, had revised their earlier enthusiasm: Joseph Ratzinger and Jerome Hammer, OP. As the views of these theologians-cum-curial prefects were influential in shaping the response that the Holy See would eventually offer, they deserve to be addressed.

Ratzinger and Hammer's responses evidenced the influence of the former Council *peritus* Henri de Lubac, SJ. According to de Lubac, although Conferences could be useful to the bishops' ministry within their respective nations and in fostering the relationship of the College as a whole, "Nevertheless, strictly speaking, that is, in its full meaning, based on Scripture, episcopal collegiality, which succeeds that of the Twelve, is essentially universal— and on the other hand, a collective act is not in itself a collegial act. Consequently, it is not said that the bishops carry out their responsibility 'collegially' in their conference, but that they carry it out 'conjointly.'"[6] Ratzinger and Hammer further argued that an enhanced role for Episcopal Conferences could lead to resurgence in the kind of ecclesio-nationalism that had once given birth to Gallicanism. To this they added that bishops might succumb to the bureaucratic weight of their respective conferences and become more functionaries of an institution than the vicars of Christ they are empowered to be for the churches in their care.[7]

In 1985, an extraordinary Synod of Bishops requested that John Paul II establish a commission to study and resolve the issue. In 1998, his resolution was offered: *Apostolos Suos*. In this document, issued *motu proprio*, the Holy Father's reasoning substantially mirrored that of Ratzinger and Hammer. He concluded that while bishops "jointly exercise the episcopal ministry for the good of the faithful of the territory of the conference" (no. 20), this "exercise of the episcopal ministry never takes on the collegial nature proper to the actions of the order of Bishops as such, which alone holds the supreme power over the whole Church. In fact, the relationship between individual Bishops and the College of Bishops is quite different from their relationship to the bodies set up for the above-mentioned joint exercise of certain pastoral tasks" (no. 12).[8]

> The organizations formed by the Bishops of a certain territory (country, region, etc.) and the Bishops who are members of them share a relationship which, although presenting a certain similarity, is really quite different from that which exists between the College of Bishops and the individual Bishops. The binding effect of the acts of the episcopal ministry jointly exercised within Conferences of Bishops and in communion with the Apostolic See derives from the fact that the latter has constituted the former and has entrusted to them, on the basis of the sacred power of the individual Bishops, specific areas of competence. (no. 13)

In this instance, the pope specifically had in mind the *munus regendi* (office of governance) of "the diocesan Bishop and the Bishops equivalent to them in law" (no. 19) and their legitimate, free exercise of this office (no. 20). Bishops do more than govern their churches. They are also teachers of the faith who must proclaim the truth "so that the message of Christ enlightens and guides people's consciences in resolving new problems arising from changes in society" (no. 22). When such a proclamation receives the unanimous consent of all the bishops of "a determined territory," they may promulgate it in the name of their Conference. When such unanimity is lacking, however, "the Bishops of a Conference cannot issue a declaration as authentic teaching of the Conference to which all the faithful of the territory would have to adhere, unless it obtains the *recognitio* of the Apostolic See, which will not give it if the majority requesting it is not substantial" (no. 22).

Apostolos Suos has not been without its critics. It has been criticized for having gone out of its way to avoid the comparisons made at the Council between Conferences and regional synods of bishops, for making Conferences' authority into nothing more substantial than either the aggregate authority of its member bishops or the authority of a papal teaching—for which the creation of Conferences was entirely unnecessary. While one may argue that a papal *recognitio* does not bestow a new (and greater) authority upon a Conference's action, but merely recognizes the authority inherent to that act, another may counterargue that the very process for obtaining a *recognitio* suggests the opposite.[9] *Apostolos Suos* would appear to support such a retort: "The *recognitio* of the Holy See serves furthermore to guarantee that, in dealing with new questions posed by the accelerated social and cultural changes characteristic of present times, the doctrinal response will favor communion and not harm it, and will rather *prepare an eventual intervention of the universal magisterium*" (AS 22; my emphasis). With such an eventuality clearly stated, how far off the mark could its critics be, especially since the late Holy Father chose to promulgate *Apostolos Suos*, not in collegial association with his brother bishops, but *motu proprio*?

ii. *The Synod of Bishops and Primacy*. The Synod of Bishops, envisioned by the Council itself as a means of realizing its teaching on collegiality, was established by Paul VI in 1965 with the *motu proprio Apostolica Sollicitudo*. Reflecting on the development of the Synod, Archbishop Emeritus of San Francsico and former President of the US Conference of Catholic Bishops John Quinn has stated, "Today's synods seem distant from the ideal set forth in the council decree on bishops: 'Acting on behalf of the whole catholic episcopate, it [the Synod] will show that all the bishops in hierarchical communion participate in the care of the whole church.'"[10] Quinn was not alone in raising this objection, which continues to resonate almost two decades later. What is more, he would not have been alone in raising it back in 1965.

Apostolica Sollicitudo was not received enthusiastically by many bishops at the Council, and this for two reasons. First, the Holy Father established it *motu proprio*, which these bishops saw as violating the collegial spirit of the Council, which was still open. Second, the Synod established by *Apostolica Sollicitudo* was not what the Council had envisioned. It was not a standing synod with deliberative authority, but an occasional gathering of representative bishops for a limited period of time and with strictly

consultative powers. The Holy See establishes the Synod's sched-
ule, agenda, and participants.[11] Further, whatever the Synod pro-
duces is given to the Holy Father to be used at his discretion.[12] In
short, the Synod's authority is explicitly subjected to the primatial authority of the Roman Pontiff. It is not an *effective* exercise
of collegiality—not unless the Holy Father chose to attribute this
degree of authority to it.

In the years since the Synod's establishment, there has been
no essential change in this status quo. This state of affairs concerning an organ envisioned by the Council as a way of affecting
its mind on the fundamentally collegial nature of ecclesial governance is an example of what ARCIC had in mind when it asked
whether the teaching of the Second Vatican Council regarding the
collegiality of bishops had been implemented sufficiently.

iii. *The Confusion of "Time Honored" Institutions: The Roman
Curia and the Bishops.* ARCIC had other issues on its mind as
well. One in particular concerned the relationship between the
bishops and the Roman Curia, specifically the degree to which
this relationship reflects the Council's understanding of primacy
as being rooted in, and at the service of, episcopal collegiality. Two
apostolic constitutions, *Regimini Ecclesiae Universae* (1967) and
Bonus Pastor (1988), were issued to affect this understanding.
While these constitutions did produce some tangible results, that
the reform of the Curia remains a priority item for the Catholic
Church is evidence that a good deal of work remains to be done.

The Curia is a practical arm of the bureaucratic structure of
the Holy See, and as such can be of great service to the communion of the Church of churches. This rightly stated, the Curia, as
it is presently constituted, always runs the real risk of seeing itself
as a *tertium quid.* When this happens, in place of the dogmatic
structure comprised of the Roman Pontiff and his brother bishops,
that is, the College with its head, there emerges a new, threefold
structure: the pope, the episcopate, and the Roman Curia. This
makes it possible for the Curia to understand itself as exercising
oversight and authority over even the College of Bishops, as if
it were somehow an extension of the primatial authority of the
pope. To the degree that this is so, and is reflected in the policies
and actions of the Curia, it obscures and diminishes both the doctrine and the reality of episcopal collegiality.[13]

This, together with what was observed above concerning Episcopal Conferences and the Synod of Bishops, makes it possible for one to see the primatial *episcope* of the Roman Pontiff as separate from the *episcope* of the bishops and even of the College. This present state of the relationship between primacy and *episcope* continues to make the pope appear to be more than a pope. Addressing this imbalance is at the heart of ARCIC's call, both for the sake of Christian unity and for the sake of our authenticity as Catholics.

2. The Importance of Recovering the Council's Mind: Receiving Vatican II as Key to an Authentically Roman Catholic Response to ARCIC

The key to achieving such harmony between primacy and episcopacy, and so arriving at the point where we can offer an authentic, positive response to ARCIC, is to receive Vatican II's understanding of collegiality as *the* ground for understanding the primacy of the Roman Pontiff. The process for such a reception would require three steps: (1) to articulate clearly both the Council's mind on this matter and its implications for the relationship between the Roman Pontiff and his brother bishops; (2) to realize the principal means by which the Council intended to begin making its mind a reality, namely Episcopal Conferences and the Synod of Bishops; and (3) to address those time-honored institutions that, at least in their present form, compromise our reception of the Council and, with it, frustrate our response to ARCIC.

a. Primatial Episcope in Collegiality. As this topic was discussed at length in chapter 2, one need only recall the heart of this teaching here: that the primacy is rooted in the episcopate.

For the Bishop of Rome, as for all the bishops, everything derives from one and the same sacrament (episcopacy), from one and the same mission of building up and maintaining the communion of the Church of churches, and from one and the same power given for the sake of this mission. This power is properly exercised in different ways, according to the office that each bishop receives within the College. In the case of the Bishop of Rome, the dimension of the *solicitudo universalis*, which is his as a bishop, extends to a special degree, while always remaining within the sacramental grace of the episcopate.[14]

i. *Three Aspects.* From this "heart," three aspects of the Council's teaching come to the fore. The first is straightforward: the *episcope* proper to the Roman Pontiff as Vicar of Christ and shepherd of the Universal Church is not of a different *kind* than that had by every bishop, who is the "visible principle and foundation of unity" of a local church (cf. LG 23). It is of a different *degree*, and belongs to him by virtue of the fact that he is the Bishop of Rome and, as such, the head of the College of Bishops, who in communion with "the successor of Peter, the Vicar of Christ, the visible Head of the whole Church, govern the house of the living God" (LG 18).[15]

The second aspect pertains to the manner in which the primacy is rooted in collegiality: through the sacrament of episcopal consecration (see LG 21). It is no longer possible to say with complete accuracy that the Roman Pontiff is *the* Vicar of Christ. Rather, he is Vicar of Christ *within* the collegial fellowship of all Christ's true vicars and legates: the College of Bishops (see LG 27). In this light, the fullness of his succession to Peter's primacy stands forth clearly. As Peter's primacy was established by the Lord within the collegial fellowship Peter had with his brother apostles, so too is the primacy of Peter's successor, the Roman Pontiff, established within the collegial fellowship he has with the apostles' successors, his brother bishops (see LG 22). Thus understood, the Roman Pontiff truly serves as the "permanent and visible source and foundation of the unity of faith and communion" of the whole body of bishops (LG 18), to whom the Lord entrusted the charge of proclaiming the gospel of God's kingdom to the ends of the earth.

The third aspect of the Council's teaching concerns the nature of collegiality itself. Collegiality is not a linear relationship that exists between the Bishop of Rome, on the one hand, and, on the other hand, the broader body of bishops. It is a dynamic being-in-relationship that characterizes the ways all the bishops, including the Bishop of Rome, relate to one another as members of the College and serve the communion of the entire people of God, exercising the authority proper to them as bishops in order that the Church of churches may effectively proclaim the kingdom to all the peoples among whom and for whom it is present as God's sacrament of salvation.

ii. *Three Implications.* It is important to note that this way of understanding collegiality differs from that contained in the *Preliminary Explanatory Note,* attached to *Lumen Gentium* at the command of "higher-authority." Therefore, it is worth taking a moment to tease out the implications of this difference before taking a second look at Episcopal Conferences and the Synod of Bishops as significant means for realizing the kind of harmony between primacy and episcopacy envisioned by the Council.

The first implication flows from the fact that the pope is "the successor of Peter, the Vicar of Christ, the visible Head of the whole Church" (LG 18), because, as Vatican I affirmed (see PA 2), he is the bishop of the local church of Rome that holds the primacy of love over all the churches.[16] Thus, the authority with which he presides over the communion of all the churches and their pastors is that which was bestowed upon him through episcopal ordination, nothing less and *nothing more.*

The second implication flows from the first. It is that the Roman Pontiff does not relate to his brother bishops simply as head of the College. He relates to them also as a member of the College. As John Paul II acknowledged in *Ut Unum Sint,* "The Bishop of Rome is a member of the 'college,' and the bishops are his brothers in the ministry" (UUS 95). This is true not only when, like all bishops, he acts out of concern for the welfare of the communion of the entire people of God. It is also true when the Roman Pontiff acts out of concern for the particular bonds of his own local church of Rome within the wider communion of churches, bonds that exist due to geography, history, or spiritual patrimony.

In addition to his roles as "pontiff" of the local church of Rome and Supreme Pontiff of the Church Universal, the Holy Father is also metropolitan of the Roman Province, primate of Italy, and "Patriarch of the West."[17] In his respective roles as metropolitan and primate, the Roman Pontiff coordinates with the bishops of his province and nation to promote the common good of their churches (see CD 36). In a like manner, as "patriarch" he has a distinct relationship to the bishops of the Latin Rite whose churches look to Rome for "the tradition and the faith which comes…[from] the Apostles."[18] He ensures that these bishops and their churches remain "organically united" in "their own discipline, their own liturgical usage, and their own theological and spiritual heritage" (LG 23). In all these roles, the Roman Pontiff fulfills the charge placed upon him by his episcopal consecration, in collegial unity with his brothers, to foster the communion of all the churches so that they may effectively proclaim the unity in diversity God wills all people to have as his people—as the one Body of Christ.

The final implication is that the Roman Pontiff serves the communion of the entire people of God primarily by exercising the *episcope* proper to him as, quite literally, the Bishop of Rome.

As the Council stated, it is a holy reality that "by governing well their own church as a portion of the universal Church, [the bishops] themselves are effectively contributing to the welfare of the whole Mystical Body, which is also the body of the churches" (LG 23). This is no less the case for the Bishop of Rome—though one may, perhaps, go so far as to say that it is especially the case for him. By exercising his *episcope* within the See of Sts. Peter and Paul, the Roman Pontiff guarantees that the local church of Rome continues both to share in the identity of the Church of the apostles and to realize catholic unity with every local church that lives, under the *episcope* of its own pastor, in that same faith—within the province of Rome, the state of Italy, the Latin West, and, ultimately, the communion of all God's people in all their churches.

It is with the above in mind that a second look may be taken at the collegial nature of Episcopal Conferences and the Synod of Bishops as a means by which a more genuine harmony between primacy and episcopacy may begin to be realized, for the sake of both our communion as Catholics and the communion we desire with *all* the people of God.

b. *Primacy and Episcopacy in Search of Collegial Harmony.* Pending new, direct action by Pope Francis, in the light of *Apostolica Sollicitudo*, the Code of Canon Law, and *Apostolos Suos*, it would appear that all questions regarding the collegial nature of Episcopal Conferences and the Synod of Bishops have been settled. However, when these same questions are considered in the light of Vatican II, as Pope Francis seems to be doing, something new emerges: both Conferences and Synod as true, effective instances of the collegial leadership that bishops must exercise for the welfare of their sisters and brothers among God's people.

i. *Recovering the Council's Mind.* A clear grasp of the Council's mind on this issue may be had in the light of its discussion of the schema that would become *Christus Dominus*. In their initial debate, the majority of the bishops revealed an understanding of collegiality as an integral part of the Church's doctrinal heritage. One bishop suggested that the schema be titled "The Practice of Collegiality." Suggestions from other bishops followed this line, including a proposal to begin the decree with a chapter treating the life of the local church and proceed from there with chapters on the relationship of the local church to metropolitan province, the Episcopal Conference, and finally the Holy See. Key to this and other like proposals was an understanding of communion (*koinonia*) that admitted a variety of expressions between those of the local church and the Church Universal.[19]

These contributions corresponded with those made by bishops from the Eastern Catholic Churches, particularly the Melkite patriarch, Maximos IV Saigh. In a wide-ranging criticism of the schema, he called for the establishment of a Supreme Council of the Church, after the pattern of the permanent synods of the Eastern Churches. This was to be a permanent institution to assist the Roman Pontiff, to which all *Roman* institutions (e.g., the Curia) would be subject. Along this same line, Cardinal Alfrink of Utrecht suggested a permanent Council of Bishops as a sign of the collegial leadership of the whole Church, and as an instrument of carrying out this leadership. This would express the collegial character of the supreme government of the Church apart from an Ecumenical Council. This permanent Council "would also in a way centralize ecclesiastical government, which was not unimportant in view of a certain decentralization brought about by the Episcopal Conferences."[20] It is with these suggestions in mind that one should hear *Christus Dominus* when it states that

> bishops chosen from various parts of the world, in ways and manners established or to be established by the Roman pontiff, render more effective assistance to the supreme pastor of the Church in a deliberative body which will be called by the proper name of Synod of

Bishops. Since it shall be acting in the name of the entire Catholic episcopate, it will at the same time show that all the bishops in hierarchical communion partake of the solicitude for the universal Church. (CD 5)

The difference between the bishops' understanding of collegiality and that given in the *Nota* attached to *Lumen Gentium* emerges clearly. Whereas the *Nota* described collegiality as a reality effected solely at the discretion of the Roman Pontiff, in both *Lumen Gentium* and *Christus Dominus*, the bishops described it as a dynamic relationship that exists between all the College's members, not simply between the body of bishops, on the one hand, and the Bishop of Rome, on the other hand. It is within this dynamic that the primacy finds its raison d'être: to serve the bishops' collegial unity, so that they may serve the communion of the Church and its proclamation of the kingdom. It is this understanding of collegiality that enables the Catholic Church to begin to realize the harmony needed between primacy and episcopacy and, what is more, find the voice it needs to respond to ARCIC. An excellent first step in this direction would be to recognize Episcopal Conferences and the Synod of Bishops as inherently effective, and not merely affective, expressions of collegiality.

ii. *The Collegiality of Episcopal Conferences.* Any discussion of Conferences as effective expressions of collegiality must admit to the validity of John Paul II's statement in *Apostolos Suos*, that at "the level of particular Churches grouped together by geographic areas…, the Bishops in charge do not exercise pastoral care jointly with collegial acts equal to those of the College of Bishops" (no. 10). True enough, but this statement does not answer the question of whether Conferences, as admittedly partial gatherings of the College's members, may act in an *effectively* collegial fashion—a question to which the Catholic Church, on the basis of Vatican II, may offer a resounding yes.[21]

Three arguments can be made in favor of this yes. The first of these treats canon 753, of the revised Code of Canon Law:

Although the bishops who are in communion with the head and members of the college, whether individually or joined together in conferences of bishops or in particular councils, do not possess infallibility in teaching, they are authentic teachers and instructors of the faith for the Christian faithful entrusted to their care; the Christian faithful are bound to adhere with religious submission of mind to the authentic magisterium of their bishops.

In this light, it is difficult to deny that the canon accords a genuine, effective teaching authority to Episcopal Conferences per se.

The second argument draws a parallel between the present Conferences of Bishops and the particular, regional councils of the early Church, which are still recognized to exercise a proper, authentic magisterium. It was with this in mind that the Council chose to speak of Episcopal Conferences and the Synods of the early Church in the same breath, and this regardless of their establishment as (respectively) permanent or temporary bodies—as if the *munus docendi* bestowed upon their members as a gift of the Spirit for the good of the Church of churches required further specific, canonically established forms in order to be effective. Therefore, to deny that Conferences do not effectively exercise their own proper, authentic magisterium would, in effect, deny the mind of the Council as the Council expressed its mind in the very documents it produced.[22]

The third argument is more speculative and depends upon the two preceding arguments: in a true theological sense, collegiality is partially and analogously verified when a group of bishops come together to serve the unity of the entire Church by their joint ministry. Since collegiality includes the power of the episcopal body to teach, it would follow, at least *prima facie*, that Conferences, as partial meetings of the College, exercise the office of teaching. This exercise of these bishops' magisterium seeks to make the truth of the gospel accessible and applicable in the lives of the faithful. This necessarily implies that a Conference will propose the one faith, albeit with different accents and nuances, in ways that correspond with the churches' differing cultural and historical situations. Since the Church's universal teaching authority cannot adequately serve the diverse pastoral needs of the churches in every nation and region of the world, it is essential that there be a pastoral teaching agency intermediate between the individual bishop in his local church and the Holy See.[23]

Key to all these arguments is the concept of communion that permeates the ecclesiology of the Council and, with it, the Council's teaching on episcopacy. Communion is an ontological reality in the Church, and the collegial unity of the bishops is a specific manifestation of this communion. It finds its full expression in an ecumenical Council, but it is also present in other legitimate assemblies of bishops. Thus, whenever a particular assembly of bishops, for example, a Conference, teaches something pertaining to the Church's faith, their message is not without effective authority, even though the historical event of the gathering cannot be the final guarantee of the truth of that declaration. The response of the faithful, therefore, should be a "religious submission of mind," on the one hand, and on the other hand, a prudent waiting for the authentication of the teaching through its reception by the faithful in all their churches—a dynamic not unlike that of the Church's reception of any authentic teaching of its faith.[24] In such instances, not only is a *recognitio* of the Holy See necessary, but asserting its necessity would effectively deny the legitimate authority that bishops possess in their own right as successors of the Apostles and vicars of Christ.[25] For this reason, Pope Francis's remarks in *Evangelium Gaudium* ring with a genuine sense of urgency:

> The Second Vatican Council stated that, like the ancient patriarchal Churches, episcopal conferences are in a position "to contribute in many and fruitful ways to the concrete realization of the collegial spirit." Yet this desire has not been fully realized, since a juridical status of episcopal conferences which would see them as subjects of specific attributions, including genuine doctrinal authority, has not yet been sufficiently elaborated. Excessive centralization, rather than proving helpful, complicates the Church's life and her missionary outreach. (no. 32)

Episcopal Conferences are genuine, effective expressions of collegiality. They exercise a pastoral office, intended to bring the one faith of the Church to bear upon issues particular to the diverse, lived situations of specific local groupings of the faithful.[26] The manner in which the faithful receive these teachings helps to clarify and authenticate their genuineness as faithful applications of the Church's faith, and for such acts a *recognitio* from the Holy See cannot be considered necessary. No doubt, these points fly in the face of *Apostolica Sollicitudo* and the current *Codex Iuris Canonici*. They do, however, reflect the manner in which the Council sought to receive anew (or "re-receive," in the language of ARCIC) collegiality at the less-than-universal level of the Church's life, and doing so would not only bring the Catholic Church closer to the vision espoused by ARCIC, but closer as well to its more authentic heritage.

iii. *Collegiality and the Synod of Bishops*. In his address commemorating the fiftieth anniversary of the institution of the Synod of Bishops, Pope Francis remarked on how

> *synodality*, as a constitutive element of the Church, offers us the most appropriate interpretive framework for understanding the hierarchical ministry itself. If we understand, as Saint John Chrysostom says, that "Church and Synod are synonymous," inasmuch as the Church is nothing other than the "journeying together" of God's flock along the paths of history towards the encounter with Christ the Lord, then we understand too that, within the Church, no one can be "raised up" higher than others. On the contrary, in the Church, it is necessary that each person "lower" himself or herself, so as to serve our brothers and sisters along the way.

The Holy Father went on to note where the Petrine primacy entrusted to him as Bishop of Rome stands within this "interpretative framework": as a primacy-in-collegality as the service of the Church of churches.

> I am persuaded that in a synodal Church, greater light can be shed on the exercise of the Petrine primacy. The Pope is not, by himself, above the Church; but within it as one of the baptized, and within the College of Bishops as a Bishop among Bishops, called at the same time—as Successor of Peter—to lead the Church of Rome which presides in charity over all the Churches.[27]

How can we bridge the gap—the gap between the form in which Pope Paul VI instituted the Synod and the form that Pope Francis (in terms that echo those used by ARCIC in *The Gift of Authority*)[28] clearly sees it both can and should take? We can get there by following a line of reasoning that resembles the one followed above regarding the full collegial authority of Episcopal Conferences, even if in this instance what is being considered is an effective manifestation of collegiality at the universal level.

When considering the development of the way the Synod is explicated by the Holy See, from its establishment by *Apostolica Sollicitudo* through its consideration in *Pastores Gregis*, the 2003 apostolic exhortation that John Paul II published following the Tenth Ordinary General Assembly of the Synod of Bishops in 2001, two sets of questions come to mind: (1) Is the Synod of Bishops an expression of collegiality? To what extent does the College of Bishops exercise its authority in the synodal process, or does the Synod act solely as a participation in papal power, that is, as an advisory body to the pope? (2) Does the Synod truly represent the entire Catholic episcopate? Related to this, in what sense can the Synod be said to speak for the entire body of bishops throughout the world?[29]

In answer to the first set of questions, one may begin by noting that although the Synod was established by a papal *motu proprio* rather than by an act of the Council, it emerged from the Council's discussion of episcopal collegiality. Thus, it would seem difficult to deny that it is an exercise, or at least a sign or expression, of precisely that collegiality. Early in his papacy, John Paul II himself did not deny it. Although in *Pastores Gregis* he spoke of the Synod as an *affective* expression of collegiality (see *Pastores Gregis* 58), twenty-one years earlier he described it as "a singularly excellent display of episcopal collegiality to the Church—and is, in a particular way, its effective instrument."[30]

In what particular way is the Synod such an instrument? It is such as a true and authentic, but partial, expression of collegiality. Collegiality is not a univocal reality. There are different and dynamic grades or degrees of collegiality ranging from the partial—such as the Synod—to the full—such as an ecumenical Council. Further, both collegiality's affective and effective aspects are necessarily complementary, and all expressions of collegiality are themselves rooted in one and the same reality: the grace of episcopal ordination. Therefore, even when the Synod is acting in a consultative mode, it is theologically and existentially acting in a collegial manner. If the Synod were given a deliberative mandate by the pope, the origin of its authenticity would *not* be found in its having been delegated by the pope, but in the sacramental grace of the episcopacy itself, strengthened by the consent or reception of the rest of the episcopate.[31]

The Synod's representative character flows from this. The Synod represents the College of Bishops (and, indeed, the communion of the Church of churches itself) in a reduced, but nevertheless legitimate way. Given that several councils lacked anything near the full complement of bishops, it must be admitted that any collegial body can designate a representative group of its members to express the opinion of the entire College. This could happen concretely in the case of the Synod. If it did, it would be possible to speak of the Synod as a true and legitimate representation of the College, and its acts, in the strict sense, as acts of the College.[32] As John Paul II expressed it in *Pastores Gregis*,

> The bishops assembled in Synod represent in the first place their own Churches, but they are also attentive to the contributions of the Episcopal Conferences which selected them and whose views about questions under discussion they then communicate. They thus express the recommendation of the entire hierarchical body of the Church and finally, in a certain sense, the whole Christian people, whose pastors they are. (no. 58)

With all this background in mind, a considered response can be offered to the question of whether "the teaching of the Second Vatican Council regarding the collegiality of bishops [has] been implemented sufficiently" (GA, no. 57).

3. A Considered Response: Primacy-in-Collegiality at the Service of Communion

In light of the above discussion, the answer is *not yet*. This lack of sufficient implementation, however, is not due to any expressed desire to deny collegiality its due. Rather, it is due to our ongoing struggle to grasp the Council's mind: what exactly is collegiality, and how is it related to the primacy we claim as proper to the Roman Pontiff as St. Peter's successor?

As noted above, the current situation is complicated by two factors. First, Vatican II did not explicitly reconcile its renewed teaching on collegiality with the primacy defined at Vatican I. Second, attempts to effect such a reconciliation have been frustrated by efforts, both during and since the Council, to treat collegiality as a servant of, or an adjunct to, the primacy. These efforts are exemplified by the way collegiality was treated in the *Nota* and by the ways those institutions intended by the Council to embody collegiality, namely Episcopal Conferences and the Synod of Bishops, have been stunted in their development, practically at the moment of their conception. However much these assemblies of bishops may affectively exhibit collegiality's spirit, they continue to lack the ability proper to themselves to exercise it effectively.

If the Catholic Church wants to implement the Council's teaching on collegiality sufficiently, we need to recover its mind on the truly and fully collegial of Episcopal Conferences and the Synod. The theological basis of just such a recovery has been provided. Two questions remain: How does this harmonize with what both Vatican Councils taught concerning primacy? Further, does this harmonization sufficiently respond to ARCIC?

With respect to the first question, the Roman Pontiff is, as Vatican I taught, "the permanent principle…visible foundation" (PA, intro.) of the unity of the episcopate because, as Vatican II demonstrated, his primacy is rooted in the bishops' collegial unity as true successors of the apostles and of their College. Thus, if the central purpose of the primacy of the Roman Pontiff is to confirm his brother bishops in their own faith and life of charity, then the primacy is rightly understood and correctly executed to the degree that it unites and strengthens the College in faith and communion. It is the strength and unity of the bishops that indicates the strength and effectiveness of the primacy.[33] As St. Gregory the Great once stated, "My honor is the honor of the whole Church. My honor is the steadfast strength of my brethren. Then do I receive true honor, when it is denied to none of those to whom honor is due."[34]

To this may be added that such strength and unity (and honor) is measured, in part, by the degree to which the bishops are effectively able to care for the communion of the Church of churches. Whenever and in whatever form bishops gather as members of the College to exercise *episcope* on behalf of the communion of God's people, even in a communion as small as a metropolitan province, their collegial unity is effectively present to the faithful. Both as member and head of their College, the Bishop of Rome bears a special responsibility to ensure that this is the case. By so doing, he not only vindicates their legitimate authority, but also his own (see LG 27).

Does this understanding of the primacy compromise the Roman Pontiff's freedom to exercise the juridical power proper to him as Supreme Pontiff? Not at all. This is intrinsic to his primacy, and remains so. What this understanding does do is demand that two aspects of primacy's juridical power be distinguished, aspects that, especially since Vatican I, have been conflated: the *facilitative* and *interventionist* exercises of primacy, that is, between the ordinary ministry of the Roman Pontiff whereby he "confirms his brothers" in the proper exercise of their ministry, and the extraordinary acts as the "great bridge builder" (*Pontifex Maximus*) by which he intervenes in the affairs of churches whose bishops have not effectively addressed threats to ecclesial unity. Making this distinction does not imply the creation of new canons to which appeal may be made against exercises of the primacy. That would limit the primacy in ways contrary to both Councils' teachings. Rather, it responds effectively to the perception that the conflation of these aspects of the primacy has so favored the latter as to have forgotten the former. Until this distinction becomes evident, not just in rhetoric but also in policy and practice, ecumenical overtures toward other Christian communities that seek to restore full visible unity to the one Church of Christ under the primacy of the Bishop of Rome are not likely to be effective.[35]

Would what was stated above be so effective, insofar as ARCIC is concerned? In *The Gift of Authority*, ARCIC reiterated its long-standing position that

> the "pattern of complementary primatial and conciliar aspects of *episcope* serving the *koinonia* of the churches

needs to be realised at the universal level." The exigencies of church life call for a specific exercise of *episcope* at the service of the whole Church. In the pattern found in the New Testament one of the twelve is chosen by Jesus Christ to strengthen the others so that they will remain faithful to their mission and in harmony with each other (see the discussion of the Petrine texts in *Authority in the Church II*, 2–5). (GA, no. 46)

As the one who continues in this service of primacy, it belongs to the Roman Pontiff to strengthen those who succeed the apostles in their mission, the bishops (cf. GA, no. 46; A-II, nos. 6–9), in order that they, in turn, may serve the communion of all God's people (cf. GA, no. 37). A recovery and implementation of Vatican II's mind on collegiality as I have discussed it above, together with a renewal of the primacy along these same lines, would be in harmony with this.

"Do the actions of bishops reflect sufficient awareness of the extent of the authority they receive through ordination for governing the local church?" (GA, no. 57)

What I have just said regarding the Roman Pontiff's universal jurisdiction might suggest the answer to be no. Then, the decision several years ago by Fabian Bruskewitz, then bishop of Lincoln, Nebraska, to excommunicate those faithful of his local church belonging to Call to Action, which counts a few of his brother bishops as members, might suggest that some bishops act with a bit too much awareness of their authority of governance. Perhaps it would be more appropriate to say that the question we face is whether bishops' actions reflect a sufficient awareness of their *munus regendi*'s proper object, which is to maintain the unity of the church they shepherd as a church within the broader communion of the Church of churches.

How does a bishop govern the people of God entrusted to his care as vicar and legate of Christ (see LG 27)? He does so by acting in ways that reflect both episcopacy's diachronic and synchronic foci: to maintain his local church in communion both with the faith of the apostles and with the other local churches that profess that same faith, in the ever-expanding bonds of communion from which the one Church of Jesus Christ arises. Thus, a bishop's actions must reflect the awareness of the extent to which his actions can work both *ad aedificationem* and *ad destructionem ecclesiae ecclesiarum*, and so shepherd his local church in such a way that, within its own communion of living faith and in communion with other churches throughout the world, it continues to proclaim the one faith, living and laboring in catholic unity for the communion of all people in Christ as the people of God.

This is a far more fundamental question than whether the actions of bishops reflect an awareness of the authority given them in episcopal ordination to govern their local churches. It is to ask whether they are aware that this authority—and the power to use this authority—was given for a purpose, and that any exercise of that authority on their part must respect that purpose, which is to preserve their local churches as churches *in communion*, in both the diachronic and synchronic senses of the term. There is ample enough reason for bishops to be so aware via the teachings of Vatican II. The question is, will they? To answer that, a word must be said about the primacy.

Will primacy admit to such an awareness by the bishops? The primacy-in-collegiality recovered by Vatican II would certainly permit it, and in terms consistent with ARCIC. Such a primacy would neither demand that bishops wait on word from the Holy See when confronted by questions they can answer themselves, nor permit bishops to act as though they were accountable only to a higher authority (see LG 27), and not also to those with whom they share the "duty...to promote and to safegaurd the unity of faith and the discipline common to the whole church" (LG 23). Instead, it would call bishops to exercise their *episcope* as both the legitimate pastors of the churches they shepherd and brothers in that ministry. The welfare of the Church of churches depends upon it. As ARCIC stated,

> The charism and function of *episcope* are specifically connected to the *ministry of memory*, which constantly renews the Church in hope. Through such ministry the Holy Spirit keeps alive in the Church the memory of what God did and revealed, and the hope of what God

237

will do to bring all things into unity in Christ. In this way, not only from generation to generation, but also from place to place, the one faith is communicated and lived out. This is the ministry exercised by the bishop, and by ordained persons under the bishop's care, as they proclaim the Word, minister the sacraments, and take part in the administering of discipline for the common good. The bishops, the clergy and the other faithful must all recognise and receive what is mediated from God through each other. (GA, no. 30)

"Has enough provision been made to ensure consultation between the Bishop of Rome and the local churches prior to the making of important decisions affecting either a local church or the whole Church?" (GA, no. 57)

In terms of canonically definable provisions, no. No such provisions are named in the documents of Vatican Councils I or II or the Code of Canon Law. In moral terms, though, one may answer yes, and draw upon Vatican II's understanding of the primacy's collegial ground to do so. Such consultation would be entirely consistent with the "form of government established by Christ the Lord," which the Holy Spirit "unfailingly preserves," in part, through the primatial ministry of the Roman Pontiff (LG 27).

As discussed above, collegiality is effectively present in the bishops' governance of the Church in various ways. It is present in partial or full assemblies of the College. It is also present when the bishops of a nation or region of the world gather in collegial unity to govern the particular churches they pastor. Finally, it is present when bishops, as "vicars and ambassadors of Christ" (LG 27), govern "the portion of the People of God committed to their care" (LG 23). Therefore, for the Bishop of Rome *not* to so consult his brother bishops would be for him to treat them as though they were *his* vicars and not the "heads of the people whom they govern" (LG 27) and the "body of pastors" charged by Christ to announce the gospel throughout the whole world (LG 23). In short, it would be for the Holy Father to act contrary to the expressed will of Christ for his Church. A canon to this effect may be welcome not only by our Anglicans, but a good many Catholics.

Perhaps, though, it is enough to recall "that bishops by divine institution have succeeded to the place of the apostles, as shepherds of the Church, and he who hears them, hears Christ, and he who rejects them, rejects Christ and Him who sent Christ" (LG 20).

As both Vatican I and II declared, the bishops' powers are "not destroyed by the supreme and universal power, but on the contrary it is affirmed, strengthened and vindicated by it" (LG 27, citing PA 3). Therefore, consulting the Church's bishops would be the least the Holy Father could do were he to exercise his primatial ministry in this way, especially if he were to invoke the charism of infallibility when teaching on a matter of faith outside of an ecumenical Council. This is something to which ARCIC paid particular attention.

> Every solemn definition pronounced from the chair of Peter in the church of Peter and Paul may...express only the faith of the Church. Any such definition is pronounced *within* the college of those who exercise *episcope* and not outside that college. Such authoritative teaching is a particular exercise of the calling and responsibility of the body of bishops to teach and affirm the faith. When the faith is articulated in this way, the Bishop of Rome proclaims the faith of the local churches. It is thus the wholly reliable teaching of the whole Church that is operative in the judgement of the universal primate. In solemnly formulating such teaching, the universal primate must discern and declare, with the assured assistance and guidance of the Holy Spirit, in fidelity to Scripture and Tradition, the authentic faith of the whole Church, that is, the faith proclaimed from the beginning. It is this faith, the faith of all the baptised in communion, and this only, that each bishop utters with the body of bishops in council. It is this faith which the Bishop of Rome in certain circumstances has a duty to discern and make explicit. This form of authoritative teaching has no stronger guarantee from the Spirit than have the solemn definitions of ecumenical councils. (GA, no. 47)

The primacy-in-collegiality recovered by Vatican II stands in harmony with ARCIC's expressed mind. Without fear of compromising the freedom to act inherent to the primacy, we may receive this vision in terms faithful to our Catholic Tradition.

When the Bishop of Rome solemnly defines a matter of faith *ex cathedra*, he "is not pronouncing judgment as a private person, but as the supreme teacher of the universal Church, in whom the charism of infallibility of the Church itself is individually present" (LG 25). At that moment, he speaks nothing other than the faith of the Church of churches. Consulting his brother bishops before delivering such a judgment is most certainly an appropriate means for investigating revelation and giving it an "apt expression" (LG 25). While it is reasonable to acknowledge the possibility that the Roman Pontiff *may* have to act without such a broad consultation, in light of the Council's teaching on collegiality it should not be the ordinary way of making even such admittedly extraordinary acts. This would be entirely in accord with the Church's divine constitution, which the Roman Pontiff, as successor of Peter, has been charged by Christ to preserve and promote.

As the bishops are the corporate persons of the churches they lead, so too is the Bishop of Rome the corporate person of their collegial unity. His primacy is exercised precisely within that unity. From this place, he is capable of representing to the world the faith and evangelical mission of the entire Body of Christ. As ARCIC said, citing St. Augustine of Hippo,

> After all, it is not just one man that received the keys, but the Church in its unity. So this is the reason for Peter's acknowledged preeminence, that he stood for the Church's universality and unity, when he was told, *To you I am entrusting*, what has in fact been entrusted to all. I mean to show you that it is the Church which has received the keys of the kingdom of heaven. Listen to what the Lord says in another place to all his apostles: *Receive the Holy Spirit*; and straight away, *whose sins you forgive, they will be forgiven them; whose sins you retain, they will be retained* (Jn 20.22–23). This refers to the keys, about which I said, *whatever you bind on earth shall be bound in heaven* (Mt 16.19). But what was

said to Peter…Peter at that time stood for the universal Church (*Sermon 295, On the Feast of the Martyrdom of the Apostles Peter and Paul*). (GA, no. 46)

Of course, in consulting the bishops, the Bishop of Rome is looking for the faith, not of the bishops as private persons, but of the people of God whom they serve, as Pope Francis clearly demonstrated during the recent Extraordinary Synod on the Family, when he both asked bishops to canvas the opinions of the *sensus fidelium* of their respective local churches on a range of topics and further invited married couples from around the world to address the Synod on their lived experience of the sacramental grace of marriage. It is to this broader consultation that ARCIC turned, when it asked,

"Is there at all levels effective participation of clergy as well as lay people in emerging synodal bodies?…How is the variety of theological opinion taken into account when such decisions are made?" (GA, no. 57)

By the term *synodal bodies*, ARCIC meant organized gatherings where all the faithful demonstrate that they "walk together in Christ" along a "common way" (GA, no. 34). The issue here is whether and to what extent the Catholic Church is actively committed to the effective participation not only of bishops, but indeed of the entire people of God in bodies that determine the Church's life and mission. This issue includes their participation not only in bodies exercising governance of the Church, but also in bodies engaged in the discernment of specific truths of our Christian faith (cf. GA, nos. 43, 47). This is not an easy question to answer—though not for lack of sufficient ground in *Lumen Gentium*.

In *Lumen Gentium*, the Council acknowledged the essential role played by all the faithful in the building up of Christ's Body as a living proclamation of God's kingdom (see LG 7). In the section on the hierarchy, it spoke of priests as "prudent cooperators of the Episcopal order, who are united with the body of bishops and who "serve the good of the whole Church according to their vocation and the grace given to them" (LG 28). Later, it spoke in even stronger terms with regard to the laity. In a section dedicated entirely to the vocation of the laity, it declared,

> The laity are gathered together in the People of God and make up the Body of Christ under one head. Whoever they are they are called upon, as living members, to expend all their energy for the growth of the Church and its continuous sanctification, since this very energy is a gift of the Creator and a blessing of the Redeemer.
>
> The lay apostolate, however, is a participation in the salvific mission of the Church itself. Through their baptism and confirmation all are commissioned to that apostolate by the Lord Himself....
>
> Upon all the laity, therefore, rests the noble duty of working to extend the divine plan of salvation to all men of each epoch and in every land. Consequently, may every opportunity be given them so that, according to their abilities and the needs of the times, they may zealously participate in the saving work of the Church. (LG 33)

In this light, one might expect to see the clergy and, more especially, the laity actively included in discussions of the life and mission of the Church at every level of the Church's life. There have been and are examples of this. Unfortunately, the unspoken assumption that the Holy Spirit operates in the Church primarily, if not exclusively, through the mediation of hierarchical authorities who act *in persona Christi* to mold and rule the people of God has led to a failure on the part of bishops to articulate more fully a theology of lay ministry and develop practices of communal discernment.[36] Thus, it must be said that, while the Catholic Church's hierarchical authorities say they are committed to promote such participation, including statements from Pope Francis calling for the greater participation of the women, we as a Church are still very much in our infancy regarding the full inclusion of the lay women and men (to say nothing of presbyters and deacons) in any body that effectively determines the course of the Church's life and mission.

This does not imply, however, that we are as yet incapable of answering ARCIC's call for such inclusion. As was noted above, there is ample ground for enabling a positive response even now, and this even with respect to the discernment and definition of specific truths of our Christian faith, such as when the Roman Pontiff in collegial unity with the churches' bishops exercises the Church's charism of infallibility.

Mention was made of the significant role that the bishops play in the exercise of this charism by the Bishop of Rome as the representatives, or corporate persons, of their churches. Such representation possesses far more than mere practical importance: since the bishop is likely to know what the faithful of his church think on a particular issue, the Holy Father consults him. Rather, it is a representation of doctrinal importance. It is a concrete instance of the *sensus fidei* in which the bishops literally speak the faith of the Church, precisely as that faith is understood and lived by *all* the faithful of the churches they shepherd. In this light, one must say that when the Holy Father would consult the bishops before exercising the Church's charism of infallibility, he is, in a very real and profound sense, consulting the *sensus fidelium* of the entire people of God concerning that faith in which they, under the guidance of the Holy Spirit, cannot err. Thus, when he subsequently delivers such a solemn definition, he is speaking nothing other than what the Church, "from the Bishops down to the last of the lay faithful," already believes: "the faith [was] given once and for all to the saints," which the faithful penetrate "more deeply with right thinking" and apply "more fully in its life" (LG 12).

Throughout this process, clergy and laity play a significant role. This is the case not only with regard to the discernment of a particular article of the faith, but also with regard to that article's eventual reception as an authentic teaching of the gospel. For, as Vatican II taught, "To these definitions the assent of the Church can never be wanting, on account of the activity of that same Holy Spirit, by which the whole flock of Christ is preserved and progresses in unity of faith" (LG 25). Recognition of this significant role demands that it be given concrete expression at every level of our communion, including the universal. It would give us the courage to exorcise the specter of Gallicanism from our ecclesial imagination. It would allow us to enter more deeply into the process of genuine renewal called for at Vatican II. Finally, it would enable us to answer ARCIC's call for a clergy and laity that are effectively

243

engaged in the life and mission of the Church, "especially in situations of challenge," when the "exercise of teaching authority in the Church…requires the participation, in their distinctive ways, of the whole body of believers, not only those charged with the ministry of memory" (GA, no. 43).

In this light, it is reasonably sufficient to say that the manner by which the Roman Pontiff would—even should—consider the diversity of theological opinions when exercising his primacy would be in accord with the dynamic of discernment outlined above. Such diversity arises from the many ways all the faithful seek to penetrate the faith "given once and for all to the saints" and apply it to the concrete reality of life within the churches. With an eye toward the history of Vatican I and II, one may say that it was precisely such a diversity that, seemingly against all odds, checked the efforts of extreme ultramontanism, fostered the recovery of collegiality, and, as reviewed here, reasserted the significance of the laity for the life and mission of the Church. Therefore, without prejudice against the freedom inherent to the primacy, it would be entirely proper for the Roman Pontiff to engage in this process of consultation, intervening only when the process's dynamic threatens ecclesial unity, and then only in a way that evidently respects the collegial bonds existing between himself and the bishops. Such an approach would be in harmony with Vatican II's vision of the primacy and, what is more, in harmony with ARCIC's vision of the relationship between authority and freedom of conscience:

> The exercise of authority in the Church is to be recognised and accepted as an instrument of the Spirit of God for the healing of humanity. The exercise of authority must always respect conscience, because the divine work of salvation affirms human freedom. In freely accepting the way of salvation offered through baptism, the Christian disciple also freely takes on the discipline of being a member of the Body of Christ. Because the Church of God is recognised as the community where the divine means of salvation are at work, the demands of discipleship for the well-being of the entire Christian community cannot be refused. There is also a discipline required in the exercise of authority.

Those called to such a ministry must themselves submit to the discipline of Christ, observing the requirements of collegiality and the common good, and duly respect the consciences of those they are called to serve. (GA, no. 49)

"In supporting the Bishop of Rome in his work of promoting communion among the churches, do the structures and procedures of the Roman Curia adequately respect the exercise of *episcope* at other levels?" (GA, no. 57)

Reception of Vatican II's understanding of the primacy as a primacy-in-collegiality would enable us, on the basis of our Catholic Tradition, to respond to ARCIC's call for "a primacy that will even now help.…the Church on earth to be the authentic catholic *koinonia.…*[and] an effective sign for all Christians as to how this gift of God builds up that unity for which Christ prayed" (GA, no. 60). In order for this to occur, we must turn our attention toward several time-honored institutions that, in their present form, threaten to compromise our reception of the Council and with it our ability to respond to ARCIC. These institutions are (1) the Roman Curia, (2) the College of Cardinals, (3) titular bishops, and (4) the selection of bishops.

1. The Roman Curia: As was noted above, the Roman Curia always runs the real risk of seeing itself as a *tertium quid* between the pope and the bishops. In the light of a history in which this risk often became a reality, one should not wonder at the numerous calls for the Curia's reform before Vatican II, not to mention afterward.[37] If the Catholic Church desires to receive the Council's teaching on the primacy and the ARCIC's call for a primacy other Christians could accept, then further steps must be taken to reform the Roman Curia in ways that hold it accountable to the Council's ecclesiological vision.

Where to begin? Archbishop Quinn offered a number of suggestions, all of which remain very much on the proverbial table: (1) the creation of a congregation that would have overall control of the Curia's various departments; (2) the inclusion of lower clergy, in particular fewer bishops, and more laypeople in full-time curial positions; (3) term limits for curial officials; (4) a reform of the way curial officials are selected, for example, greater and more open consultation with bishops regarding the fitness of a person for curial service; (5) the creation of two Curiae: one to serve the Church Universal, the other to serve the Latin churches of the West.[38] The adoption of any of these would, without doubt, change the Curia as it has come to be known. Regardless of the structures adopted, unless the kind of ressourcement that guided the Council likewise guides the work of curial reform, the genuine aggiornamento so many Catholics (and not a few of our ecumenical partners) desire for this reform will be stillborn.[39]

One must admit, of course, that no number of steps will lead us to the creation of the perfect Curia. The primacy is an evolving institution. Therefore, the Curia must evolve as well, particularly now in its service to a renewed primacy-in-collegiality. The critical issue is whether this reform will take place according to the expressed mind of the Council, or continue on as though the Council had never happened.

2. The College of Cardinals: One day after a mass at St. Anthony Shrine in Boston, a woman asked me, "Why did you refer to Cardinal Law [then archbishop of Boston] as 'our bishop, Bernard,' and not 'our cardinal archbishop, Bernard,' as my pastor does?" After pointing out that this is the formula in the *Sacramentary* and that, technically, he is the *bishop* of Boston, she responded, "But isn't he a cardinal?" "Yes," I replied. I then went on to explain what a cardinal is, noting, almost in passing, that he was cardinal-priest of Santa Susanna. "If he's the archbishop of Boston, how can that be? It doesn't make any sense, does it?"

No, it doesn't make any sense, at least not within the context of Vatican II's teaching on collegiality, and this in two respects: (1) the manner in which bishops belong to the College, and (2) the fraternal relationship that exists among the members of the College.

Collegiality does not admit to degrees of belonging. This applies even to the Roman Pontiff. He is no more a member of the College because he is its head than is any other bishop. The existence of the *College* of Cardinals, though, would suggest otherwise. It is a college within a college, which due to the honors afforded its members, for example distinctive dress and the privilege of electing the next Pope, effectively makes the College of Bishops appear to be a body of second rank.[40] This situation becomes even more problematic when one considers that whereas the College of Bishops exists *de jure divino*, the College of Cardinals is an institution of entirely human origin. If we are actually to receive collegiality as an existential, and not merely a theoretical, reality, then the existence of the cardinalate as a *collegium* must be addressed.

In the light of the fraternal bond that exists among the members of the College, the College of Cardinals fares no better. To put it succinctly, how can those whom the Council declares vicars and legates of Christ for the churches they shepherd also hold titles as clergy of the local church of Rome and its suburbicariate? Of course the titles cardinal-deacon, -priest, and -bishop are strictly honorary, but how does the bestowing of such titles honor the ministry of those who are the Bishop of Rome's *brothers*? As my inquiring Bostonian observed, it doesn't make any sense. We need to consider what the cardinalate signifies today, perhaps even to the point of reconsidering it completely.

3. Titular Bishops: The phenomenon of the titular bishop is a long-accepted staple of Catholic life. A significant number of bishops—those assigned to curial or diplomatic posts and all auxiliary bishops—are titular bishops. Some of these bishops even bear the title "cardinal." Doubtless, many perform invaluable service to the Church, and quite a few have gone on to lead churches, including the church of Rome. For all this, however, the continued existence of their office is a significant obstacle to our reception of Vatican II's renewed theology of the episcopate and its understanding of the Church as a true communion of churches.

How so? In three ways: first, it transforms what is fundamentally a sacramental ministry into an honorary or administrative title. This reinforces the impression, widespread in many quarters of the Church as well as civil society, that ecclesial structures are more concerned with rank and domination than with ecclesial service. Second, it trivializes the relationship between a bishop and his local church. How can one speak meaningfully of a bishop's "communion" with a nonexistent community? Finally, the appointing of bishops to titular sees justifies a great lacuna in our renewed ecclesiology: the necessary connection between the College of Bishops and the communion of churches.[41]

As was noted in chapter 2, the Council's recovery of the patristic concept of collegiality proved essential to its moving beyond the theology of *Mystici Corporis*. Yet, the Council recovered only half of that patristic concept. For the Church fathers, it was not, as *Lumen Gentium* 22 taught, merely the facts of ordination and communion that established one as a member of the body of bishops. It was also the fact that one was ordained to serve a specific local church, and so was received as a brother in that service. Of course, one may argue that granting the title of a now defunct see to a bishop is a respectful nod to the fathers' instincts, providing that bishop with an occasion to serve the Church Universal. However, it is difficult to argue that such a nod truly respects the fathers' faith, especially when the issue at hand is the filling curial and diplomatic posts. If we wish to renew our understanding of episcopacy's sacramental dignity and its significance for the Church of *churches*, then we must recover the necessary connection between the College of Bishops and the churches they shepherd—the churches from which communion the one Church of Jesus Christ arises.

4. The Selection of Bishops: Unlike the phenomenon of titular bishops, the current practice whereby the Roman Pontiff selects virtually all bishops of the Latin Rite is of recent origin. Only with the 1917 Code of Canon Law (can. 329, §2) did the general law of the Church declare the pope to have such a power. It is a practice that is incompatible with the renewed ecclesiology of Vatican II, and an ecumenical dead-end.

This continued, current practice belongs not to the ecclesiology of *Lumen Gentium*, but to that of *Mystici Corporis*; not to an understanding of the Church as a Church of churches, but to that of the Church as a monolithic, quasi-monarchical institution ruled by a Sovereign Pontiff through appointed and dependent local lords. To whatever degree collegiality is operative in this process, it may be said to be only *affectively*, rather than *effectively* so—to say nothing of involvement by clergy and laity, which, for all practical purposes, is nothing indeed. If the Catholic Church is to bring harmony between its polity and its theology, then the practice of centralizing episcopal appointments in Rome must be reformed, and in ways that deliberately reflect the ecclesiological vision of Vatican II.

This is not a call for the Holy See to disassociate itself from the selection process, nor a veiled call for the direct elections of bishops by the clergy and laity of local churches, after the manner of Western democracies. Rather, it is a call for a process—or various processes, which make practical as well as theological sense to those involved in them—that recognizes the inherent ecclesial dignity of the local church, confirms the vital connection between a bishop and the people he represents as well as shepherds, and affirms the importance of a church's clergy and laity being effectively involved in the selection of the one who will lead them in faith. If the faithful, through the exercise of the supernatural sense of the faith, have a role to play in receiving God's word and discerning God's will, then the Church cannot overlook the contributions of the faithful in the choice of church leadership.[42]

Diversity of practice is not disunity. Rather, it accurately reflects the diversity of the local churches that make up the one Church.[43] Moreover, it even more accurately responds to the concerns of our ecumenical partners, including the Anglican Communion, who are not desirous of surrendering the right to choose their local episcopal leadership. It is unreasonable to believe that Anglicans will submit to the current Roman practice, or that they will accept a primacy that continues to claim the right to supersede legitimate diversity in the name of unity, even when unity is not at stake. Far more than by words, it is by actions that the Catholic Church will demonstrate that Anglicans need not be so concerned, and no action would be more convincing than for the Catholic Church to reform its own house.

In our present situation, it is vital that we recognize the old ultramontane outlook and the popular instruction to which it gave rise have never disappeared. This has only compounded the confusion and attendant contention we Catholics experience as we struggle to resolve Vatican II's lack of clarity over practical relationships between the power of the College of Bishops and that of the Roman Pontiff. If we wish to find a way through this impasse, we must engage in a critical, dispassionate study of the institutions set up to embody Vatican II. We must make the Council's mind our own, and allow its teachings to enter our life as the people of God. Only then will we be free from the out-of-date attitudes of recent centuries,[44] further the process of renewal initiated by the Council, and, as we make our own the ecumenical aspirations of our sisters and brothers from other ecclesial traditions, be able to offer others what we have only just begun to re-receive: a primacy-in-collegiality capable of being "an effective sign for all Christians as to how this gift of God builds up that unity for which Christ prayed" (GA, no. 60).

IV. CONCLUSION

> Simon, Simon, listen! Satan has demanded to sift all of you like wheat, but I have prayed for you that your own faith may not fail; and you, when once you have turned back, strengthen your brothers. (Luke 22:31–32)

The Petrine primacy of the Roman Pontiff is indeed a particular, unique expression of the ministry of *episcope*. For all its particularity, though, it is and remains a ministry of episcopacy, which like all expressions of this ministry—and, indeed, every ministry in the Church of churches that the Spirit gives *ad aedificationem* and *ad destructionem ecclesiae ecclesiarum*—finds its example in the person of Jesus Christ, who came among us as one who serves.

Ministry as service, leadership as service, authority as service....Anyone who has worked for any amount of time in any Church community, regardless of its ecclesial Tradition, is familiar with such language. As one churchman and theologian long acquainted with ecumenical dialogue once quipped to me, "Remember, whenever people in authority start speaking the language of service, what they are really talking about is power." Indeed, I have often found this to be the case, but to the extent that we remember that any and every power given by the Spirit is not given for lordship. Rather, it is given so that those entrusted with it may have the strength they need to follow the Lord's example of bending low to meet people in their needs. If this was the case for Peter, how much more must it be for anyone who would claim to be his successor?

How can we Catholics realize this anew within our Church? We can do it by receiving the grace to renew the papacy, the primatial office of the Roman Pontiff and all other offices that exist to assist him in his ministry, according to the mind of Vatican Council II. In this way, the primacy may be seen not only by Catholics, but also by all our sisters and brothers in Christ as a service that strengthens those whom the Spirit has called and empowered to lead us in faith, especially those entrusted with the apostolic ministry of *episcope*—and what is more, as a service to every one of us, in the integrity of all our churches, within the rich diversity of our ecclesial traditions.

"FEED MY SHEEP…": PRIMATE OF THE CHURCH OF CHURCHES

[Jesus] said to him the third time, "Simon son of John, do you love me?" Peter felt hurt because he said to him the third time, "Do you love me?" And he said to him, "Lord, you know everything; you know that I love you." Jesus said to him, "Feed my sheep."

—John 21:17

Christ, having been lifted up from the earth has drawn all to Himself. Rising from the dead He sent His life-giving Spirit upon His disciples and through Him has established His Body which is the Church as the universal sacrament of salvation. Sitting at the right hand of the Father, He is continually active in the world that He might lead men [*sic*] to the Church and through it join them to Himself and that He might make them partakers of His glorious life by nourishing them with His own Body and Blood. Therefore the promised restoration which we are awaiting has already begun in Christ, is carried forward in the mission of the

Holy Spirit and through Him continues in the Church in which we learn the meaning of our terrestrial life through our faith, while we perform with hope in the future the work committed to us in this world by the Father, and thus work out our salvation.

—Vatican Council II, *Lumen Gentium* 48

When the churches, through their exercise of authority, display the healing and reconciling power of the Gospel, then the wider world is offered a vision of what God intends for all creation. The aim of the exercise of authority and of its reception is to enable the Church to say "Amen" to God's "Yes" in the Gospel.

—ARCIC II, *The Gift of Authority*, no. 50

I. INTRODUCTION

When they had finished breakfast, Jesus said to Simon Peter, "Simon son of John, do you love me more than these?" He said to him, "Yes, Lord; you know that I love you." Jesus said to him, "Feed my lambs." A second time he said to him, "Simon son of John, do you love me?" He said to him, "Yes, Lord; you know that I love you." Jesus said to him, "Tend my sheep." He said to him the third time, "Simon son of John, do you love me?" Peter felt hurt because he said to him the third time, "Do you love me?" And he said to him, "Lord, you know everything; you know that I love you." Jesus said to him, "Feed my sheep." (John 21:15–17)

As both Vatican Councils I and II demonstrate, how one understands the mystery of the Church determines the way one understands every aspect of the Church's faith and mission, including the Petrine primacy of the Roman Pontiff. This is more evident in the teachings of Vatican II. The Council's mission-driven understanding of the communion (*koinonia*) of God's people as

253

a Church of *churches* provided the appropriate context for it to re-receive the patristic concept of episcopal collegiality and, with this in mind, develop a theology of papal primacy as primacy-in-collegiality at the service of that communion.

In the wake of the Council, this was the ecclesiological path that Catholic theologians took with their Anglican counterparts as members of ARCIC. When seen in this light, the current debate in Catholic circles regarding the proper relationship between the local church and the Church Universal becomes all the more significant, for its resolution will not only determine our own reception of the Council's mind on the proper relationship between primacy and episcopacy. It will also, as ARCIC observed, determine our ability to offer the primacy truly as "a gift to be received by all the churches," a gift that even now can "assist the Church on earth to be the authentic catholic *koinonia* in which unity does not curtail diversity and diversity does not endanger but enhance [the] unity" (GA, nos. 47, 60) of the people whom God has established in Christ as the sacrament of humanity's salvation (cf. LG 1, 48).

II. ARCIC ON THE PRIMACY OF PETER'S CHAIR AMONG THE CHURCHES

A. The Twofold "Amen" of the Believer and the Church

As the Commission stated explicitly in the introduction to *The Final Report*, "Fundamental to all our statements is the concept of koinonia (communion)" (FR, intro., §4). This was especially the case in all its statements on authority in the Church, which, as the Commission noted in its third statement *The Gift of Authority*, exists for the sake of humanity's "Amen" to the "Yes" God spoke to us, once and for all, in Jesus Christ (GA, no. 8).

By the work of the Holy Spirit, the "life-giving obedience of Jesus Christ calls forth" every believer's "'Amen' to God the Father" (GA, no. 10). When a believer offers this "Amen," a "further dimension is always involved: an 'Amen' to the faith of the Christian community" (GA, no. 12). Thus, the believer is caught up and "incorporated into an 'Amen' of faith, older, deeper, broader, richer than the individual's 'Amen' to the Gospel" (GA, no. 13). This is the "Amen" of the Church, which all believers offer by following Christ in communion with one another in their local churches. Within the communion of their churches, believers, "by the grace of the Spirit, together with all believers of all times and all places," inherit the "faith of the Church in the communion of saints" (GA, no. 13), and, by means of the gifts whereby the Spirit maintains the Church in faithful obedience to the gospel of its Lord and his mission (cf. A-I, nos. 3, 5), effectively proclaim God's saving work (cf. FR, intro., §7)—God's "Yes" to all people of all times and all places in Jesus Christ.

B. *Episcope* in Collegiality at the Service of the Church of Churches

At the nexus of this dynamic of communion stand those who exercise the ministry of *episcope*, that is, bishops. By means of this "pastoral authority" that the Spirit bestows upon them "for the effective exercise of *episcope* within a local church" (GA, no. 36), the bishops maintain the communion believers have with one another and with the saints. This they do by exercising *episcope* in a synodal fashion, in other words, enabling believers to "walk together" (from the Greek *syn-hodos*, meaning "common way") in one mind and heart in Christ (cf. GA, no. 34).

> Through such ministry the Holy Spirit keeps alive in the Church the memory of what God did and revealed, and the hope of what God will do to bring all things into unity in Christ. In this way, not only from generation to generation, but also from place to place, the one faith is communicated and lived out. This is the ministry exercised by the bishop, and by ordained persons under the bishop's care, as they proclaim the Word, minister the sacraments, and take their part in administering discipline for the common good. The bishops, the clergy and

the other faithful must all recognise and receive what is mediated from God through each other. (GA, no. 30)

As communion in and with Christ is not limited to a local church, but necessarily draws all local churches into ever wider bonds of communion with one another, so too is the ministry of *episcope* that bishops exercise not limited to their respective local churches. Through their communion with each other, which "is expressed through the incorporation of each bishop into a college of bishops," bishops serve communion both "within and among local churches."

Bishops are, both personally and collegially, at the service of communion and are concerned for synodality in all its expressions. These expressions have included a wide variety of organs, instruments and institutions, notably synods or councils, local, provincial, worldwide, ecumenical. The maintenance of communion requires that at every level there is a capacity to take decisions appropriate to that level. When those decisions raise serious questions for the wider communion of churches, synodality must find a wider expression. (GA, no. 37)

C. Primacy-in-Collegiality at the Service of the Church of Churches

It is precisely here, within the wider communion of churches, that universal primacy finds its significance for ARCIC. This is a primacy, modeled on the ministry of Peter among his brother apostles (see A-II, no. 9), that has been providentially established for the sake of the Church's communion (see A-II, nos. 11–13), and that may be exercised by the bishop who succeeds to the chair of Peter within the local church of Peter and Paul, the Bishop of Rome. When he does exercise it, specifically with regard to the Church's faith, the Bishop of Rome does so from within the College of Bishops "and not from outside that college."

Such authoritative teaching is a particular exercise of the calling and responsibility of the body of bishops to teach and affirm the faith. When the faith is articulated in this way, the Bishop of Rome proclaims the faith of the local churches. It is thus the wholly reliable teaching of the whole Church that is operative in the judgement of the universal primate. In solemnly formulating such teaching, the universal primate must discern and declare, with the assured assistance and guidance of the Holy Spirit, in fidelity to Scripture and Tradition, the authentic faith of the whole Church, that is, the faith proclaimed from the beginning. It is this faith, the faith of all the baptised in communion, and this only, that each bishop utters with the body of bishops in council. It is this faith which the Bishop of Rome in certain circumstances has a duty to discern and make explicit. (GA, no. 47)

Thus, for ARCIC, the Petrine primacy of the Roman Pontiff is truly a primacy-in-collegiality at the service of the Church of *churches*. It is exercised both from within, in his person, and in the name of the College of Bishops. Speaking to the Church, they together shepherd that faith that the people of God, "from the beginning," have professed and proclaimed within their churches. Thus, the primacy does not stifle Christian freedom. Rather, it calls each believer to exercise his or her freedom by freely taking on "the discipline of being a member of the Body of Christ"—a discipline to which the Roman Pontiff, together with every member of the College, is called to submit himself, observing "the requirements of collegiality and the common good," and duly respecting the consciences of all those he has been called to serve as, together, they walk in Christ and utter their "Amen" to the saving "Yes" God spoke, once and for all, in him (GA, no. 49).

III. A ROMAN CATHOLIC RESPONSE

The decades since the close of Vatican II have witnessed an ongoing debate within Roman Catholic ecclesiology regarding the proper relationship between the local church and the Church Universal. As this debate has a direct bearing upon how one understands the primacy of the Roman Pontiff, it should be asked, Which resolution would allow us to answer ARCIC's call for a primacy that "will already assist the Church on earth to be the authentic catholic *koinonia* in which unity does not curtail diversity, and diversity does not endanger but enhance unity?" (GA, no. 60).

A. A Primacy at the Service of the Church of Churches

As was noted earlier, not only the "adequate harmonization of primacy and episcopacy," but also the like harmonization of the Church Universal and the local church is widely considered to be *one of the most pressing theological tasks of the Church today*. This is a task to which a great many Catholic theologians have offered a response, including a former occupant of Peter's chair, Pope Emeritus Benedict XVI. These responses tend to fall into the sides represented in the Joseph Ratzinger/Walter Kasper debate: those who support Ratzinger's position and hold the ontological priority of the Universal Church to be "almost self-evident,"[1] and those who, following the thought of Henri de Lubac, support Kasper in asserting that a "universal church which would have a separate existence, or which someone imagined as existing outside the particular churches, is a mere abstraction."[2] I do not intend to resolve the debate here. Rather, I ask which of these positions provides the context from which the Catholic Church may effectively respond to ARCIC's call for a primacy that "will already assist the Church on earth to be the authentic catholic *koinonia* in which unity does not curtail diversity, and diversity does not endanger but enhances unity" (GA, no. 60). It is without doubt the latter.

If the Church Universal arises from the communion of local churches, then the Petrine primacy of the Roman Pontiff stands forth as a true primacy-in-collegiality at the service of communion. This is the one mystery of the Church of which Vatican II stated, "This Church constituted and organized in the world as a society, subsists in the Catholic Church, which is governed by the successor of Peter and by the Bishops in communion with him" (LG 8). Within this communion of God's people, the Roman

Pontiff possesses the primacy by virtue of the fact that he is, first and foremost, the Bishop of Rome. As Vatican I taught, "'The holy and most blessed Peter...lives' and presides and 'exercises judgment in his successors,' the bishops of the holy Roman see, which he founded and consecrated with his blood," for "whoever succeeds to the chair of Peter obtains by the institution of Christ himself, the primacy of Peter over the whole church" (PA 2). In an ecclesiology of communion, the primacy of the Roman Pontiff is thus rooted in the collegial relationship he has with his brother bishops as successors of the apostles and of their collegium, their College, which Christ established to teach, govern, and sanctify the communion of all his people in the diversity of their churches. To assert the contrary is to resurrect the vision of *Mystici Corporis* and, with it, an understanding of the primacy fundamentally at odds with the Council's mind and the far richer deposit of our Catholic faith.

B. Primacy and the College of Bishops

Seen in this light, the *episcope* exercised by Rome's bishop on behalf of the communion of God's people is the same as that exercised by every bishop for the sake of his local church. It is the exercise of the threefold charge (*munus*) he received in his episcopal consecration: to teach, to sanctify, and to govern the people of God as a Vicar of Jesus Christ (see LG 21). Thus, the primatial *episcope* he possesses as Peter's successor differs only in degree, not in kind, from the *episcope* of his brother bishops as successors of the apostles. This primatial *episcope* does not destroy the "proper, ordinary and immediate" authority of the Roman Pontiff's brothers. Rather, it affirms, strengthens, and vindicates their authority (see LG 27), ensuring that they have the freedom and opportunity to exercise it both individually, for the sake of their respective churches, and collegially, for the sake of the degrees of communion their churches share nationally, regionally, and universally. As Vatican II stated,

> For it is the duty of all bishops to promote and to safeguard the unity of faith and the discipline common to the whole Church, to instruct the faithful to love for the

whole mystical body of Christ, especially for its poor and sorrowing members and for those who are suffering persecution for justice's sake, and finally to promote every activity that is of interest to the whole Church, especially that the faith may take increase and the light of full truth appear to all men. And this also is important, that by governing well their own church as a portion of the universal Church, they themselves are effectively contributing to the welfare of the whole Mystical Body, which is also the body of the churches. (LG 23)

In this way, the Petrine primacy of the Roman Pontiff reveals itself to be "a permanent and visible source and foundation of unity of faith and communion" of the entire College of Bishops (LG 18) and, what is more, the permanent principle and visible foundation for the "unity of faith and communion" of "the whole multitude of believers" (PA, intro.).

C. Papal Primacy and the People of God

The proclamation of the gospel and the sanctification of all people as God's people is not the sole property of the Church's pastors, not even the Roman Pontiff. It belongs to the Church in all its members, for "just as Christ carried out the work of redemption in poverty and persecution, so the Church is called to follow the same route that it might communicate the fruits of salvation to men" (LG 8) and be "a sacrament or as a sign and instrument both of a very closely knit union with God and of the unity of the whole human race" (LG 1). This applies to the bishops; it applies to the clergy; it applies in an especial way to the laity.

The laity are gathered together in the People of God and make up the Body of Christ under one head. Whoever they are they are called upon, as living members, to expend all their energy for the growth of the Church and its continuous sanctification, since this very energy is a gift of the Creator and a blessing of the Redeemer.... Thus every layman, in virtue of the very gifts bestowed upon him, is at the same time a witness and a living

instrument of the mission of the Church itself "according
to the measure of Christ's bestowal" (Eph. 4:7). (LG 33)

Therefore, as "the Vicar of Christ [and] the visible Head of the whole
Church" (LG 18), it falls to the Roman Pontiff in a special way
to ensure that the *sensus fidelium* is effectively present whenever
and wherever the unity in faith and mission are at stake. This is
particularly true for the exercise of infallibility, including when
undertaken by the Roman Pontiff. When, in his role "as the supreme
teacher of the universal Church, in whom the charism of infallibility
of the Church itself is individually present" (LG 25), it is vital that
he consult the faithful, as represented in the persons of their pastors,
whose faith and ministry is rooted in the churches, for

> the entire body of the faithful, anointed as they are
> by the Holy One, cannot err in matters of belief. They
> manifest this special property by means of the whole
> peoples' supernatural discernment in matters of faith
> [*supernaturali sensu fidei totius populi*] when "from the
> Bishops down to the last of the lay faithful" they show
> universal agreement in matters of faith and morals. That
> discernment in matters of faith is aroused and sustained
> by the Spirit of truth. It is exercised under the guidance
> of the sacred teaching authority, in faithful and respect-
> ful obedience to which the people of God accepts that
> which is not just the word of men but truly the word of
> God. Through it, the people of God adheres unwaver-
> ingly to the faith given once and for all to the saints, pen-
> etrates it more deeply with right thinking, and applies it
> more fully in its life. (LG 12)

This is a primacy that is rooted squarely in collegiality and is at
the service of the communion of the Church of churches. This is
a primacy that fosters Christian freedom and calls God's people,
in all their churches, to exercise "right judgment" and apply the
faith "more fully to life." This is a primacy that, in the light of the
mystery of the Church, recognizes the limits of its own legitimate
freedom. Finally, this is a primacy, wholly true to the richness of

our renewed identity as Catholics, that will enable us to answer ARCIC's call for

> a primacy that will even now help to uphold the legiti-
> mate diversity of traditions, strengthening and safe-
> guarding them in fidelity to the Gospel. It will encourage
> the churches in their mission. This sort of primacy will
> already assist the Church on earth to be the authentic
> catholic *koinonia* in which unity does not curtail diver-
> sity, and diversity does not endanger but enhances unity.
> It will be an effective sign for all Christians as to how
> this gift of God builds up that unity for which Christ
> prayed. (GA, no. 60)

One further question remains: what will be required of us Catholics to make our response a reality?

III. THE COSTLY CALL TO CHRISTIAN UNITY

As those who facilitate processes by which organizations seek to envision and enflesh new futures know, to move from vision to reality three things must be identified and, like the legs of a stool, stand in balance with one another: (1) a clear vision for the future; (2) an honest assessment of the ability to realize that future; and (3) a willingness to pay the price needed to actualize that ability and realize the vision. This balancing act applies to every visioning process, no matter whether those engaged in the process represent sacred or secular interests, for if its legs are not so balanced then its dreams will be dashed and reality will become far less than that for which anyone had hoped.

In the preceding pages and chapters, we Catholics have encountered each of the first two legs in the process of envision-ing a primacy that, even now, may assist the Church here on earth to be the authentic catholic communion that God wills to use to bring about that unity for which Christ prayed, the unity of all people as God's people. We have listened to ARCIC's vision of this primacy, and, in the light of this vision, we have also assessed our own ability to realize this future. In the process we have discovered that what ARCIC calls us to is nothing less than our truest selves as Catholics—which should not be surprising, since the very foundations upon which our ecclesial Tradition is built derive from the very same deposit of faith (*depositum fidei*) from which Anglicans draw nourishment for their own life of discipleship. As the Anglican–Roman Catholic Joint Preparatory Commission identified this rich deposit,

> We record with great thankfulness our common faith in God our Father, in our Lord Jesus Christ, and in the Holy Spirit; our common baptism in the one Church of God; our sharing of the holy Scriptures, of the Apostles' and Nicene Creeds, the Chalcedonian definition, and the teaching of the Fathers; our common Christian inheritance for many centuries with its living traditions of liturgy, theology, spirituality, Church order, and mission.[3]

The ways our communions have diverged from this common inheritance "since the sixteenth century have arisen not so much from the substance of this inheritance as from our separate ways of receiving it."[4] In a very real sense, what ARCIC is doing is calling both Anglicans and Catholics to receive anew this inheritance and so be true to who we are, in order that the unity we already have in Christ, by virtue of our common baptism, may be fully realized in our visible communion in faith and mission. In part, this entails our receiving anew the Petrine primacy of the Roman Pontiff, to engage in "a progressive deepening in the understanding of the truth that was revealed once and for all,"[5] in order to understand more fully "how this gift of God builds up that unity for which Christ prayed" (GA, no. 60) with all who are in him.

A. ARCIC's Vision as Our Own

What must we do to realize this vision? We need to arrive at a deeper, more explicitly stated understanding of the episcopal nature of the primacy and of how this roots the one who exercises it precisely within the unity of the College of Bishops. We must acknowledge the manifold ways in which collegiality is at work, not just between the Bishop of Rome as head of the College and the great body of bishops, but between the bishops themselves as they care for the communion of the churches they shepherd as the one Church of Jesus Christ, present in every corner of the world as the sacrament of humanity's "Amen" to God's "Yes" in Jesus Christ. Such an acknowledgment, effectively realized, reveals the primatial ministry of the Roman Pontiff to be that of a true Pontifex Maximus, who supports, affirms, strengthens, and vindicates the ministry of his brother pontiffs as they build bridges of reconciliation and communion within and among the churches, "especially for its poor and sorrowing members and for those who are suffering persecution for justice's sake" (LG 23).

The realization of such a primacy enables all God's people, "from the Bishops down to the last of the lay faithful" (LG 12), to exercise the gifts with which the Spirit has empowered them and walk together as ministers of reconciliation and effective witnesses of God's kingdom. For this to happen, concrete steps must be taken to address every area of our life where resistance to this vision may be found: canons that treat the Synod of Bishops as a prop for the primacy and Episcopal Conferences as expressions of only affective collegiality; a Roman Curia that acts with an inflated sense of its proper authority; the cardinalate as a college within *the* College; the gap existing between the College of Bishops and the Church of *churches* they shepherd, a lacuna perpetuated by the ecclesiological non sequitur of *titular* bishops; and a process of selecting bishops that makes them appear to be vicars of the Holy Father, rather than vicars of Christ. If we address these and, certainly, many more dark corners of our ecclesial life, we shall begin the process of receiving what Vatican II bequeathed us: a renewed primacy capable of serving the renewed Church to which the Spirit of Pentecost has called us—and that ARCIC desires.

B. Making the Vision a Reality

What is the price, though? To receive and realize the vision of Vatican II, and in so doing respond to ARCIC's call, demands something more from us. From precisely within the shakiness of our present situation, as we struggle to make the mind of the Council our own and respond to the ecumenical aspirations of our sisters and brothers in Christ, we must surrender the old ultra-montane outlook of the maximizing minority of Vatican I (and Vatican II, for that matter) and the popular instructions to which it gave rise that made the pope appear to be more than a pope. We must engage in a critical and dispassionate study of the institutions set up to embody and carry forward the vision of Vatican II, so that this vision may genuinely enter into the life of the one people of God in all their many and diverse churches.[6]

This is the process in which we are presently engaged—*only* fifty-plus years after the Council—as we strive and struggle to receive anew the Petrine primacy of the Roman Pontiff as a primacy-in-collegiality at the service not only of our Catholic communion, but also of the communion of all those whom the Spirit calls to be members of the people of God. Moreover, this is a process that will find its resolution only to the degree that we permit ourselves to live out the implications of this *re*-reception in the here and now of our discipleship.

Undoubtedly, this is an immense task that we cannot possibly do on our own (see UUS 96). It is, instead, a task in which we must engage with all those who draw upon the rich deposit of the Christian faith for the nourishment to live as the Lord's disciples. Thus, with our minds and hearts open to the same Spirit that inspired St. John Paul II to write *Ut Unum Sint*, we must make our own the graced openness that his successor, Pope Francis, expressed in the presence of Patriarch Bartholomew during his 2015 pilgrimage to Jerusalem, where the one and the same Lord was "lifted up" in order to draw humankind to himself:

> Every time we reflect on the future of the Church in the light of her vocation to unity, the dawn of Easter breaks forth! Here I reiterate the hope already expressed by my predecessors for a continued dialogue with all our brothers and sisters in Christ, aimed at finding a means of exercising the specific ministry of the bishop of Rome which, in fidelity to his mission, can be open to a new situation and can be, in the present context, a service

of love and of communion acknowledged by all. (cf. *Ut Unum Sint* 95–96)

IV. FINAL THOUGHTS: A GIFT FOR ALL CHRISTIANS

For over fifty years the question of the primacy of the Bishop of Rome has been an essential theme, not only in the theological dialogues in which the Catholic Church is engaging with other Christians, but also more generally within the ecumenical movement as a whole. Thus, the responses that "church leaders and their theologians" offered St. John Paul II's appeal in *Ut Unum Sint*—and have continued to offer his successors—stand upon a well-established foundation of reflective, ecumenical inquiry, one that challenges not only "the other Churches and Ecclesial Communities," but also the Catholic Church itself to take "a fresh look at this ministry of unity" (UUS 89). Among these responses is the consensus of the Anglican–Roman Catholic International Commission—a significant achievement awaiting a response of its own.

What will our response, the response of the Catholic Church, be? While one cannot predict the future, even in this present time of waiting, the breadth and depth of ARCIC's consensus begs a question of its own: If this consensus was accepted by the Catholic Church as consonant with the integrity of its faith, then what must the Catholic Church do (and indeed, *must* do, as the integrity of its faith would itself demand such action) for the universal primacy it claims for the Bishop of Rome to become "a service of love and communion acknowledged by all" Christians as a gift for their unity as Christ's one and undivided Body?

Quite a question! In the critical, faithful light of the consensus achieved by ARCIC, eight aspects of current Catholic teaching regarding the nature and proper exercise of the Petrine primacy of the Roman Pontiff stand in need of further development and necessary reform. These aspects are the following:

1. Catholicism's understanding of the primacy in light of the Petrine texts and...

2. The connection between St. Peter and the local church of Rome
3. The relationship between primacy and collegiality
4. The significance of the local bishop for the life of the local church and its communion with other local churches
5. The significance of collegiality for the exercise of the primacy
6. The relationship between primatial *episcope* and the *sensus fidelium* for discerning the Church's *sensus fidei*
7. The significance of certain time-honored institutions for the realization of a renewed primacy-in-collegiality
8. The significance of the relationship between the Church Universal and the local church for the renewal of the primacy

As we have seen, these eight points may be divided among the three charges the Lord put to Simon bar Jonah when he established him as *Cephas*—Peter, "the Rock"—upon whom he would build his Church: "You are Peter," "Strengthen your brothers," and "Feed my sheep." Let us begin, as we did above, with the significance of the apostle's new name: *Cephas*, Peter, "the Rock."

A. You Are Peter

Everything that the Catholics have had to say regarding the primacy of the Bishop of Rome has depended upon our traditional beliefs that (1) the Lord established the apostle Peter as "first" (*primus*, primate) among the apostles and that (2) this primacy has been faithfully preserved in the apostolic succession of Rome's bishops— beliefs that have gone largely without any critical consideration of their scriptural and historical grounds. ARCIC calls us to rectify this situation. What is more, by means of the consensus it achieved on these beliefs, it has provided us with the foundations necessary for this much-needed work. What might its results be?

1. The Petrine Texts: What emerges is an understanding of the primacy as a reality fundamentally rooted in the grace of forgiveness, through which God's power appears as mercy and thus as the true foundation of the Church. As this grace was not given to the apostle Peter alone, but was granted to him by the Lord in the company of his brother apostles, the specifically *Petrine* character of the Roman Pontiff's primacy finds its significance within the communion he shares with the apostles' successors, that is, the bishops and, what is more, the communion (*koinonia*) they have with all God's people. In this light, the Petrine primacy of the Roman Pontiff finds its purpose in strengthening the faith-filled "Amen" of the Church's pastors and faithful, in all their churches, "so that they will remain faithful to their mission and in harmony with each other" (GA, no. 46, citing A-II, nos. 2–5).

2. The Petrine Primacy and the See of Rome: Two answers emerge from an examination of the connection between the See of Rome and the primacy of its bishop. The first is that it is the primacy of the local church of Rome within the communion of churches that "carries and explains the primacy of the Roman pontiff."[7]

The Roman Church was preeminent within the wider Church of churches even before Sts. Peter and Paul visited it. The preaching and martyrdom of these apostles enhanced its preeminence even more, establishing it as *the* touchstone of faith for all the churches. As the *episcope* credited to St. Linus as Rome's first bishop developed into an established and recognizable office, the one who exercised it came to be seen as representing the Petrine strength of Rome's faith to all the churches in a singular way. Other churches may have claimed a Petrine heritage, but only the local church of Rome was acknowledged to be the one over which the apostle still presided in the person of its bishop.

The second answer flows from the first, namely that the Roman Pontiff succeeds to Peter's primacy as one who re-presents the apostle through his own ministry as the *Bishop* of Rome. He does this in two ways. First and foremost, he does this locally when, as bishop of the church of Rome, he teaches, sanctifies, and governs that portion of the people of God entrusted to his care as the Body of Christ (see CD 11), in order that it may be "a sacrament or as a sign and instrument both of a very closely knit union with God and of the unity of the whole human race" (LG 1). Second, he does this universally when, as head of the College of Bishops, he confirms, nourishes, and strengthens both the collegial unity of his brother bishops as successors of the apostles and the communion of the churches they shepherd as the one Church of Jesus Christ. In both of these instances, the nature of the authority that the Roman Pontiff exercises as St. Peter's successor is one and the same. It is that of a bishop. Were his authority something more or other than that of a bishop, then he would be more than a pope and, what is more, something other than the apostle Peter's true successor.

B. Strengthen Your Brothers

This chapter considered the third through the seventh aspects of Catholic teaching on the primacy for which ARCIC calls for further development. Of these five aspects, the first was the most significant: the relationship between primacy and collegiality. In a very real sense, the way this relationship is understood conditions the way everything that follows from it is likewise understood: the significance of the local bishop for the life of his church and its communion with other churches; the significance of collegiality for the exercise of the primacy; the relationship between primatial *episcope* and the *sensus fidelium* in the discernment of the Church's *sensus fidei*; and the significance of certain time-honored institutions for the realization of a renewed primacy-in-collegiality.

1. Primacy-in-Collegiality at the Service of Communion: Collegiality was the key ecclesiological concept of Vatican II. With it, the Council was able not simply to receive the definitions of Vatican I, but to do so in a manner far more in tune with that Council's mind than had been the case since its close. For all that, however, collegiality itself has had an uneven reception, one that threatens, at least in the immediate future, a genuine renewal of the primatial magisterium and jurisdictional authority of the Bishop of Rome. This is a state of affairs that ARCIC would have us address.

In the decades between the Councils, theologies that saw the primacy in terms that were largely static, heavily juridical, and maximizing were in ascendancy. These tended to see the primacy as an authority different not only in degree, but also *in kind* from that had by the bishops, who functioned in effect as vicars of the Holy Father in the dioceses, curial offices, or diplomatic posts to which he (officially, at least) assigns them. Collegiality enabled Vatican II to see the Roman Pontiff and the bishops as being in a dynamic relationship. By virtue of their common episcopal ordination, they formed a *college* that succeeded the College of Apostles. The bishops were the pope's *brothers*. They were vicars of Christ within their churches, exercising an authority as proper to them as was the primacy he held as bishop of the local church of Rome, which differed only in degree, not in kind, from that of his brothers.

This was a clear break with the recent past, to be sure, but it was a break done in fidelity to the far richer inheritance of the Church's deposit of faith. Yet, there were many bishops at Vatican II who, for many reasons, were uneasy with this break, including some who were able to exercise the influence necessary to obscure it enough to ensure that their own preconciliar approach to the primacy would not only *not* be forgotten, but would continue to play an active role in the Church's life. The net result of this influence is our present, somewhat muddled state of affairs in which collegiality, rather than being seen as the primacy's proper context, has instead too often been seen as effectively contextualized by it.

Into this state of affairs ARCIC calls the Catholic Church to address this postconciliar confusion by recovering the mind of Vatican II and, as a consequence of this recovery, realizing the nascent institutions by which they hoped to bring that mind to life: Episcopal Conferences and the Synod of Bishops. Certainly, such an effective recovery will not please every Catholic. However, it will challenge us Catholics to be truer to our doctrinal heritage than we have been since the Council's close—a heritage that belongs not to us alone, but to all those whom the Lord desires to unite to himself as a living proclamation of his Father's kingdom of justice, love, and peace for all peoples.

2. The Local Bishop within the Church of Churches: ARCIC asked whether the actions of bishops reflect sufficient awareness of the extent of the authority they receive through ordination for governing the local church. The question is more complex than it appears at first glance, for the authority given a bishop at his ordination for the governance of a local church has a necessarily universal dimension: the communion of his church within that communion of churches from which the one Church of Jesus Christ arises. Thus, I rephrased the question, asking whether the bishops' actions reflect a sufficient awareness on their part of the proper object of their charge of governance (*munus regendi*): to maintain the communion of the church they shepherd as a church in communion.

Vatican II offers more than enough reason for the bishops to be aware of their responsibilities as Christ's vicars among the people they shepherd. The more fundamental question is whether they will so act, and what is more, if they attempt to do so, will their primate permit it? Without a doubt, the primacy-in-collegiality recovered by Vatican II would permit it, and in terms consistent with ARCIC. Such a primacy would neither demand that bishops wait on word from the Holy See when confronted by questions they can answer themselves, nor permit them to act as though they were accountable to the Holy Father alone, and not also to those with whom they share the "duty...to promote and to safeguard the unity of faith and the discipline common to the whole church" (LG 27). Instead, it would call all the bishops to exercise their *episcope* both as the legitimate pastors of the churches they shepherd and as brothers in that ministry. As ARCIC stated,

> The charism and function of *episcope* are specifically connected to the *ministry of memory*, which constantly renews the Church in hope. Through such ministry the Holy Spirit keeps alive in the Church the memory of what God did and revealed, and the hope of what God will do to bring all things into unity in Christ. In this way, not only from generation to generation, but also from place to place, the one faith is communicated and lived out. This is the ministry exercised by the bishop, and by ordained persons under the bishop's care, as they proclaim the Word, minister the sacraments, and take part in the administering of discipline for the common good. The bishops, the clergy and the other faithful must all recognise and receive what is mediated from God through each other. (GA, no. 30)

3. Collegiality and the Exercise of the Primacy: The issue here concerns consultation of the bishops by the Roman Pontiff prior to his making important decisions affecting either a local church or the Church Universal. Although no explicit provisions have been made to ensure this, there is ample reason in the Council to expect that such consultation would—and should, in normal circumstances—take place. Just as the Roman Pontiff is the corporate person of the College of Bishops, so too are the bishops the corporate persons of the churches they shepherd. When making decisions of import named above, he should consult them, especially when the decision would involve the exercise of infallibility. For such consultation is a principle means by which the Roman Pontiff would be able to ascertain the *sensus fidelium* in all the churches, in order that he may be able to give voice to the *sensus fidei*, which alone is capable of binding all God's people in one mind and heart in Christ.

4. Primacy and the *Sensus Fidelium*: As I mentioned earlier, when consulting the bishops as representatives of their churches, the Bishop of Rome is looking for the faith, not of the bishops as private persons, but of the people who comprise the local communions of God's people whom they serve, the clergy (i.e., priests and deacons) and the laity. When exercising his primatial magisterium on matters of faith, such discernment of the *sensus fidelium* on the part of the Holy Father is not an option. It is a genuine necessity.

In *Lumen Gentium*, Vatican II acknowledged the essential role played by all the faithful in the building up of Christ's Body as a living proclamation of God's kingdom (see LG 7). In the section on the hierarchy, it spoke of priests as "prudent cooperators of the Episcopal order," who are united with the "body of bishops" and who "serve the good of the whole Church according to their vocation and the grace given to them" (LG 28). It spoke in even stronger terms with regard to the laity.

> The lay apostolate, however, is a participation in the salvific mission of the Church itself. Through their baptism and confirmation all are commissioned to that apostolate by the Lord Himself. Moreover, by the sacraments, especially holy Eucharist, that charity toward God and man which is the soul of the apostolate is communicated and nourished....Upon all the laity, therefore, rests the noble duty of working to extend the divine plan of

salvation to all men of each epoch and in every land. Consequently, may every opportunity be given them so that, according to their abilities and the needs of the times, they may zealously participate in the saving work of the Church. (LG 33)

In this light, it is incumbent on the Roman Pontiff to ensure that clergy and laity are engaged in the life and mission of the Church, including via participation in bodies capable of effectively expressing what ARCIC calls the Church's *synodality*, that is, our walking together in the Lord (see GA, no. 34). Concomitant with this, it is vital that he also ensure that the diversity of theological opinion has the opportunity to be heard. This diversity arises from the dynamic process whereby the faithful penetrate the *sensus fidei* and apply it to the concrete reality of their lives within the churches. Therefore, without prejudice against either the freedom inherent to the primacy or its responsibility for proclaiming the faith once and for all delivered to the saints, it is entirely proper for the Roman Pontiff to allow this process to follow its due course, intervening only at such time as it threatens ecclesial unity, and then in such a way as to respect the collegial bonds existing between himself and the bishops. Such an approach would be completely in harmony with Vatican II's vision of the primacy and, what is more, in harmony with ARCIC's vision of the relationship between authority and freedom of conscience.

5. Time-Honored Institutions and the Realization of Primacy-in-Collegiality: Although ARCIC identified only the significance of the Roman Curia for the realization of a primacy-in-communion, I identified three other time-honored institutions that, in their present form, compromise our reception of Vatican II, and so our ability to respond to ARCIC's call for "a primacy that will even now help...the Church on earth to be...an effective sign for all Christians as to how this gift of God builds up that unity for which Christ prayed" (GA, no. 60). These institutions are (1) the College of Cardinals, a *de jure humano* institution that often obscures the significance of the College of Bishops, which exists *de jure divino*, for the unity of the Church in its life and mission; (2) titular bishops, whose offices of auxiliary bishops, curial officials, and career diplomats compromise the necessary connection between the College of Bishops and the communion of churches that was so essential to the ecclesiology of the Church fathers; (3) the present practice whereby the Roman Pontiff, with few exceptions, appoints the bishops in communion with him, which, in addition to perpetuating the belief that the bishops are vicars of the pope, is simply an ecumenical dead end.

It is vital that we recognize that the old ultramontane outlook and the popular teachings and, indeed, devotions to which it gave rise have not disappeared, and that this has only compounded our struggle to resolve Vatican II's lack of clarity over practical relationships between the power of the College of Bishops and that of the Roman Pontiff. If we wish to find a way through this present impasse, we must engage in a critical and dispassionate study of the institutions set up to embody Vatican II. We must make the Council's mind our own, and allow it to enter into the lives of the people of God. Only then shall we be free from the ecclesiological attitudes of recent centuries to further our renewal of the primacy and so be able to offer all Christians the gift of a primacy-in-collegiality capable of being "an effective sign…as to how this gift of God builds up that unity for which Christ prayed" (GA, no. 60).

C. Feed My Sheep

This chapter considered the significance of the current debate over the proper relationship between the local church and the Church Universal for a renewal of the primacy that is, at once, in harmony with both Vatican II and ARCIC. Such a consideration is no mere academic exercise. It has practical import. As both Vatican Councils I and II (as well as their respective aftermaths) demonstrate, how one understands the Church determines the way one understands every aspect of the Church's faith and mission, including Roman primacy. Therefore, without seeking to resolve the present debate, I asked which of its poles better enables us to answer ARCIC's call for a primacy that "will already assist the Church on earth to be the authentic catholic *koinonia* in which unity does not curtail diversity, and diversity does not endanger but enhances unity" (GA, no. 60): those who hold the ontological priority of the Universal Church to be virtually self-evident, or those who assert that the Church Universal arises from the communion of local churches? I contended that it is the latter.

Seen in the light of a Church of churches from which the Church Universal arises from the communion of local churches, the Petrine primacy of the Roman Pontiff stands forth as a true primacy-in-collegiality in the service of communion, as was taught by Vatican II. This is a primacy that fosters Christian freedom and calls God's people, in all their churches, to exercise "right judgment" and apply the faith "more fully to life." This is a primacy that recognizes the limits of its own legitimate freedom, as these limits are identified and understood in the light of the one mystery of the Church that, in Peter, it was instituted by the Lord to serve. Finally, this is a primacy, wholly true to the richness of our renewed identity as Catholics, that will enable us as Church to answer ARCIC's call for

> a primacy that will even now help to uphold the legitimate diversity of traditions, strengthening and safeguarding them in fidelity to the Gospel. It will encourage the churches in their mission. This sort of primacy will already assist the Church on earth to be the authentic catholic *koinonia* in which unity does not curtail diversity, and diversity does not endanger but enhances unity. It will be an effective sign for all Christians as to how this gift of God builds up that unity for which Christ prayed. (GA, no. 60)

D. An Immense Task We Cannot Do on Our Own

There is one conclusion that should be drawn. It is, of course, that the process of our receiving a renewed Petrine primacy of the Roman Pontiff is an immense task that we cannot possibly accomplish on our own. It is a task in which we must be engaged with all our sisters and brothers in Christ in whose company we desire to receive it anew as a gift of God for the building up of that unity for which *our* Lord prayed—unity not solely for the sake of those who are already in Christ, but also for the sake of the kingdom of God, "that the world may know that you have sent me" (GA, no. 33).

It is tempting to understand this necessity in purely practical terms. In a word, if we desire to live in a communion with other Christians that is served by a papacy that, even now, as ARCIC put it, will "assist the Church on earth to be the authentic catholic *koinonia* in which unity does not curtail diversity, and diversity does not endanger but enhances unity" (GA, no. 60), then we should work together with them in order to make this vision a reality. There is a certain undeniable logic to this. Yet, it is more important to understand the envisioning of such a papacy as a necessary appeal to us for an exercise of intellectual honesty—to say nothing of the virtue of Christian humility.

Every and any particular interpreter's ecclesial commitments influence what is perceived as an adequate representation of the early Church.[8] We Catholics are, to be more precise, *Roman* Catholics and, precisely as such, we have been interpreting both the significance of St. Peter within that reality and, what is more, the ongoing ecclesial implications of that significance for a very long time—and not without a degree of prejudice. Therefore, if we seek to understand more fully what the apostle signifies for us today, as disciples who desire "that unity for which Christ prayed" (GA, no. 60), then it is imperative for us to seek that understanding in communion with those whom we recognize as our sisters and brothers in the Lord. Only by so doing shall we accept ARCIC's fundamental challenge to us, which, as history testifies, is a challenge we have never fully set aside: "that Roman Catholics be open to and desire a re-reception of the exercise of primacy by the Bishop of Rome and the offering of such a ministry to the whole Church of God" (GA, no. 62). What is more, only then shall we, together with our sisters and brothers in the Anglican Communion, allow the communion we already have in Christ to bear the kingdom's fruit. As ARCIC stated quite clearly at the conclusion of *The Gift of Authority*,

> When the real yet imperfect communion between us is made more visible, the web of unity which is woven from communion with God and reconciliation with each other is extended and strengthened. Thus the "Amen"

which Anglicans and Roman Catholics say to the one Lord comes closer to being an "Amen" said together by the one holy people witnessing to God's salvation and reconciling love in a broken world. (GA, no. 63)

Where to begin? Earlier in *The Gift of Authority*, ARCIC offers us, Anglicans and Catholics alike, a way. "Theological dialogue must continue at all levels in the churches"; however such dialogue "is not of itself sufficient" (GA, no. 58). It is imperative that we enter into a dialogue of *life*, that we begin "walk[ing] together" (GA, no. 34) in order to make "more visible the *koinonia* we already have" (GA, no. 58). For the sake of this communion (*koinonia*), and of the communion it was established by the Lord to create among all peoples, "Anglican and Roman Catholic bishops should find ways of cooperating and developing relationships of mutual accountability in their exercise of oversight. At this new stage we have not only to *do* together whatever we can, but also to *be* together all that our existing *koinonia* allows" (GA, no. 58; emphases in original).

> Such cooperation in the exercise of *episcope* would involve bishops meeting regularly together at regional and local levels and the participation of bishops from one communion in the international meetings of bishops of the other. Serious consideration could also be given to the association of Anglican bishops with Roman Catholic bishops in their *ad limina* visits to Rome. Wherever possible, bishops should take the opportunity of teaching and acting together in matters of faith and morals. They should also witness together in the public sphere on issues affecting the common good. Specific practical aspects of sharing *episcope* will emerge from local initiatives. (GA, no. 59)

To this list, one may add a series of other suggestions that would take into account the sort of "local initiatives" that clergy, religious, and laity not only may do, but have already been doing for decades. After all, it is unity among all faithful Anglicans and Catholics, and not simply among their respective bishops, that is our desired end.

"But will it work?" This is a constant question I hear among those with whom I have shared ARCIC's achievements and echoed its challenges. Will it work? More fundamental is the question, "Do we have faith enough to be willing to try it?" If not, then, at least for the immediate future, the work for unity between the Anglican Communion and the Catholic Church will be as dead as the pulp upon which this book is printed—not to mention the small forest felled to produce ARCIC's agreed statements. At a more personal level, not to have—and not to exercise—such faith would be for us to betray the very heritage we claim by virtue of that faith, which at Vatican II not only committed itself to the work for Christian unity, but also declared itself impelled to do so by its own identification with the one Church of Jesus Christ (see LG 8).

In its final analysis, the call that our participation in the ARCIC dialogue makes to us is nothing less than the call to be true to our identity as Church—the faith-filled heritage we share with one another as Catholics; the communion we must strengthen with Anglicans as our sisters and brothers in the Lord; our vocation as Christians to proclaim the kingdom of God. "Above all, how will the Roman Catholic Church address the question of universal primacy as it emerges from 'the patient and fraternal dialogue' about the exercise of the office of the Bishop of Rome to which John Paul II has invited 'church leaders and their theologians'?" (GA, no. 57; citing UUS 96). With faith and hope in the Lord who speaks to us through them. There is no other way.

NOTES

CHAPTER 1

1. Cf. J. T. P. Bury, ed., *The New Cambridge Modern History*, vol. 10, *The Zenith of European Power 1830–1870* (Cambridge: Cambridge University Press, 1971), 9ff.

2. See Roger Aubert et al., *The Church in a Secularized Society*, vol. 5 of *The Christian Centuries*, trans. P. E. Cruncan et al. (New York: Paulist Press, 1978), 5ff.; also, Herman Pottmeyer, *Towards a Papacy in Communion: Perspectives from Vatican Councils I & II*, trans. Matthew J. O'Connell (New York: Crossroad, 1998), 36ff.

3. See *Pastor Aeternus* (PA), introduction: "And since the gates of hell are trying, if they can, to overthrow the Church, make their assault with a hatred that increases day by day against its divinely laid foundation, we judge it necessary, with the approbation of the Sacred Council, and for the protection, defense and growth of the Catholic flock, to propound the doctrine concerning the institution, permanence and nature of the sacred and apostolic primacy, upon which the strength and coherence of the whole Church depends."

4. "Decree Opening the Council," in Norman P. Tanner, *Decrees of the Ecumenical Councils*, vol. 2 (Washington, DC: Georgetown University Press, 1990), 802.

5. See Robert Auber et al., *The Church in the Age of Liberalism*, vol. 7 of *The History of the Church*, trans. Peter Becker (New York: Crossroad, 1981), 315.

6. Joseph de Maistre, "Letter to the Count of Blacas," in *Correspondence*, vol. 4 (Lyon, 1821), 428, cited in Pottmeyer, *Towards a Papacy in Communion*, 54.

7. Joseph de Maistre, *Du Pape*, 2nd ed. (Lyons: Rusand; Paris: Libraire Ecclesiastique, 1821), 123, as cited in Klaus Schatz, *Papal Primacy: From Its Origins to the Present*, trans. John A. Otto and Linda M. Malone (Collegeville, MN: Liturgical Press, 1996), 148.

8. Ibid., 151.

9. Ibid., 152.

10. See Margaret O'Gara, *Triumph in Defeat: Infallibility, Vatican I, and the French Minority Bishops* (Washington, DC: The Catholic University of America Press, 1988), 68–85.

11. When the book was published, three months before the Council opened, it engendered no small amount of controversy. The papal nuncio in Paris had attempted to bribe its publisher to gain the galley proofs. When it appeared, he sent a copy to Rome immediately with a note denouncing it as "unscholarly hackwork." (August Hasler, *How the Pope Became Infallible: Pius IX and the Politics of Persuasion*, trans. Peter Heinegg [Garden City, NY: Doubleday, 1981], 99.) During the Council, Pius himself referred to Maret as a "viper" (ibid., 83).

12. See O'Gara, *Triumph in Defeat*, 160–63, for a summary of Maret's argument.

13. Richard Gaillardetz, *Teaching with Authority: A Theology of the Magisterium in the Church*, vol. 41, Theology and Life Series (Collegeville, MN: Liturgical Press, 1997), 212.

14. See Margaret O'Gara, "Three Successive Steps toward Understanding Papal Primacy in Vatican I," *The Jurist* 64 (2004): 209.

15. Gian Domenico Mansi, *Sacrorum conciliorum nova et amplissima collection*, vol. 52 (Paris: H. Welter, 1927), 338, as cited in Jean-Marie Tillard, *The Bishop of Rome*, trans. John de Satgé (Wilmington, DE: Michael Glazier, 1983), 129–30 (henceforth Mansi 52); see also Jean-Marie Tillard, "The Jurisdiction of the Bishop of Rome," *Theological Studies* 40 (1979): 5.

16. Mansi 52, 678, as cited in Tillard, *The Bishop of Rome*, 130; of note, Bishop Bravard refused to enter the aula for the final vote on *Pastor Aeternus* on July 18, 1870, and he never published the decree in his diocese (see O'Gara, *Triumph in Defeat*, 7, 198).

17. To compare the schema referred to by the bishops here

and what they eventually passed, see O'Gara, *Triumph in Defeat*, 257–69.

18. Mansi 52, 1108D–1109A, as cited in Patrick Granfield, *The Limits of the Papacy: Authority and Autonomy in the Church* (New York: Crossroad, 1987), 62.

19. Mansi 52, 1140, as cited in Tillard, *The Bishop of Rome*, 28.

20. Mansi 52, 1310, cited in Tillard, "The Jurisdiction of the Bishop of Rome," 8.

21. Mansi 52, 1105, as cited in Tillard, "The Jurisdiction of the Bishop of Rome," 9.

22. See Tillard, "The Jurisdiction of the Bishop of Rome," 8.

23. Mansi 52, 1104, as cited in Tillard, "The Jurisdiction of the Bishop of Rome," 11. My emphases.

24. Zinelli, in Mansi 52, 1109–10, cited in Tillard, "The Jurisdiction of the Bishop of Rome," 11–12. My emphases.

25. Mansi 52, 1105, as cited in Tillard, *The Bishop of Rome*, 136.

26. See Tillard, *The Bishop of Rome*, 137. Tillard noted, "The official interpretation of the word 'immediate' is not maximalizing, but vague. Based on the certainty that anything which goes against the divine works *ad destructionem Ecclesiae*, it infers that the very nature of the Roman primacy and of the will of Christ for his Church themselves imposes such limits as are essential." Thus, "we are concerned [here] with a divine right whose charge (*munus*) requires it to be at the service of the divine right of the other bishops. It is for this reason—a point too seldom grasped—that the crucial problem is how to display clearly the specific quality of service inherent in the primacy, rather than the exact nature of the power that goes with it." In other words, if the power (*potestas*) inherent to the primacy is for the sake of continuing St. Peter's charge (*munus*) to serve the unity of the Church, then it is to this charge—and to the nature of the service it calls upon the Roman Pontiff to render the Church as its Supreme Pontiff—that one must look in order to discern primacy's proper limits.

27. Francis Sullivan, *Magisterium: Teaching Authority in the Catholic Church* (Mahwah, NJ: Paulist Press, 1983), 90–91.

28. It is remarkable how closely Terreni's understanding of papal infallibility anticipated what was defined by Vatican I. For a summary of Terreni's argument, see Sullivan, *Magisterium*, 92–93.

29. O'Gara, *Triumph in Defeat*, 194.

30. I am indebted to Francis Sullivan for this approach to the question in *Magisterium*.

31. Citing Pope St. Hormisdas's letter of 517, to the bishops of Spain (cf. Henry Denzinger, *Enchiridion symbolorum, definitionum et declarationum de rebus fidei et morum*, no. 171).

32. For the full text of the passage from which this was drawn, see Denzinger, *Enchiridion*, no. 466.

33. Mansi 52, 1214, as cited in Pottmeyer, *Towards a Papacy in Communion*, 95.

34. NB: Pottmeyer noted that in his explanation of this text, Bishop Gasser did state that the possible objects of infallible statements may include "those truths which are necessarily required in order that the deposit of revelation may be truly preserved, rightly expounded, and effectively determined, even though these truths are not revealed as such" (95, citing Mansi 52, 1226 B). One may see here an affirmation of the dogma of the immaculate conception, defined sixteen years earlier by Pius IX. Pottmeyer continued, "According to the information provided by Gasser, the precise determination of this so-called 'secondary object' of infallibility was to be made only in the Second Constitution on the Church, because the scope of the infallibility of the church and that of the Pope is the same" (95, citing Mansi 52, 1226 F; 1316 CD). This omission is significant on two counts. First, it underscores the point made in the text that, when he speaks *ex cathedra*, the Holy Father possesses "that infallibility which the divine Redeemer willed his Church to enjoy in defining doctrine concerning faith or morals," and not some other, separate charism of infallibility unique to him. Second, it leaves open the question as to the degree of assent that the faithful must offer definitions of such a secondary nature.

Of course, this second Constitution was never passed. Therefore, "the question of the 'secondary object' of infallibility remained open at the end of the council. In order however, to leave the question open and not to limit infallibility to revealed truths, the text of the definitions used the words 'to be held' instead of 'to be believed'" (Pottmeyer, 96). With an eye toward the ecumenical dialogue begun with the Anglican Communion a century later, one may well ask whether this nuance in the text of *Pastor Aeternus* itself opened a door for Catholics to address Anglican concerns regarding reception of extrabiblical, papally defined dogmas without compromising the integrity of the teaching of *Pastor Aeternus* itself.

35. See O'Gara, *Triumph in Defeat*, 160–63.

36. The Articles were drawn up on order of King Louis XIV in support of his battle with Pope Innocent XI over the nomination of French bishops. The Articles stated the (1) kings are not subject to the pope, (2) ecumenical councils supersede the pope's authority, (3) the pope must respect the customs of the local church, and (4) papal decrees do not bind unless accepted by the entire Church. Their enduring influence may be attributed to the belief (see the decree *Frequens* of the Council of Constance) that, in the life and faith of the Church, bishops mattered.

37. The Articles had been condemned three years earlier by Pope Alexander VIII with *Inter Multiplices*. As the timeline indicates, the pope's condemnation was without effect. What caused the king to rescind the Articles? In effect, the king got what he wanted from Alexander's successor, Innocent XII.

38. See Sullivan, *Magisterium*, 103.

39. See Pottmeyer, *Towards a Papacy in Communion*, 97–98.

40. See Hasler, *How the Pope Became Infallible*, 189. According to Hasler, 20 percent of the bishops boycotted the final session.

41. Cited in Tillard, *The Bishop of Rome*, 138–39. In a letter to Pius IX, the bishops summarized Bismarck's points: "1. The Pope may assume episcopal rights in every diocese and substitute his own episcopal power. 2. Episcopal jurisdiction is absorbed by papal jurisdiction. 3. The Pope no longer exercises certain reserved, limited rights as in the past, but he is the repository of full and entire episcopal power. 4. The Pope in general replaces each bishop individually. 5. The Pope at his own discretion entirely may at any time take over the bishop's place in dealings with the government. 6. The bishops are no more than instruments of the Pope, his agents without any responsibility of their own. 7. Bishops in relation to governments have become in fact the agents of a foreign sovereign, of a sovereign, indeed, who through his infallibility is more perfectly absolute than any absolute monarch in the world."

42. Cited in Tillard, *The Bishop of Rome*, 139–40.

43. Cited in ibid., 140–41.

44. Ibid., 141.

45. Ibid., citing Victor Germain, *Catéchisme*, 130–32, Quebec 1941.

46. See Pottmeyer, *Towards a Papacy in Communion*, 104–9.

47. See O'Gara, *Triumph in Defeat*, 215.

48. Due to the seizure of Rome by the forces of the *Risorgimento*, Pius declared the indefinite prorogation of the Council. It would not be declared officially concluded until 1960.

CHAPTER 2

1. John XXIII, "Opening Speech to the Council," in *The Documents of Vatican II*, ed. Walter M. Abbott, trans. Joseph Gallagher (New York: Guild Press, America Press, Association Press, 1966), 715.

2. John XXIII, "Address at St. Paul Outside the Walls," in *Council Daybook: Vatican II, Session 1; Session 2*, ed. Floyd Anderson (Washington, DC: National Catholic Welfare Conference, 1965), 2.

3. Xavier Rynne, *Vatican Council II* (New York: Farrar, Straus and Giroux, Inc., 1968), 4.

4. For an excellent, concise treatment of this period, see John O'Malley, "The Long Nineteenth Century," in *What Happened at Vatican II* (Cambridge, MA: Belknap Press, 2008), 53–92.

5. John XXIII, "Opening Speech to the Council," 715.

6. Cited in Giuseppe Alberigo, "The Announcement of the Council: From the Security of the Fortress to the Lure of the Quest," in *History of Vatican II*, vol. 1, *Announcing and Preparing Vatican Council II*, ed. Giuseppe Alberigo, English edition by Joseph A. Komonchak (Maryknoll, NY: Orbis,1995), 24.

7. Ibid.

8. John XXIII, "Opening Speech to the Council," 715.

9. Giuseppe Ruggieri, "Beyond an Ecclesiology of Polemics: The Debate on the Church," in *History of Vatican II*, vol. 2, *The Formation of the Council's Identity: First Period and Intercession, October 1962–September 1963*, ed. Giuseppe Alberigo, English edition by Joseph A. Komonchak (Maryknoll, NY: Orbis, 1997), 331–37. See also O'Malley, *What Happened at Vatican II*, 152–59.

10. See Aloys Grillmeier, "Chapter I: The Mystery of the Church," trans. Kevin Smyth, in *Commentary on the Documents of Vatican II*, vol. 1, ed. Herbert Vorgrimler, trans. Kevin Smyth et al. (New York: Herder and Herder, 1967), 138–40.

11. See Komonchak, "Towards an Ecclesiology of Communion," in *History of Vatican II*, vol. 4, *Church as Communion: Third Period and Intercession, September 1964–September 1965*, ed. Giuseppe Alberigo, English edition by Joseph A. Komonchak (Maryknoll, NY: Orbis, 2004), 43.

12. See John O'Malley, "Trent and Vatican II: Two Styles of Church," in *From Trent to Vatican II: Historical and Theological Investigations*, ed. Raymond Bulman and Frederick Parrella (New York: Oxford University Press, 2006), 315.

13. See Aloys Grillmeier, "Chapter II: The People of God," trans. Kevin Smyth, in Vorgrimler and Smyth, *Commentary on the Documents of Vatican II*, 1:154.

14. Cf. *Dei Verbum* (DV): "This tradition which comes from the Apostles develop in the Church with the help of the Holy Spirit. For there is a growth in the understanding of the realities and the words which have been handed down. This happens through the contemplation and study made by believers, who treasure these things in their hearts (see Luke 2:19, 51) through a penetrating understanding of the spiritual realities which they experience, and through the preaching of those who have received through Episcopal succession the sure gift of truth. For as the centuries succeed one another, the Church constantly moves forward toward the fullness of divine truth until the words of God reach their complete fulfillment in her" (no. 8). These complimentary passages from the Council's only two dogmatic constitutions illustrate the fundamental importance of reading the Council as a whole, as opposed to a collection of documents only temporally related to one another.

15. See O'Malley, "Trent and Vatican II," 315.

16. See LG 10: "Therefore all the disciples of Christ, persevering in prayer and praising God, (see Ac 2, 42–47) should present themselves as a living sacrifice, holy and pleasing to God. (see Rm 12, 1) Everywhere on earth they must bear witness to Christ and give an answer to those who seek an account of that hope of eternal life which is in them (see 1 Pt 3, 15)."

17. See Grillmeier, "Chapter II: The People of God," 185.

18. See Joseph Komonchak, "Ministry and the Local Church," *The Catholic Theological Society of America Proceedings* 36 (1981): 58–62.

19. See Giles Routhier, "'Église localé' ou 'Église particulière': querelle sémantique ou option théologique?" *Studia Canonica* 25 (1991): 277–334; also Patrick Granfield, "The Local Church as a Center of Communication and Control," *The Catholic Theological Society of America Proceedings* 35 (1980): 256–63, and Gianfranco Ghirlanda, "Universal Church, Particular Church, and Local Church at the Second Vatican Council and in the New Code of Canon Law," in René Latourelle, *Vatican II: Assessment and Perspectives Twenty-Five Years After (1962–1987)*, 3 vols. (New York: Paulist Press, 1988–89), 2:233–71.

20. See J. M. R. Tillard, "The Local Church within Catholicity," *The Jurist* 52 (1992): 448–51.

21. Hervé-Marie Legrand, "Revaluation of Local Churches: Some Theological Implications," trans. Francis McDonagh, in *The Unifying Role of the Bishop*, vol. 71, *Concilium: Religion in the Seventies*, ed. Edward Schillebeeckx (New York: Herder and Herder, 1972), 57.

22. See Sabbas Kilian, "The Meaning and Nature of the Local Church," *The Catholic Theological Society of America Proceedings* 35 (1980): 251.

23. See Joseph Komonchak, "The Local Realization of the Church," in *The Reception of Vatican II*, ed. Giuseppe Alberigo et al. (Washington, DC: The Catholic University of America Press, 1987), 77–78.

24. "The Final Report," *Origins* (December 19, 1985): 448. Although the precise sense in which the Synod understood communion has been the subject of debate (see Massimo Faggioli, *Vatican II: The Battle for Meaning* [Mahwah, NJ: Paulist Press, 2012], 83–90), that communion was central to the Council is accepted. For a sense of how significant it was for the development of the Council's mind, see Ladislas Orsy, *Receiving the Council: Theological and Canonical Insights and Debates* (Collegeville, MN: Liturgical Press, 2009), 1–15.

25. It is tempting to see this image as affirming a preconciliar, pyramidial ecclesiology, with the pope at the apex of the Church.

When in *Sacrosanctam Concilium* the Council spoke of the "hierarchic and communal nature of the liturgy" (nos. 26–32), though, it spoke of the Church as manifesting itself as an *ordered* communion with a diversity of ministries. The image was the Church as the Body of Christ, which, animated by the Spirit, receives its life from the triune God, who is ordered as a communion of coequal persons. It is in this sense that the Council began chapter 3 of *Lumen Gentium*, asserting that Christ established a diversity of offices for the building up of his Church, particularly—but not exclusively—the office of bishop (cf. Richard Gaillardetz, *The Church in the Making: Lumen Gentium, Christus Dominus, Orientalium Ecclesiarum*, Rediscovering Vatican II, ed. Christopher Bellitto [New York: Paulist Press, 2006], 72–74). This is another instance of keeping in mind the fundamental importance of reading the Council as a whole.

26. See also O'Malley, *What Happened at Vatican II*, 173–85.

27. Karl Rahner et al., "Chapter III: The Hierarchical Structure of the Church, with Special Reference to the Episcopate," trans. Kevin Smyth, in Vorgrimler and Smyth, *Commentary on the Documents of Vatican II*, 1:189–90.

28. See ibid., 191.

29. See Francis A. Sullivan, *From Apostles to Bishops: The Development of the Early Episcopacy in the Early Church* (New York: Newman Press, 2001), 217.

30. See Karl Rahner et al., "Chapter III: The Hierarchical Structure of the Church," 186–93.

31. "The canonical mission of bishops can come about by legitimate customs that have not been revoked by the supreme and universal authority of the Church, or by laws made or recognized by that authority, or directly through the successor of Peter himself; and if the latter refuses or denies apostolic communion, such bishops cannot assume any office" (LG 24).

32. See Tillard, *The Bishop of Rome*, trans. John de Satgé (Wilmington, DE: Michael Glazier, 1983), 38–39.

33. See ibid., 152–53.

34. See ibid., 40–41.

35. As Bishop Zinelli stated, "It must be admitted that the power of the sovereign pontiff is in reality (*realiter*) of the same kind as that of the bishops (*esse eadem speciem ac potestatem*

episcoporum). Why not, then, use the same word to indicate the quality of jurisdiction exercised by the popes and by the bishops, and why not speak of episcopal power in the bishops and of the supreme episcopal power in the sovereign pontiff?" (Mansi 52, 1104, as cited in Jean-Marie Tillard, "The Jurisdiction of the Bishop of Rome," *Theological Studies* 40 [1979]: 11).

36. "This power of the Supreme Pontiff by no means detracts from that ordinary and immediate power of episcopal jurisdiction, by which bishops, who have succeeded to the place of the apostles by appointment of the Holy Spirit, tend and govern individually the particular flocks which have been assigned to them. On the contrary, this power of theirs is asserted, supported and defended by the Supreme and Universal Pastor; for St. Gregory the Great says: 'My honor is the honor of the whole Church. My honor is the steadfast strength of my brethren. Then do I receive true honor, when it is denied to none of those to whom honor is due.'"

37. See Patrick Granfield, *The Limits of the Papacy* (New York: Crossroad, 1987), 58.

38. Cf. LG 27: The "proper, ordinary and immediate" jurisdiction of a bishop within his church "is ultimately regulated by the supreme authority of the Church, and can be circumscribed by certain limits, for the advantage of the Church or of the faithful." While it may be assumed that the "supreme authority" referred to here is that of the Roman Pontiff, LG 22 is not so restrictive.

39. See Granfield, *The Limits of the Papacy*, 85.

40. Ibid., 41.

41. See Tillard, *The Bishop of Rome*, 40.

42. See Richard Gaillardetz, *Witnesses to the Faith: Community, Infallibility, and the Ordinary Magisterium of Bishops* (Mahwah, NJ: Paulist Press, 1992), 157.

43. See ibid., 160–61.

44. See Tillard, *The Bishop of Rome*, 159–61.

45. Suenens, in José de Broucker, *The Suenens Dossier: The Case for Collegiality* (Notre Dame, IN: Fides, 1970), 36, as cited in Granfield, *The Limits of the Papacy*.

46. John XXIII, "Opening Speech to the Council," 715.

47. Lukas Vischer, "The Reception of the Debate on Collegiality," in *The Reception of Vatican II*, ed. Giuseppe Alberigo et

al. (Washington, DC: The Catholic University of America Press, 1987), 235–36.

48. Ibid., 236–41.

49. John Quinn, *The Reform of the Papacy: The Costly Call to Christian Unity* (New York: Crossroad, 1999), 111–13.

50. In his biography of Paul VI, Peter Hebblethwaite described how the pope consulted several bishops and spent many sleepless nights pouring over the schema, to convince himself that collegiality did not contradict the definitions of *Pastor Aeternus*; see *Paul VI: The First Modern Pope* (New York: Paulist Press, 1993), 384–92.

51. See Hermann Pottmeyer, *Towards a Papacy in Communion: Perspectives from Vatican Councils I & II* (New York: Crossroad, 1998), 112–17.

52. See Luis Antonio G. Tagle, "The 'Black Week' of Vatican II (November 14–21, 1964)," in *History of Vatican II*, vol. 4, *The Church as Communion: Third Period and Intercession September 1964–September 1965*, ed. Giuseppe Alberigo, English edition by Joseph A. Komonchak (Maryknoll, NY: Orbis, 2003), 387. Also O'Malley, *What Happened at Vatican II*, 240–46.

53. See Yves Congar, "A Last Look at the Council," in *Vatican II by Those Who Were There*, ed. Alberic Stacpoole (London: Geoffrey Chapman, 1986), 346.

54. See Tagle, "The 'Black Week' of Vatican II (November 14–21, 1964)," 436–43. As Tagle noted, for all their efforts to hem in collegiality, the minority that sought the NEP only succeeded in muddying matters even more. Yet, having gotten what they wanted, they did make the most of it.

CHAPTER 3

1. John Quinn, *The Reform of the Papacy: The Costly Call to Christian Unity* (New York: Crossroad, 1999), 114–15.

2. Theodore Hesburgh, "Letter of Invitation," in *Toward Vatican III: The Work That Needs to Be Done*, ed. David Tracy et al. (New York: Seabury Press, 1978), 3.

3. See Joseph Komonchak, "Vatican II as an 'Event,'" in *Vatican II: Did Anything Happen?* ed. John O'Malley (New York:

Continuum, 2007), 24–51, for a thorough discussion of Vatican II as an "event" in the life of the Church and, indeed, the modern world. As Komonchak put it, "'Event' I take to represent a different category; I mean it not in the sense of a simple occurrence, but in the sense of a 'noteworthy' occurrence, one that has consequences" (27), not the least consequence being the ongoing debate over how properly to understand the Council, with respect to both the history that preceded it (a history that, indeed, we are re-reading in the light of what the Council taught) and the still-developing future that it inaugurated.

As the book's other contributors make clear, for all that may rightly be said regarding the Council's continuity with the past, Vatican II also broke with that past. It did do so, though, not by way of repudiation, but in order to initiate the new Pentecost that John XXIII had called for and the "signs of the times" demanded. The Council's literary output alone bears witness to this intention. As O'Malley himself said, "Those 16 decrees seem like a spectacularly long-winded way of saying, 'Nothing is happening here. Business as usual'" ("Vatican II: Did Anything Happen?" in O'Malley, *Vatican II: Did Anything Happen?* 60). For a further discussion of the Council's embrace of reform with a view toward renewing the Church's apostolic identity, see Gerald O'Collins, "Does Vatican II Represent Continuity or Discontinuity?" *Theological Studies* 73 (2012): 768–94.

4. See Hermann Pottmeyer, "A New Phase in the Reception of Vatican II: Twenty Years of Interpretation of the Council," in *The Reception of Vatican II*, ed. Guiseppe Alberigo et al. (Washington, DC: The Catholic University of America Press, 1987), 27.

5. For a brief history of this struggle, see Massimo Faggioli, "Vatican II: The History and the Narratives," *Theological Studies* 73 (2012): 749–67.

6. This is not to say that these and similar questions are impossible to answer, nor is it to say that there is not a growing consensus among scholars on, if not the precise hermeneutic through which answers may be found, then at least the principles that should guide the development of such a hermeneutic. As Richard Gaillardetz has noted, such a hermeneutic must go beyond the juxtaposition of discrete passages in an effort to discern the emerging theological vision that is evident in the conciliar

documents as a whole [see *The Church in the Making:* Lumen Gentium, Christus Dominus, Orientalium Ecclesiarum, *Rediscovering Vatican II,* ed. Christopher Bellitto (New York: Paulist Press, 2006), xviii]. For a brief review of various attempts to develop such a hermeneutic (and their various results), see Massimo Faggioli, *Vatican II: The Battle for Meaning* (New York: Paulist Press, 2012), 125–33. See Ormond Rush, *Still Interpreting Vatican II: Some Hermeneutical Principles* (Mahwah, NJ: Paulist Press, 2004), for the principles that guide the presentations and arguments of this book, i.e., that the Council's mind may be discerned by both a (1) diachronic and (2) synchronic reading of its texts (i.e., the texts in the light of both their historical development and their relationship to one another) and (3) a consideration of how these texts have been—and, indeed, continue to be—received in the light of the Church. See also Rush, "Towards a Comprehensive Interpretation of the Council and its Documents," *Theological Studies* 73 (2012) 547–69.

7. See Hermann Pottmeyer, "A New Phase in the Reception of Vatican II," 27.

8. John XXIII, "Opening Speech to the Council," in *The Documents of Vatican II,* ed. Walter M. Abbott, trans. Joseph Gallagher (New York: Guild Press, America Press, Association Press, 1966), 715.

9. Joseph Ratzinger, "The Primacy of Peter and the Unity of the Church," in *Called to Communion: Understanding the Church Today,* trans. Adrian Walker (San Francisco: Ignatius Press, 1996), 48.

10. Quinn, *The Reform of the Papacy,* 114–15.

11. See Tillard, *The Bishop of Rome,* 44.

12. "I am persuaded that in a synodal Church, greater light can be shed on the exercise of the Petrine primacy. The Pope is not, by himself, above the Church; but within it as one of the baptized, and within the College of Bishops as a Bishop among Bishops, called at the same time—as Successor of Peter—to lead the Church of Rome which presides in charity over all the Churches." Address of His Holiness Pope Francis, given in Rome during the *Ceremony Commemorating the 50th Anniversary of the Synod of Bishops,* October 17, 2015, http://w2.vatican.va/content/

francesco/en/speeches/2015/october/documents/papa-francesco
_20151017_50-anniversario-sinodo.html.

13. *Ecclesiae Sanctae*, no. 41, 1: "Bishops of countries or territories which do not yet have an episcopal conference according to the norms of the Decree *Christus Dominus* are to see to its establishment as soon as possible, and to the drawing up of its statutes which are to be confirmed by the Apostolic See," http://w2.vatican.va/content/paul-vi/en/motu_proprio/documents/hf_p-vi_motu-proprio_19660806_ecclesiae-sanctae.html.

14. Ladislas Orsy argues persuasively to the negative in "Episcopal Conferences: *Communio* Among the Bishops," in *Receiving the Council: Theological and Canonical Insights and Debates* (Collegeville, MN: Liturgical Press, 2009), 16–34.

15. See Tillard, *The Bishop of Rome*, 44–45. See Pope Francis's remarks in *Evangelium Gaudium*, 32. NB: those remarks will be taken up later in chapter 8.

16. At the time this debate began, Kasper was bishop of Rottenberg-Stuttgart.

17. For a review of the debate, see Kilian McDonnell, "The Ratzinger/Kasper Debate: The Universal Church and the Local Churches," *Theological Studies* 63 (2002): 227–50.

18. Joseph Ratzinger, "The Origin and Essence of the Church," in *Called to Communion*, 44. NB: this position reiterated the basic line of argument taken by the CDF in 1992 in its *Letter to the Bishops of the Catholic Church on Some Aspects of the Church Understood as Communion*: "The Church of Christ, which we profess in the Creed to be one, holy, catholic and apostolic, is the universal Church, that is, the worldwide community of the disciples of the Lord, which is present and active amid the particular characteristics and the diversity of persons, groups, times and places. Among these manifold particular expressions of the saving presence of the one Church of Christ, there are to be found, from the times of the Apostles on, those entities which are in themselves Churches, because, although they are particular, the universal Church becomes present in them with all its essential elements" (no. 7). "The universal Church is therefore the *Body of the Churches*. Hence it is possible to apply the concept of communion *in analogous fashion* to the union existing among

particular Churches, and to see the universal Church as a *Communion of Churches*" (no. 8). "In order to grasp the true meaning of the analogical application of the term *communion* to the particular Churches taken as a whole, one must bear in mind above all that the particular Churches, insofar as they are *'part of the one Church of Christ,'* have a special relationship of *'mutual interiority'* with the whole, that is, with the universal Church, because in every particular Church *'the one, holy, catholic and apostolic Church of Christ is truly present and active.'* For this reason, *'the universal Church cannot be conceived as the sum of the particular Churches, or as a federation of particular Churches.'* It is not the result of the communion of the Churches, but, in its essential mystery, it is a reality *ontologically and temporally* prior to every *individual* particular Church*"* (no. 9). Emphases in original. Available online in English at http://www.vatican.va/roman_curia/congregations/ cfaith/documents/rc_con_cfaith_doc_28051992_communionis -notio_en.html. It is for this reason that I do not treat the *Letter* in the text above. For a concise, excellent critique of the *Letter* itself within the fuller context of the debate concerning the meaning of the Church as communion, see Bernard P. Prusak, *The Church Unfinished: Ecclesiology through the Centuries* (New York: Paulist Press, 2004), 302–12.

19. Cf. Joseph Ratzinger, "The Origin and Essence of the Church," 44.

20. Walter Kasper, "On the Church: A Friendly Response to Cardinal Ratzinger," *America* 184 (April 23–30, 2001): 10.

21. Ibid., 11.

22. See Avery Dulles, "Ratzinger and Kasper on the Universal Church," *Inside the Vatican* 20 (June 4, 2001): 13: "The ontological priority of the Church universal appears to me to be almost self-evident, since the very concept of a particular (i.e., local, in the context of this book) church presupposes a universal Church to which it belongs, whereas the concept of the universal Church does not imply that it is made up of distinct particular churches."

23. Cited by Kasper in "On the Church," 13; source not given.

CHAPTER 4

1. Introduction, no. 1, to Anglican–Roman Catholic International Commission, *The Final Report* (London: SPCK and Catholic Truth Society, 1982), 5. All future references to the documents contained in *The Final Report* will be cited according to the internal ordering of the documents themselves, unless otherwise noted.

2. "The Common Declaration by Pope Paul VI and the Archbishop of Canterbury: Rome, Saint Paul Without-the-Walls, 24 March 1966," in *The Final Report*, 117–18.

3. Michael Ramsey, *The Gospel and the Catholic Church* (London, 1936), 227–28, cited in J. Robert Wright, "Anglicans and the Papacy," in *A Pope for All Christians: An Inquiry into the Role of Peter in the Modern Church*, ed. Peter J. McCord (New York: Paulist Press, 1976; London: The Catholic Book Club, 1978), 183.

4. See "An Anglican Comment on Papal Authority in the Light of Recent Developments," in *Authority in the Anglican Communion: Essays Presented to Bishop John Howe*, ed. Stephen Sykes (Toronto: Anglican Book Centre, 1987), 237. The first two periods had been named by him already in "Anglicans and the Papacy," 184. These essays played a major role in the development of this discussion, particularly that of Bishop John Hind, "Primacy and Unity: An Anglican Contribution to a Patient and Fraternal Dialogue," in *Petrine Primacy and the Unity of the Church: "Toward a Patient and Fraternal Dialogue,"* ed. James F. Puglisi (Collegeville, MN: Liturgical Press, 1999), 35–58, which helped to guide me through the writings of Anglicanism's early apologists.

5. Hind, "Primacy and Unity," 38.

6. Ibid., 39, citing J. Ussher or Ps. Ussher, *A Body of Divinity; or the Sum and Substance of the Christian Religion*, first published 1645, as quoted in *Anglicanism: The Thought and Practice of the Church of England, Illustrated from the Religious Literature of the Seventeenth Century*, ed. P. E. More and F. L. Cross (London: SPCK, 1962), 69.

7. Hind, "Primacy and Unity," 39, as cited in Norman Sykes, *Old Priest and New Presbyter: The Anglican Attitude to Episcopacy, Presbyterianism and Papacy since the Reformation* (New York: Cambridge University Press, 2008), 177.

8. See the *Litany* in the first and second prayer books of King Edward I. This prayer was later eliminated in the prayer book promulgated during the reign of Elizabeth I in 1559.

9. This was included in Article 36, of the *Forty-Two Articles* of 1553, and in Article 37, of the *Thirty-Nine Articles* of 1563/71 and 1662.

10. *Apology of the Church of England*, trans. Anne Lady Bacon (London: SPCK, 1852), 153–54.

11. Hind, "Primacy and Unity," 40, quoting William Laud, *The Works, II: Conference with Fisher*, Library of Anglo-Catholic Theology (Oxford: John Henry Parker, 1849), 346.

12. Hind, "Primacy and Unity," 40, quoting Laud, *Conference with Fisher*, 186.

13. Hind, "Primacy and Unity," 40, quoting Laud, *Conference with Fisher*, 208.

14. Hind, "Primacy and Unity," 41, citing John Bramhall, *Schism Guarded*, section 1, chapter 1, as quoted in More and Cross, *Anglicanism*, 66, no. 28.

15. Hind, "Primacy and Unity," 42, as cited by Sykes, *Old Priest and New Presbyter*, 199–200.

16. Of course, Catholic recusancy was not the only opposition to the reformed Church of England. Some Protestants believed that the Reformation had not gone far enough. For them, it was not enough to throw off the pope. The Church needed to be thoroughly purified of all traces of "popish religion." This *Puritan* opposition came to a head during the reign of Charles I when, following the establishment of the English Commonwealth and, with Charles's execution, the Lord Protectorate, it disestablished the Church. This change was reversed with the Restoration of the monarchy under Charles II.

17. See Hind, "Primacy and Unity," 44.

18. These institutions, together with the archbishop of Canterbury, comprise the recognized "Instruments of Unity" of the Anglican Communion.

19. NB: none of the decisions or documents produced by these commissions are understood to be canonically binding on the provinces until the provinces choose to adopt them—and not all the provinces have done so. In fact, some provinces have explicitly chosen to reject them, particularly with respect to the Anglican

Covenant. Thus, how the provinces will eventually resolve these issues remains an open question.

20. Resolution 49, cited in Hind, "Primacy and Unity," 47.

21. See ibid.

22. See *The Virginia Report* (Harrisburg, PA: Morehouse Publishing, 1999), 27. An online version of the report is available at http://www.anglicancommunion.org/media/150889/report-1.pdf.

23. See ibid., 21. As the former archbishop of Canterbury Rowan Williams said in a BBC interview directly following the extraordinary meeting of primates at Lambeth Palace on October 18, 2003, "Our Communion depends a great deal on relationships rather than rules."

24. Ibid., 38–39.

25. Ibid., 43.

26. Michael Ramsey, *The Gospel and the Catholic Church* (London, 1936), 227–28, cited in Wright, "Anglicans and the Papacy," 183.

27. See http://w2.vatican.va/content/francesco/en/homilies/2016/documents/papa-francesco_20160125_vespri-conversione-san-paolo.html.

28. Wright, "Anglicans and the Papacy," 184, citing *Doctrine in the Church of England* (London, 1938), 125–26. The italicized words belong to Wright's citation.

29. Wright, "Anglicans and the Papacy," 185–87, citing *Holy Cross Magazine* (July 1967): 2–5; cf. *American Church News* (Pelham Manor, NY), September 27, 1967, and *The Little Chronicle* (Mt. Sinai, NY), LII:2, November 1970.

30. Wright, "Anglicans and the Papacy," 184–85, citing *Church Times* (London), July 8, 1966 and February 10, 1967. Wright noted that he conflated the quotations for the purposes of his essay.

31. The text of the apostolic constitution *Anglicanorum Coetibus* is available online in English translation at http://w2.vatican.va/content/benedict-xvi/en/apost_constitutions/documents/hf_ben-xvi_apc_20091104_anglicanorum-coetibus.html.

32. See Joint Statement by the archbishop of Westminster and the archbishop of Canterbury, available online at http://rowanwilliams.archbishopofcanterbury.org/articles.php/

1007/joint-statement-by-the-archbishop-of-westminster-and
-the-archbishop-of-canterbury. See also the personal, pastoral
response of Christopher Hill, then bishop of Guildford, available
online at http://oldsite.hereford.anglican.org/news/54/personal
-ordinariates-response-of-the-bishop-of-guildford.aspx.

33. Hind, "Primacy and Unity," 52.

34. Stephen W. Sykes, "The Papacy and Power: An Anglican
Perspective," in *Church Unity and the Papal Office: An Ecumenical Dialogue on John Paul II's Encyclical* Ut Unum Sint, ed. Carl
E. Braaten and Robert W. Jenson (Grand Rapids, MI: William B.
Eerdmans Publishing Company, 2001), 59–75.

35. ARCIC II, *The Gift of Authority: Authority in the Church
III* (London, Toronto, New York: Catholic Truth Society, Anglican
Book Centre, Church Publishing, Inc., 1999), §47.

CHAPTER 5

1. "The Malta Report: Report of the Anglican–Roman Catholic Joint Preparatory Commission," 4, in Anglican–Roman Catholic
International Commission, *The Final Report* (London: SPCK and
Catholic Truth Society, 1982), 109.

2. *Authority in the Church I* (henceforth A-I) was approved by
the Commission during its Venice Meeting, August 24–September
2, 1976. It was subsequently published, with permission of the
communions' respective authorities, on January 20, 1977. *Authority in the Church II* (henceforth A-II), together with *Elucidations,*
henceforth *Eluc.*), was approved by the Commission during its
final meeting at Windsor Castle, January 7–11, 1981. These were
published as part of *The Final Report* (FR), permission for which
was granted in January of the following year.

3. "The Common Declaration by Pope Paul VI and the
Archbishop of Canterbury: Rome, Saint Paul Without-the-Walls,
24 March 1966," in *The Final Report*, 118.

4. Schuyler Brown, "Koinonia as the Basis of New Testament Ecclesiology?" *One in Christ* 12 (1976): 159.

5. Ibid., 165.

6. Ibid., 159.

7. "The Common Declaration by Pope Paul VI and the Archbishop of Canterbury: Rome, Saint Paul Without-the-Walls, 24 March 1966," 117–18.

8. FR, no. 49. This goes to confirm what was already acknowledged in *The Malta Report*, 20, where, after calling for "a serious theological examination…on the nature of authority with particular reference to its bearing on the interpretation of the historic faith to which both our Communions are committed," all four of the subjects singled out for attention pertained, either directly or indirectly, to Roman Catholic teaching regarding the nature and exercise of primatial *episcope*.

9. A-I, no. 1: "The confession of Christ as Lord is the heart of the Christian faith. To him God has given all authority in heaven and on earth. As Lord of the Church he bestows the Holy Spirit to create a communion of men [*sic*] with God and with one another. To bring this *koinonia* to perfection is God's eternal purpose. The Church exists to serve the fulfillment of this purpose when God will be all in all."

10. A-I, no. 3: "The common life in the body of Christ equips the community and each of its members with what they need to fulfil this responsibility [i.e., to serve the fulfillment of 'God's eternal purpose to be all in all']: they are enabled so to live that the authority of Christ will be mediated through them. This is Christian authority: when Christians so act and speak, men perceive the authoritative word of Christ."

11. A-I, no. 8: "Since each bishop must ensure that the local community is distinctively Christian he has to make it aware of the universal communion of which it is a part."

12. A-I, no. 12: "On the basis of this analogy the First Vatican Council affirmed that this service was necessary to the unity of the whole Church. Far from overriding the authority of the bishops in their own dioceses, this service was explicitly intended to support them in their ministry of oversight. The Second Vatican Council placed this service in the wider context of the shared responsibility of all the bishops."

13. A-I, no. 18; see also no. 20: "The bishops are collectively responsible for defending and interpreting the apostolic faith. The primacy accorded to a bishop implies that, after consulting his fellow bishops, he may speak in their name and express their mind."

As here presented, the primatial *episcope* enables the bishop so endowed to act, one may say (though ARCIC I did not), as a corporate person, i.e., as representing in his own person, by virtue of his office, the entire College of Bishops. This does not imply that the primate can so act only when there is unanimity among the bishops. As history attests, a lack of just such unanimity may itself warrant primatial intervention. What is more, it does not imply that the *episcope* of a primate is essentially greater than that of his brother (*sic*) bishops. It does imply, however, that when the primate does so act, it is with nothing more than the *episcope* of one charged to protect and promote the *koinonia* of the Church. In short, he does so with the *episcope* of a bishop, whose office occasionally demands that he confirm his brothers' mind according to the apostolic faith that they are responsible to correctly interpret and steadfastly defend.

14. A-I, no. 21: "If primacy is to be a genuine expression of *episcope* it will foster the *koinonia* by helping the bishops in their task of apostolic leadership both in their local church and in the Church universal. Primacy fulfils its purpose by helping the churches to listen to one another, to grow in love and unity, and to strive together towards the fullness of Christian life and witness; it respects and promotes Christian freedom and spontaneity; it does not seek uniformity where diversity is legitimate, or centralise administration to the detriment of the local churches. A primate exercises his ministry not in isolation but in collegial association with his brother bishops. His intervention in the affairs of a local church should not be made in such a way as to usurp the responsibility of its bishop."

15. A-I, no. 22: "Although primacy and conciliarity are complimentary elements of *episcope* it has often happened that one has been emphasized at the expense of the other, even to the point of serious imbalance. When churches have been separated from one another, this danger has been increased. The *koinonia* of the churches requires that a proper balance be preserved between the two with the responsible participation of the whole people of God."

16. *Eluc.*, no. 8: "The Commission does not...say that what has evolved historically or what is practiced by the Roman see is necessarily normative: it maintains only that visible unity requires

the realization of a 'general pattern of the complementary primatial and conciliar aspects of episcope' in the service of the universal 'koinonia of the churches' (para. 23)."

17. *Eluc.*, no. 8: "Anglicanism has never rejected the principle
and practice of primacy. New reflection on it has been stimulated
by the evolving role of the archbishop of Canterbury within the
Anglican Communion. The development of this form of primacy
arose precisely from the need for a service of unity in the faith
in an expending communion of Churches. It finds expression in
the Lambeth Conferences convoked by successive archbishops of
Canterbury which originated with requests from overseas provinces for guidance in matters of faith. This illustrates a particular relationship between conciliarity and primacy in the Anglican
Communion."

18. *Eluc.*, no. 8: "The history of our separation has underlined
and continues to underline the necessity for this proper theological balance [between the fruitful diversity with the *koinonia* of
local churches and the unity in essentials that must mark the universal *koinonia*], which has often been distorted or destroyed by
human failings or other historical factors (cf. para. 22)."

19. It is important to note that a "presumption" in favor of
Roman primacy is not the same thing as a commitment to Roman
primacy, much less a commitment to the degree of primacy with
which Vatican I (supposedly) declared as necessarily belonging to
the bishop of Rome as the divinely appointed successor of Peter
and supreme, infallible pontiff on the Church Universal. What the
Commission was building here was an openness to the possibility
of a universal primacy exercised by the bishop of Rome on behalf
of full *koinonia* between the churches of the Anglican Communion and the communion of the Catholic Church. This openness
was not open-ended, of course. If the Commission was to respect
its own methodology of listening to the voice of Christ speaking
in and through the richness of one another's ecclesial Traditions,
then Catholic doctrine concerning the primacy of the bishop of
Rome could not be ignored, but no more could Anglican concerns
over this doctrine. In a very real sense, what the Commission can
be said to have been doing was discerning the true/truer nature
of the Catholic doctrine of papal primacy via the process of the
Anglican reception of it—a process the product of which would,

in its turn, entail a *re*-reception of papal primacy on the part of Catholicism. More will be said on this point below when ARCIC II's agreed statement *The Gift of Authority* is discussed. It has been raised here only to illustrate that the work of the Commission was more nuanced and more balanced than many of its critics had given (and continue to give) it.

20. *Eluc.*, no. 8: "The Commission has already pointed to the possibilities of mutual benefit and reform which should arise from a shared recognition of one universal primacy which does not inhibit conciliarity—a 'prospect (which) should be met with faith, not fear' (Co-Chairmen's Preface). Anglicans sometimes fear the prospect of over-centralization, Roman Catholics the prospect of doctrinal incoherence. Faith, banishing fear, might see simply the prospect of the right balance between a primacy serving the unity and a conciliarity maintaining the just diversity of the *koinonia* of all the churches."

21. It is worth noting that, in this same section, the Commission stated, "Although Paul was not among the Twelve, he too was conspicuous for the leadership which he exercised with an authority received from the Lord himself, claiming to share with Peter and others parallel responsibility and apostolic authority (Gal. 2:7–8; 1 Cor. 9:1)." This observation calls to mind two points. The first reaches back to *Authority in the Church I*, and is a recognition of both the importance and, moreover, the legitimacy of charismatic leadership within the *koinonia* (cf. A-I, no. 4). Long before he met any of the Twelve, including and especially Peter, Paul was an active preacher of the gospel and an effective leader within the emerging Gentile-Christian community. The second point is that made in the section from which it comes in *Authority in the Church II*, i.e., that Peter's leadership existed neither apart from nor over those who, like himself, were called to be apostles. Rather, it was fixed precisely in their company—in communion with them. What leadership he exercised within the nascent *koinonia*, it was by nature the very same kind of leadership, the very same kind of *episcope*, which he shared with his brothers. First, foremost and always, Peter was an apostle of the Lord.

22. NB: the Commission cited A-I, no. 12, in support of this statement.

23. I.e., that Roman primacy exists *ex ipsius Christi Domini institutione seu iure divino*.

24. A-II, no. 14: "However, given recent developments in the Roman Catholic understanding of the status of other Christian churches, this particular difficulty may no longer be an obstacle to Anglican acceptance, as God's will for his Church, of a universal primacy of the bishop of Rome such as has been described in the first Statement on Authority (para. 23)."

25. A-II, no. 15: "In the past, Roman Catholic teaching that the bishop of Rome is universal primate by divine right or law has been regarded by Anglicans as unacceptable. However, we believe that the primacy of the bishop of Rome can be affirmed as part of God's design for the universal *koinonia* in terms which are compatible with both our traditions."

26. A-II, no. 16: "In both our communions, [jurisdiction] is given for the effective fulfilment of office and this fact determines its exercise and limits. It varies according to the specific functions of the *episcope* concerned. The jurisdictions associated with different levels of *episcope* (e.g., primates, metropolitans and diocesan bishops) are not in all respects identical. The use of the same juridical terms does not mean that exactly the same authority is attributed to all those exercising *episcope* at different levels. Where a metropolitan has jurisdiction in his province this jurisdiction is not merely the exercise in a broader context of that exercised by a bishop in his diocese: it is determined by the specific functions which he is required to discharge in relation to his fellow bishops."

27. "Concern for the universal Church is intrinsic to all episcopal office; a diocesan bishop is helped to make this concern a reality by the universal jurisdiction of the universal primate. But the universal primate is not the source from which diocesan bishops derive their authority, nor does his authority undermine that of the metropolitan or diocesan bishop. Primacy is not an autocratic power over the Church but a service in and to the Church which is a communion in faith and charity of local churches" (A-II, no. 19); cf. no. 21: "The purpose of the universal primate's jurisdiction is to enable him to further catholicity as well as unity and to foster and draw together the riches of the diverse traditions of the churches. Collegial and primatial responsibility for preserving the distinctive life of the local churches involves a proper respect

for their customs and traditions, provided these do not contradict the faith or disrupt communion. The search for unity and concern for catholicity must not be divorced."

28. A-II, no. 20: "Although the scope of universal jurisdiction cannot be precisely defined canonically, there are moral limits to its exercise: they derive from the nature of the Church and the universal primate's pastoral office."

29. This point was made by J. Robert Wright in "An Anglican Comment on Papal Authority in the Light of Recent Documents," in *Authority in the Anglican Communion: Essays Presented to Bishop John Howe* (Toronto: Anglican Book Centre, 1987), 250–51.

30. This is a reference to Paul VI's statement, "There will be no seeking to lessen the legitimate prestige and the worthy patrimony of piety and usage proper to the Anglican Church when the Roman Catholic Church—this humble 'Servant of the servants of God'—is able to embrace her ever beloved Sister in the one authentic communion of the family of Christ" (*Acta Apostolicae Sedis* 62 [1970]: 753).

31. A-II, no. 23: "It is Christ himself, the Way, the Truth and the Life, who entrusts the Gospel to us and gives to his Church teaching authority which claims our obedience. The Church has a whole, indwelt by the Spirit according to Christ's promise and looking to the testimony of the prophets, saints and martyrs of every generation, is witness, teacher and guardian of the truth (cf. *Authority I*, para. 18). The Church is confident that the Holy Spirit will effectually enable it to fulfil its mission so that it will neither lose its essential character nor fail to reach its goal." The footnote appended to this last sentence reads, "This is the meaning of *indefectibility*, a term which does not speak of the Church's lack of defects but confesses that, despite all its many weaknesses and failures, Christ is faithful to his promise that the gates of hell shall not prevail against it."

32. NB: the emphases are my own. In her article "Reception as Key: Unlocking ARCIC on Infallibility," O'Gara explains this statement by the Commission. "I think that ARCIC understands reception as a part of the exercise of infallibility that functions, if you will, within the 'order of knowing.' It is the epistemological side of doctrine, as it were, just as the process of discerning the canon was the epistemological side of inspiration. Reception

is a sign or manifestation that a teaching is true; it is the means by which we discover what truth the Holy Spirit is helping the Church to understand more deeply. Reception is not an enlarged voting booth: it is the Spirit crying 'Abba' within us. We hear this in many voices that have become one. In this sense, ARCIC is simply stating in phenomenological terms what we have tended to describe only metaphysically when discussing authentic teaching" (*The Ecumenical Gift Exchange* [Collegeville, MN: Liturgical Press, 1988], 83–84). As I will discuss later with regard to *The Gift of Authority*, this understanding, not only of reception, but also of the larger issue of ecclesial authority itself as a movement of the Spirit, is essential to understanding ARCIC's mind on universal primacy. Primacy is first and foremost a gift of the Spirit, given to the Church in the service of its indefectible faith.

33. "The Church's teaching authority is a service to which the faithful look for guidance especially in times of uncertainty; but the assurance of the truthfulness of its teaching rests ultimately rather upon its fidelity to the Gospel than upon the character or office of the person by whom it is expressed. The Church's teaching is proclaimed because it is true; it is not true simply because it has been proclaimed. The value of such authoritative proclamation lies in the guidance that it gives to the faithful. However, neither general councils nor universal primates are invariably preserved from error even in official declarations (cf. *Authority I Elucidation*, para. 3)."

34. A-II, no. 26: "The Church exercises teaching authority through various instruments and agencies at various levels (cf. *Authority I*, paras. 9 and 18–22). When matters of faith are at stake decisions may be made by the Church in universal councils; we are agreed that these are authoritative (cf. *Authority I*, para. 19). We have also recognized the need in a united Church for a universal primate who, presiding over the *koinonia*, can speak with authority in the name of the Church (cf. *Authority I*, para. 23). Through both these agencies the Church can make a decisive judgment in matters of faith, and so exclude error."

35. A-II, no. 30: "This approach is illustrated by the reaction of many Anglicans to the Marian definitions, which are the only examples of such dogmas promulgated by the bishop of Rome apart from a synod since the separation of our two communions.

Anglicans and Roman Catholics can agree in much of the truth that these two dogmas are designed to affirm. We agree that there can be but one mediator between God and man, Jesus Christ, and reject any interpretation of the role of Mary which obscures this affirmation. We agree in recognizing that Christian understanding of Mary is inseparably linked with the doctrines of Christ and of the Church. We agree in recognizing the grace and unique vocation of Mary, Mother of God Incarnate (*Theotokos*), in observing her festivals, and in according her honor in the communion of saints. We agree that she was prepared by divine grace to be the mother of our Redeemer, by whom she herself was redeemed and received into glory. We further agree in recognizing in Mary a model of holiness, obedience and faith for all Christians. We accept that it is possible to regard her as a prophetic figure of the Church of God before as well as after the Incarnation. Nevertheless the dogmas of the Immaculate Conception and the Assumption raise a special problem for those Anglicans who do not consider that the precise definitions given by these dogmas are sufficiently supported by Scripture. For many Anglicans the teaching authority of the bishop of Rome, independent of a council, is not recommended by the fact that through it these Marian doctrines were proclaimed as dogmas binding on all the faithful. Anglicans would also ask whether, in any future union between our two Churches, they would be required to subscribe to such dogmatic statements. One consequence of our separation has been a tendency for Anglicans and Roman Catholics alike to exaggerate the importance of the Marian dogmas in themselves at the expense of other truths more closely related to the foundation of the Christian faith."

36. NB: the emphases are in the original text. "In our three Agreed Statements [*Eucharist Doctrine, Ministry and Ordination*, and *Authority in the Church I*] we have endeavored to get behind the opposed and entrenched positions of past controversies. We have tried to reassess what are the real issues to be resolved. We have often deliberately avoided the vocabulary of past polemics, not with any intention of evading the real difficulties that provoked them, but because the emotive associations of such language have often obscured the truth. For the future relations between our churches the doctrinal convergence which we have experienced offers hope that remaining difficulties can be resolved."

37. Cf. UR, no. 7, which was cited in the co-chairs' preface to FR (4): "There can be no ecumenism worthy of the name without interior conversion. For it is from newness of attitudes of mind, from self-denial and unstinted love, that desires of unity take their rise and develop in a mature way."

38. NB: the Commission defined what it meant here by "substantial agreement" in its 1979 *Elucidation on Eucharistic Doctrine*: "It means that the document represents not only the judgement of all its members—i.e. it is an agreement—but their unanimous agreement 'on essential matters where it considers that doctrine admits no divergence' (*Ministry*, para. 17)" (no. 2).

CHAPTER 6

1. *The Gift of Authority: Authority in the Church III* (New York: Church Publishing, 1999), no. 50 (henceforth, GA.).

2. Cf. GA, no. 6. In this light, it is worth recalling that the "unity in truth, for which Christ prayed," the restoration of which was the expressed desire of Pope Paul VI and Archbishop Michael Ramsey when they established ARCIC (cf. *The Common Declaration* in the Anglican–Roman Catholic International Commission, *The Final Report* (London: SPCK and Catholic Truth Society, 1982) [FR], 117), is not unity simply for the sake of domestic harmony within the household of the Church, but unity for the sake of the Church's mission of proclaiming the gospel. As pope and archbishop stated in the conclusion of the *Common Declaration* with which they established ARCIC, "Through such collaboration, by the Grace of God the Father and in the light of the Holy Spirit, may the prayer of Our Lord Jesus Christ for unity among His disciples be brought nearer to fulfilment, and with progress towards unity may there be a strengthening of peace in the world, the peace that only He can grant who gives 'the peace that passeth all understanding,' together with the blessing of Almighty God, Father, Son and Holy Spirit, that it may abide with all men [*sic*] for ever."

3. ARCIC II, *Church as Communion* (London: Church House Publishing and Catholic Truth Society, 1991), preface (henceforth, CC).

4. Citing "Common Declaration of Pope John Paul II and the Archbishop of Canterbury, Robert Runcie, 2 October 1989."

5. This agreed statement did include a fifth section, "Communion between Anglicans and Roman Catholics." Yet, as this section does not offer anything of further substance to the unfolding of ARCIC's understanding of *koinonia* per se, it is not treated here.

6. It is precisely with this in mind that the Commission was later able to make its own *apologia* for unity in GA, no. 33: "Jesus prayed to the Father that his followers might be one 'so that the world may know that you have sent me and have loved them even as you have loved me' (Jn 17.23). When Christians do not agree about the Gospel itself, the preaching of it in power is impaired. When they are not one in faith they cannot be one in life, and so cannot demonstrate fully that they are faithful to the will of God, which is the reconciliation through Christ of all things to the Father (cf. Col 1.20). As long as the Church does not live as the community of reconciliation God calls it to be, it cannot adequately preach this Gospel or credibly proclaim God's plan to gather his scattered people into unity under Christ as Lord and Saviour (cf. Jn 11.52). Only when all believers are united in the common celebration of the Eucharist (cf. *Church as Communion*, 24) will the God whose purpose it is to bring all things into unity in Christ (cf. Eph 1.10) be truly glorified by the people of God. The challenge and responsibility for those with authority within the Church is so to exercise their ministry that they promote the unity of the whole Church in faith and life in a way that enriches rather than diminishes the legitimate diversity of local churches."

7. Citing *Ministry and Ordination*, nos. 33, 39, in support of this statement. However, for this statement as well as for those that followed upon it, one may also look to *Authority in the Church I* and *II* and *Elucidations* for support.

8. A-I, in conjunction with *Eluc.*, 3.

9. ARCIC II alluded to this in its reference in GA, no. 46, to Pope Leo's role in the decisions of Chalcedon.

10. NB: the Commission did not exclusively associate this particular exercise of primatial *episcope* exclusively with the Bishop of Rome. The commission spoke of it as part of the duty owed by the bishop of a "principle see" to all the churches of his region. (Cf. *Eluc.*, no. 7, for the commission's discussion of such "regional

primacy.") The Bishop of Rome was one such bishop—though not *simply* one such bishop. It was precisely because he was the bishop of *Rome* that he was recognized as having a significant role to play in fostering the common mind of the Church's communion.

11. See Gavin White, "Collegiality and Conciliarity in the Anglican Communion," in *Authority in the Anglican Communion: Essays Presented to Bishop John Howe*, ed. Stephen Sykes (Toronto: Anglican Book Centre, 1987), 205–6.

12. Cf. Philip Turner, "Episcopal Authority in a Divided Church," *Pro Ecclesia* 8 (1999): 37–44.

13. Cf. *Ministry and Ordination*, no. 11, in FR, nos. 34–35.

14. Referencing Sermon 295. NB: no citation regarding the particular translation or edition of this sermon was given by the Commission.

15. "When a believer says 'Amen' to Christ individually, a further dimension is always involved: an 'Amen' to the faith of the Christian community. The person who receives baptism must come to know the full implication of participating in divine life within the Body of Christ. The believer's 'Amen' to Christ becomes yet more complete as that person receives all that the Church, in faithfulness to the Word of God, affirms to be the authentic content of divine revelation. In that way, the 'Amen' said to what Christ is *for each believer* is incorporated within the 'Amen' the Church says to what Christ is *for his Body*. Growing into this faith may be for some an experience of questioning and struggle. For all it is one in which the integrity of the believer's conscience has a vital part to play. The believer's 'Amen' to Christ is so fundamental that individual Christians throughout their life are called to say 'Amen' to all that the whole company of Christians receives and teaches as the authentic meaning of the Gospel and the way to follow Christ" (GA, no. 12).

16. "At the centre of [the] life [of the local church] is the celebration of the Holy Eucharist in which all believers hear and receive God's 'Yes' in Christ to them. In the Great Thanksgiving, when the memorial of God's gift in the saving work of Christ crucified and risen is celebrated, the community is at one with all Christians of all the churches who, since the beginning and until the end, pronounce humanity's 'Amen' to God—the 'Amen'

which the Apocalypse affirms is at the heart of the great liturgy of heaven (cf. Rev 5.14; 7.12)" (GA, no. 13).

17. Michael Ramsey, *The Gospel and the Catholic Church* (London, 1936), 227–28, cited in J. Robert Wright, "Anglicans and the Papacy," in *A Pope for All Christians: An Inquiry into the Role of Peter in the Modern Church*, ed. Peter J. McCord (New York: Paulist Press, 1976), 183.

18. All citations will be from GA, no. 47, unless otherwise noted.

19. Cf. Luke 22:32, cited in A-II, no. 5.

20. See GA, no. 41, citing A-I, no. 18, and A-II, no. 23.

21. See GA, no. 14–16: "The 'Yes' of God commands and invites the 'Amen' of believers. The revealed Word, to which the apostolic community originally bore witness, is received and communicated through the life of the whole Christian community. Tradition (*paradosis*) refers to this process. The Gospel of Christ crucified and risen is continually handed on and received (cf. 1 Cor 15.3) in the Christian churches. This tradition, or handing on, of the Gospel is the work of the Spirit, especially through the ministry of Word and Sacrament and in the common life of the people of God. Tradition is a dynamic process, communicating to each generation what was delivered once for all to the apostolic community. Tradition is far more than the transmission of true propositions concerning salvation. A minimalist understanding of Tradition that would limit it to a storehouse of doctrine and ecclesial decisions is insufficient…" (no.14).

"Tradition is a channel of the love of God, making it accessible in the Church and in the world today. Through it, from one generation to another, and from one place to another, humanity shares communion in the Holy Trinity…" (no. 15).

"Apostolic Tradition is a gift of God which must be constantly received anew. By means of it, the Holy Spirit forms, maintains and sustains the communion of the local churches from one generation to the next. The handing on and reception of apostolic Tradition is an act of communion whereby the Spirit unites the local churches of our day with those that preceded them in the one apostolic faith. The process of tradition entails the constant and perpetual reception and communication of the revealed Word of God in many varied circumstances and continually changing times. The Church's

'Amen' to apostolic Tradition is a fruit of the Spirit who constantly guides the disciples into all the truth; that is, into Christ who is the way, the truth and the life (cf. Jn 16.13; 14.6)" (no. 16).

CHAPTER 7

1. Walter Kasper, "Introduction to the Theme and Catholic Hermeneutics of the Dogmas of the First Vatican Council," in *The Petrine Ministry: Catholics and Orthodox in Dialogue*, ed. Walter Kasper, trans. the Staff of the Pontifical Council for Promoting Christian Unity (New York: Newman Press, 2006), 13, citing *Dei Verbum* 8.

2. See no. 11, in which ARCIC addressed Anglican concerns and objections to this way of describing the "right" whereby the Petrine primacy of the Roman Pontiff is said to exist: "The Roman Catholic conviction concerning the place of the Roman Primacy in God's plan for his Church has traditionally been expressed in the language of *jus divinum* (divine law or divine right). This term was used by the First Vatican Council to describe the Primacy of the 'successor in the chair of Peter' whom the Council recognized in the bishop of Rome. The First Vatican Council used the term *jure divino* to say that this primacy derives from Christ. While there is no universally accepted interpretation of this language, all affirm that it means at least that this primacy expresses God's purpose for his Church. *Jus divinum* in this context need not be taken to imply that the universal primacy as a permanent institution was directly founded by Jesus during his life on earth. Neither does the term mean that the universal primate is a 'source of the Church' as if Christ's salvation had to be channeled through him. Rather, he is to be the sign of the visible *koinonia* God wills for the Church and an instrument through which unity in diversity is realized. It is to a universal primate thus envisaged within the collegiality of the bishops and the *koinonia* of the whole Church that the qualification *jure divino* can be applied."

3. Raymond Brown, Karl Donfried, and John Reumann, eds., *Peter in the New Testament* (Minneapolis: Augsburg, 1973). The essays contained in this book, all of which address the figure

of the apostle Peter in the New Testament, originated as background for *Papal Primacy and the Universal Church*, the fifth volume of the series Lutherans and Catholics in Dialogue (Paul C. Empie and T. Austin Murphy, eds., *Papal Primacy and the Universal Church*, vol. 5, Lutherans and Catholics in Dialogue [Minneapolis: Augsburg, 1974]).

4. William Farmer and Roch Kereszty, *Peter and Paul in the Church of Rome: The Ecumenical Potential of a Forgotten Perspective*, Theological Inquiries: Studies in Contemporary and Theological Problems, ed. Lawrence Boadt et al. (New York: Paulist Press, 1990).

5. Joseph Ratzinger, "The Primacy of Peter and the Unity of the Church," in *Called to Communion: Understanding the Church Today*, trans. Adrian Walker (San Francisco: Ignatius Press, 1996), 64–65.

6. Ibid., 54–55, cited by Ratzinger as G. Schulze-Kadelbach, 'Die Stellung des Petrus in der Urchristenheit,' in *Theol. Lit.-Ztg.* 81: (1956): 1–14; citation on 4.

7. Ratzinger, "The Primacy of Peter and the Unity of the Church," 56, cited by Ratzinger as J. Jeremias, *Golgotha und der heilige Fels* (Leipzig, 1926), 74.

8. Ratzinger, "The Primacy of Peter and the Unity of the Church," 56.

9. Ibid., 63.

10. Ibid.

11. Ibid.

12. Ibid., 64–65.

13. Jean-Marie Tillard, *The Bishop of Rome*, trans. John de Satgé (Wilmington, DE: Michael Glazier, 1983), 26–27.

14. John P. Meier, "Petrine Ministry in the New Testament and the Patristic Church," in *How Can the Petrine Ministry Be a Service to the Unity of the Universal Church?* ed. James F. Puglisi (Grand Rapids, MI: Eerdmans, 2010), 14.

15. Ignatius of Antioch, "Letter to the Romans," introduction, in Ludwig Schopp et al., eds. *The Apostolic Fathers*, vol. 1, *The Fathers of the Church: A New Translation*, trans. Gerald G. Walsh (New York: Christian Heritage, Inc., 1947), 107.

16. Irenaeus of Lyon, "Against the Heretics," 3, in *The Faith of the Early Fathers*, vol. 1, selected and translated by William A. Jurgens (Collegeville, MN: Liturgical Press, 1970), 90.

17. See Tillard, *The Bishop of Rome*, 70. Much has been made of the so-called Letter of Clement, as an example of this point (cf. Robert Eno, *The Rise of the Papacy* [Wilmington, DE: Michael Glazier, Inc., 1990], 35–37). Perhaps more significant is the example provided by Tillard: when, during the *sede vacante* period between Bishops Fabian and Cornelius (AD 250/1), Roman presbyters under the leadership of Novatian wrote to St. Cyprian of Carthage regarding the re-reception of *lapsi* from the Decian persecution. "Although deprived of her bishop, the local church of Rome never supposed that this paradoxical situation excused her from her duty" (70).

18. Schatz described this extension of the primacy of the Roman Church to that of its bishop well, when he spoke of the "special reverence of early Christians for the martyrdom of Peter and Paul and its significance for the charism of the Roman community. In the definitive testimony to faith of their martyrdom, the two κορύφαοι [heads, leaders], Peter and Paul, had simultaneously handed on their faith as an enduring heritage for the Roman church (*paradosis*) and endowed it with that faith forever. Their witness to the faith, made perfect in the shedding of their blood, was handed on in the *paradosis*; their martyrdom remained present in the witness of the Roman church. Thus, for example, the letter of the Synod of Arles (314) to bishop Sylvester of Rome said of the Roman bishops: '[in them] the apostles also have their seat from day to day and...their outpoured blood (*curor*) bears continual witness to the glory of God.' If any church was proof against heretics, it had to be this one" (see Klaus Schatz, *Papal Primacy: From Its Origins to the Present*, trans. John A. Otto and Linda M. Malone [Collegeville, MN: Liturgical Press, 1996], 8). For a concise review of the historical process whereby the primacy of the Church of Rome extended to, and by the early patristic period came to be embodied by, the Bishop of Rome, see Meier, "Petrine Ministry in the New Testament and the Patristic Church," 13–33.

19. See Eusebius, *The History of the Church*, III.2, and V.6, in which Eusebius cites St. Irenaeus of Lyon's list of Roman Pontiffs. The version consulted is *The History of the Church from Christ to Constantine*, trans. G. A. Williamson, Penguin Classics (London: Penguin Books, 1965).

20. See Eno, *The Rise of the Papacy*, 26–29, where Eno noted

the consensus among most scholars that the mono-episcopacy developed gradually in Rome. There is, however, disagreement as to precisely how the community—presuming there was only one Christian community in the city—was led and what significance should be attributed to the lists of those named as early Roman bishops. Therefore, to speak of Linus as *the* Bishop of Rome, appointed by the apostles Peter and Paul themselves, would be somewhat anachronistic. The *episcope* attributed to him by later generations, whatever it may have been originally, took time to develop in the mono-episcopacy we know today. See also Meier, "Petrine Ministry in the New Testament and the Patristic Church," 28–30.

21. This movement is covered concisely in Roland Minnerath, "The Petrine Ministry in the Early Patristic Tradition," in Puglisi, *How Can the Petrine Ministry Be a Service to the Unity of the Universal Church?* 34–48.

22. Eno cites the theological consensus that while it may be presumed that Peter, together with Paul, exercised some leadership within the early Roman Christian community, it would be anachronistic to describe him as the community's first bishop: "Such a designation originates in the ill-conceived collapsing of the unique role of the apostle into the later Church office....There is the founding apostle...and after him comes the first bishop, again expressing the essential difference between the two roles and the constitutive significance of the foundational generation over against the episcopal succession for the rest of time and all the other generations which come after. So in that technical but nevertheless very important sense, Peter was not the first bishop of Rome. The little known Linus holds that honor" (18).

23. Roman Missal, Prayer over the Gifts from the Feast of the Chair of Peter.

24. Ibid., preface of Peter and Paul.

25. Ibid., preface of Apostles I.

26. Ibid., Votive Mass for a deceased pope: "God our Father, you reward all who believe in you. May your servant, N. our Pope, vicar of Peter and shepherd of your Church, who faithfully administered the mysteries of your forgiveness and love on earth, rejoice forever with you in heaven."

CHAPTER 8

1. See Michael Buckley, *Papal Primacy and the Episcopate: Towards a Relational Understanding* (New York: Crossroad, 1998), 14, referencing William Henn, "Historical-Theological Synthesis of the Relation between Primacy and Episcopacy during the Second Millennium," *Il primato del successore de Pietro: Atti del simposio teologico, Roma, dicembre 1996* (Vatican City: Libreria Editrice Vaticana, 1997), 215–20.

2. See Henn, "Historical-Theological Synthesis," 263; cited in Buckley, *Papal Primacy and the Episcopate*, 16.

3. See Hermann Pottmeyer, "A New Phase in the Reception of Vatican II: Twenty Years of Interpretation of the Council," in *The Reception of Vatican II*, ed. Guiseppe Alberigo et al. (Washington, DC: The Catholic University of America Press, 1987), 27.

4. See Francis Sullivan, "The Teaching Authority of Episcopal Conferences," *Theological Studies* 63 (2002): 472–74.

5. See Klaus Mörsdorf, "Decree on the Bishops' Pastoral Office in the Church: History of the Decree," trans. Hilda Graef, in *Commentary on the Documents of Vatican II*, ed. Herbert Vorgrimler, trans. Kevin Smyth et al., vol. 2 (New York: Herder and Herder, 1968), 179–81.

6. Henri de Lubac, *The Motherhood of the Church Followed by Particular Churches in the Universal Church*, trans. Sergia Englund (San Francisco: Ignatius Press, 1982, originally published in French under the same title, 1971), 258–59.

7. See Richard Gaillardetz, *The Church in the Making:* Lumen Gentium, Christus Dominus, Orientalium Ecclesiarum, Rediscovering Vatican II, ed. Christopher Bellitto (New York: Paulist Press, 2006), 128–29.

8. This passage continued, "The collegiality of the actions of the body of Bishops is linked to the fact that 'the universal Church cannot be conceived as the sum of the particular Churches, or as a federation of particular Churches.' 'It is not the result of the communion of the Churches, but, in its essential mystery, it is a reality ontologically and temporally prior to every individual particular Church.' Likewise the College of Bishops is not to be understood as the aggregate of the Bishops who govern the particular Churches,

nor as the result of their communion; rather, as an essential element of the universal Church, it is a reality which precedes the office of being the head of a particular Church. In fact, the power of the College of Bishops over the whole Church is not the result of the sum of the powers of the individual Bishops over their particular Churches; it is a pre-existing reality in which individual Bishops participate." This reasoning brings to light an issue for which ARCIC's call is particularly poignant. In fact, one may well say that it is *the* issue upon which our response to ARCIC rises or falls—the relationship between the Church Universal and the local churches, which shall be discussed in the next chapter.

9. See Gaillardetz, *The Church in the Making*, 130; Joseph Komonchak, "On the Authority of Bishops Conferences," *America* (September 12, 1998): 7–10; also Sullivan, "The Teaching Authority of Episcopal Conferences."

10. John Quinn, *The Reform of the Papacy: The Costly Call to Christian Unity* (New York: Crossroad, 1999), 111, citing CD 5.

11. *Apostolica Sollicitudo*, chaps. III, IV, and VI.

12. *Apostolica Sollicitudo*, chaps. II and III.

13. See John Quinn, "The Exercise of the Primacy and the Costly Call to Unity," in *The Exercise of the Primacy: Continuing the Dialogue*, ed. Phyllis Zagano and Terrance W. Tilley (New York: Crossroad, 1998), 12–13.

14. See Jean-Marie Tillard, *The Bishop of Rome*, trans. John de Satgé (Wilmington, DE: Michael Glazier, 1983), 40–41.

15. Reference to collegial governance from LG 22.

16. Cf. Ignatius of Antioch, "Letter to the Romans," in *The Faith of the Early Fathers*, ed. and trans. William Jurgens, vol. 1 (Collegeville, MN: Liturgical Press, 1970), 21–22.

17. NB: In 2006, Pope Benedict XVI ordered that the title "Patriarch of the West" be dropped from the list of papal titles, on the ground that the title lacked any real, objective historical and theological significance. A copy of the press release issued by the Pontifical Council for Promoting Christian Unity to explain this action is available (in French and Italian) at http://www.vatican .va/roman_curia/pontifical_councils/chrstuni/sub-index/index _general-docs.htm. My reference to the title in the text above is not an attempt to reopen the debate on its appropriateness— hence my placing the title within parentheses. Rather, I employ

it as a means for discussing the particular relationship that the Roman Pontiff has to the churches of the Latin Rite, as distinct from the relationship he has to the churches of the various other rites, as alluded to by the Council in LG 23.

18. Irenaeus of Lyon, "Against the Heretics," 3, in *The Faith of the Early Fathers*, vol. 1, *The Fathers of the Church: A New Translation*, ed. Ludwig Schopp et al., trans. Gerald G. Walsh (New York: Christian Heritage, Inc., 1947).

19. See Klaus Mörsdorf, "Decree on the Bishops' Pastoral Office in the Church: History of the Decree," trans. Hilda Graef, in Vorgrimler and Smyth, *Commentary on the Documents of Vatican II*, 2:170.

20. Ibid., 172–73.

21. See Sullivan, "The Teaching Authority of Episcopal Conferences," 472–93. In this article, Sullivan developed his argument with reference to Avery Dulles, "Doctrinal Authority of Episcopal Conferences," in *Episcopal Conferences: Historical, Canonical, and Theological Studies*, ed. Thomas Reese (Washington, DC: Georgetown University Press, 1989), 207–32; Ladislas Orsy, "Reflections on the Theological Authority of the Episcopal Conferences," in *Episcopal Conferences: Historical, Canonical, and Theological Studies*, 233–52; Hermann Pottmeyer, "Das Lehramt der Bischofskonferenz," in *Die Bischofskonferenz. Theologischer und juridischer Status*, ed. Hubert Müller and Hermann Pottmeyer (Düsseldorf: Patmos, 1989), 116–33. I am indebted to these sources for my argument here, to which I also add Ladislas Orsy, "Episcopal Conferences: *Communio* among the Bishops," in *Receiving the Council: Theological and Canonical Insights and Debates* (Collegeville, MN: Liturgical Press, 2009), 16–34.

22. See Orsy, "Episcopal Conferences: *Communio* among the Bishops," 20–22.

23. See Dulles, "Doctrinal Authority of Episcopal Conferences," 217–26.

24. See Orsy, "Reflections on the Theological Authority of the Episcopal Conferences," 251.

25. See Sullivan, "The Teaching Authority of Episcopal Conferences," 484–85, citing Pottmeyer, "Das Lehramt der Bischofskonferenz," 116–33, and Orsy, "Episcopal Conferences: *Communio* among the Bishops," 28.

26. See Orsy, "Episcopal Conferences: *Communio* among the Bishops," 31–33, on the doctrinal significance of affirming such an expression of unity and diversity within the churches. In particular, note Orsy's source for argument: Karl Rahner, "On the Divine Right of the Episcopate," in *The Episcopate and the Primacy*, trans. Kenneth Barker et al (New York: Herder and Herder, 1962) 105–6.

27. The pope's address is available online in English translation at http://w2.vatican.va/content/francesco/en/speeches/2015/october/documents/papa-francesco_20151017_50-anniversario-sinodo.html.

28. "In each local church all the faithful are called to walk together in Christ. The term *synodality* (derived from *syn-hodos* meaning 'common way') indicates the manner in which believers and churches are held together in communion as they do this. It expresses their vocation as people of the Way (cf. Acts 9.2) to live, work and journey together in Christ who is the Way (cf. Jn 14.6). They, like their predecessors, follow Jesus on the way (cf. Mk 10.52) until he comes again" (GA, no. 34).

29. In my treatment of the Synod, I am indebted to James Coriden, "The Synod of Bishops: Episcopal Collegiality Still Seeks Adequate Expression," *The Jurist* 64 (2004): 116–36.

30. James Coriden, "The Synod of Bishops: Episcopal Collegiality Still Seeks Adequate Expression," 126, citing Allocution, *In fine huius Synodi, AAS* 76 (1984): 297. In a discourse to the Council of the Secretary General of the Synod, John Paul II elaborated, "Certainly the Synod is the instrument of collegiality and a powerful factor of communion in a way different from an ecumenical Council. However, we speak always of an instrument that is effective, agile, opportune, and promptly at the service of all the local Churches and of their reciprocal communion....The Synod is in fact a particularly fruitful expression and a most valid instrument of episcopal collegiality, that is, of the particular responsibility of the bishops in relationship to the Bishop of Rome. The Synod is one form in which the collegiality of the Bishops is expressed.... Between the Council and the Synod there obviously exists a qualitative difference, but, nonetheless, the Synod expresses collegiality in a highly intense way, even though not equal to that realized in Council" ("Discourse to the Council of the Secretary General of

the Synod," April 30, 1983, in *AAS* 75 [1983]: 648–51; translation by Coriden).

31. See James Coriden, "The Synod of Bishops," 126–27, citing Angel Antón, "Verso un collegialità più effictiva nel Sinodo dei vescovi," *La Revista del Clero Italiano* 64 (1983): 482–98, 568–70.

32. See James Coriden, "The Synod of Bishops," 129–30, citing Antón, "Verso un collegialità più effictiva nel Sinodo dei vescovi," 567–68.

33. See Buckley, *Papal Primacy and the Episcopate*, 72.

34. *Letter to Eulogius of Alexandria*, VIII 29 (30) (MGH, Ep. 2, 31 28–30, PL 77, 933), as cited in *Pastor Aeternus* 3.

35. See Gaillardetz, *The Church in the Making*, 177–78.

36. See ibid., 150, citing John Beal, "It Shall Not Be So among You! Crisis in the Church, Crisis in Church Law," in *Governance, Accountability and the Future of the Catholic Church*, ed. Francis Oakley and Bruce Russett (New York: Continuum, 2004), 96–97.

37. For a brief history of the Roman Curia and the Council's call for its reform, cf. John Provost, "*Pastor Bonus*: Reflections on the Reorganization of the Roman Curia," *The Jurist* 48 (1988): 499–507; and John Quinn, *The Reform of the Papacy: The Costly Call to Christian Unity* (New York: Crossroad, 1999), 154–71. With regard to the Curia acting as such a *tertium quid*, cf. Gaillardetz, *The Church in the Making*, 135 and 178; and Quinn, *The Reform of the Papacy*, 157–61. See also Massimo Faggiolo, "The Roman Curia at and after Vatican II: Legal-Rational or Theological Reform?" in *Theological Studies* 76 (September 2015): 550–71, whose historical overview of this issue includes the pontificate of Pope Francis.

38. Cf. Quinn, *The Reform of the Papacy*, 171–77.

39. See also Massimo Faggiolo, "The Roman Curia at and after Vatican II: Legal-Rational or Theological Reform?" 569–71.

40. Quinn, *The Reform of the Papacy*, 143.

41. See Gaillardetz, *The Church in the Making*, 171–72.

42. See John Huels and Richard Gaillardetz, "The Selection of Bishops: Recovering the Traditions," *The Jurist* 59 (1999): 362.

43. Ibid.

44. Tillard, *The Bishop of Rome*, 42–43.

CONCLUSION

1. Avery Dulles, "Ratzinger and Kasper on the Universal Church," *Inside the Vatican* 20 (June 4, 2001): 13: "The ontological priority of the Church universal appears to me to be almost self-evident, since the very concept of a particular church presupposes a universal Church to which it belongs, whereas the concept of the universal Church does not imply that it is made up of distinct particular churches"; as cited by Kilian McDonnell, "The Ratzinger/Kasper Debate: The Universal Church and the Local Churches," *Theological Studies* 63 (2002): 235.

2. Henri de Lubac, as cited by Kasper as "*One Church*, 13"; source not given.

3. "The Malta Report: Report of the Anglican–Roman Catholic Joint Preparatory Commission," 4, in International Commission, *The Final Report* (London: SPCK and Catholic Truth Society 1982), 3.

4. Ibid., 4.

5. Walter Kasper, "Introduction to the Theme and Catholic Hermeneutics of the Dogmas of the First Vatican Council," in *The Petrine Ministry: Catholics and Orthodox in Dialogue*, ed. Walter Kasper, trans. the Staff of the Pontifical Council for Promoting Christian Unity (Mahwah, NJ: Newman Press, 2006), 13.

6. See Jean-Marie Tillard, *The Bishop of Rome*, trans. John de Satgé (Wilmington, DE: Michael Glazier, 1983), 42–43; also Giles Routhier, "Vatican II: The First Stage of an Unfinished Process of Reversing the Centralizing Government of the Catholic Church," trans. Catherine Clifford, *The Jurist* 64 (2004): 247–48.

7. Cf. PA, 3: "The Roman Church possesses a pre-eminence of ordinary power over every other Church, and…this jurisdictional power of the Roman Pontiff is both episcopal and immediate."

8. Cf. Pheme Perkins, *Peter: Apostle for the Whole Church* (Columbia, SC: University of South Carolina Press, 1994), 3.

INDEX

Index

Index

Index

Munus regendi (office of governance), 70, 220, 236
Murphy-O'Connor, Cormac, 152–153
Mystery of Church, 47, 49, 94, 253
Mystici Corporis Christi, 62–64, 67, 248

New Testament, 128, 138, 156
Nicaea, Council, 73
Non-papal period, 105, 110–119

Olivi, Peter of John, 23
On the General Council and Religious Peace (Maret), 12
Ordinary power, 16–21
"Origin and Essence of the Church, The" (Ratzinger), 94

Papal primacy: apostolic character of, 172–174; ARCIC and, 102, 197–199, 215–216, 263–264, 275; as authority for mission, 175–176; Church and, 203–205; claims to, papal, 10; College of Bishops and, 57, 88–89, 249; collegial harmony and, 226–233; collegiality and, 45, 56, 89–93, 165–170, 269–274; conciliarity and, 133, 162–165; cost of call to Christian unity and, 262–266; defining, 9–10; discerning the gift, 99–102; dispensability of, 2–3; divine right of, 140–141; dynamics of, 3; *Elucidation* and, 134–135; encounters framing, 3; engagement of all Christians and, 275–278; in *episcope*, 131–132; faith and, 98; as gift for all Christians, 266–278;

history and, 135–136; *koinonia* and, 129–130; *Lumen Gentium* and, 84; naming the gift, 1–4; objections to, 11–12; offering the gift, 187–189; past and, grasp of, 3; *Pastor Aeternus* and, 15, 86, 90; people of God and, 260–262; permanency of, 2, 13–14; Peter and, 26, 60, 73, 203–206, 267–269; providence and, 136–137; public opinion and, 36–38; reality of vision and, making, 264–266; *sensus fidelium* and, 272–273; synodality and, 170–172; Synod of Bishops and, 221–222; as theme in theological dialogues, 266; theology and, 34–36; unity and, 15; unmitigation of, 13–14; Vatican I and, 7. *See also specific council and topic on*
Papal sovereignty, 12–13. *See also* Papal primacy
Pastor Aeternus: atmosphere of development of, 13; *ex esse* clause in, 73; faith and, 28; German bishops' reply to Bismarck's opinion on, 31–32, 36; infallibility and, 22–31, 176; interpretations of, 34–37; opening of, 6–7, 13; papal primacy and, 15, 86, 90; permanency of papal primacy and, 13–14; Petrine primacy and, 85; Pius IX's opinion on, 32–34; power of keys and, 202; primatial jurisdiction and, 15–22; root of, 23–24; service of unity and, 14–15; unmitigation of papal primacy and, 13–14;

329

Index